Liberty Brought Us Here

Liberty Brought Us Here

The True Story of American Slaves Who Migrated to Liberia

Susan E. Lindsey

UNIVERSITY PRESS OF KENTUCKY

Published by the University Press of Kentucky,
scholarly publisher for the Commonwealth,
serving Bellarmine University, Berea College, Centre
College of Kentucky, Eastern Kentucky University,
The Filson Historical Society, Georgetown College,
Kentucky Historical Society, Kentucky State University,
Morehead State University, Murray State University,
Northern Kentucky University, Transylvania University,
University of Kentucky, University of Louisville,
and Western Kentucky University.
All rights reserved.

Editorial and Sales Offices: The University Press of Kentucky
663 South Limestone Street, Lexington, Kentucky 40508-4008
www.kentuckypress.com

Maps and family trees by Shellee Marie Jones.

Library of Congress Cataloging-in-Publication Data

Names: Lindsey, Susan E., 1952– author.
Title: Liberty brought us here : the true story of American slaves who
    migrated to Liberia / Susan E. Lindsey.
Description: Lexington : The University Press of Kentucky, 2020. | Includes
    bibliographical references and index.
Identifiers: LCCN 2020013203 | ISBN 9780813179339 (hardcover) | ISBN
    9780813179360 (pdf) | ISBN 9780813179346 (epub)
Subjects: LCSH: African Americans—Liberia—Biography. | Majors family. |
    Harlan family.
Classification: LCC DT633.2 .L56 2020 | DDC 966.62/020922—dc23
LC record available at https://lccn.loc.gov/2020013203

This book is printed on acid-free paper meeting
the requirements of the American National Standard
for Permanence in Paper for Printed Library Materials.

Manufactured in the United States of America.

Member of the Association
of University Presses

But they shall sit every man under his vine
and under his fig tree; and none shall make them afraid. . . .
—Micah 4:4

Contents

Contents

Preface

This is a true story.

Several years ago, I stumbled across the tale of Ben Major and the enslaved people he freed for migration to Liberia. I was stunned to learn that they had corresponded across the Atlantic Ocean for years, and—even more astonishing—that the letters from Africa still existed. The first time I read the Major letters, I was moved to tears. I sat quietly, alone, in a museum reading room and absorbed the thought that I was holding a letter written by a former slave, a brittle and faded piece of paper that had sailed across the ocean on a ship more than a century and a half earlier.

I wanted to know more. Why did Ben Major, who descended from a long line of slave owners, free his enslaved people? Did the newly emancipated people *want* to go to another country? Did they have a choice? What would life in Africa have been like for them? What was the colonization movement about? Were those who supported colonization motivated by noble or nefarious intentions?

It took more than six years to find the answers: years of digging through academic journals, books, courthouse documents, family records, private collections, archives, old newspapers, and online resources, as well as multiple trips to universities, museums, cemeteries, and dusty attics. I celebrated each new detail I uncovered and every fact I could confirm. I had embarked on an amazing journey: one that revealed the story of Ben Major and the family he freed—headed by brothers Tolbert and Austin Major—and the related story of a neighboring family of formerly enslaved people headed by the widow Agnes Harlan.

Unlike many other former slave owners of the time, Ben stayed in touch with the people he had freed, responding to their letters and sending much-needed items such as seeds, tools, books, medicine, and other supplies to help them survive and flourish in their new home in Liberia. In return, they sent coffee, peanuts, and other items to Ben and his family.

I have been inspired by this story, but I've also struggled with its meaning. Ben was clearly a decent man, a man who wanted to do what was best for himself, his family, and his formerly enslaved people. Their surviving correspondence seems to indicate that Tolbert and the others who went to Liberia respected and perhaps even cared for Ben and his family. Was such a relationship possible between formerly enslaved people and the man who had held them in bondage?

Ultimately, this is the story of a search for peace, security, and liberty—in Liberia and in frontier Illinois, where Ben and his family settled after leaving Kentucky.

In writing this book, I hope to honor the memory of the Major and Harlan families who settled in Liberia, as well as the memory of Ben Major. I also want to bring to light the story of the colonization of Liberia—a story that has been largely ignored in America. Most Liberians are aware of their country's connection to America, but few Americans know or understand their country's role in the history of Liberia.

The Major letters from Liberia—combined with extensive research—provide a unique glimpse into colonization and its impact on both the emancipators and the emancipated. This book tells the story of real people on two continents who faced tough choices, grueling circumstances, disease, hardships, loss, and death.

It is a tale worth telling.

Author's Note

A few notes about the choices I've made in writing this book: In historical documents, the names Major and Harlan are spelled in various ways, including Majors, Magers, and Magor, and Harland, Harlin, and Horland. For consistency, I have used "Major" and "Harlan" throughout the book, except in quotations from original sources. Many enslaved people were given the surnames of their owners. I have included charts that may help readers understand family relationships.

Language changes over time; what is considered correct in one decade may be inappropriate in another. I've used "black people" to refer to people of African descent and avoided "Negro" or "colored" except when quoting another source. I've avoided "African American" because one definition for the term is a citizen of the United States who is of African ancestry. Enslaved people were denied citizenship. And because this book is about people who were descended from Africans, but born in the United States, and who then migrated to Africa to live among indigenous Africans, I thought use of the term might be confusing. I've also avoided terms such as "natives" and "savages" to describe the indigenous people of Africa, except when quoting other sources.

Another note on terminology: Nineteenth-century Americans made a sharp distinction between those who advocated for the *abolition* of slavery and those who supported *emancipation* of enslaved people. Abolitionists wanted an immediate and complete end to slavery and sought to outlaw it across the United States. Emancipationists typically advocated for a more gradual end to slavery. Abolition would apply to all enslaved people; emancipation applied to one person or group of people at a time.

When quoting from the letters in the main body of the book, I have inserted missing words and corrected some spelling and punctuation to facilitate reading. I did not alter the grammar. In the appendix, however, I've reproduced the complete text of each letter in as close a form as possible to the original.

My primary objective is to tell the story of Ben Major, his family, and the formerly enslaved Major and Harlan families. Their story cannot be told outside the context of slavery, the colonization movement, the history of Liberia, and the religious beliefs of those involved. However, this book is not intended to be a comprehensive account of slavery in the United States, nor is it a history of the American Colonization Society, Liberia, or the Christian Church (Disciples of Christ). I've included an extensive bibliography for readers who want to learn more about these topics.

Finally, although this is a story about real people and real events, I have taken the liberty of recreating scenes, particularly at the start of several chapters, based on facts and historical documentation.

Major Family Chart

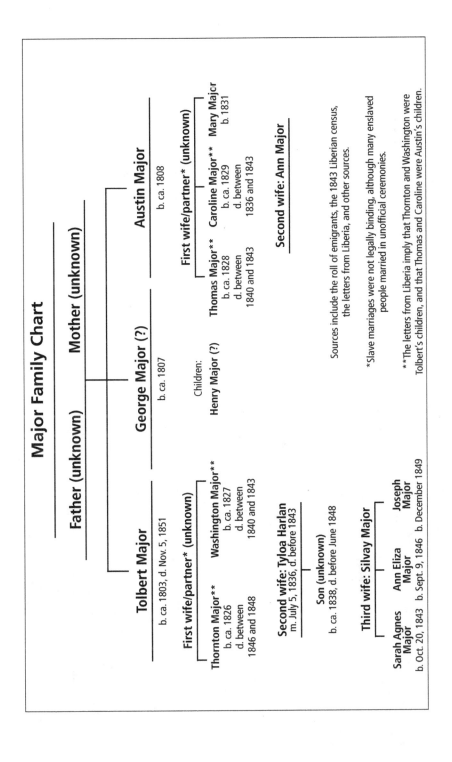

Father (unknown)   **Mother (unknown)**

Tolbert Major
b. ca. 1803, d. Nov. 5, 1851

George Major (?)
b. ca. 1807

Austin Major
b. ca. 1808

First wife/partner* (unknown)

Thornton Major**
b. ca. 1826
d. between
1846 and 1848

Washington Major**
b. ca. 1827
d. between
1840 and 1843

Second wife: Tyloa Harlan
m. July 5, 1836, d. before 1843

Son (unknown)
b. ca. 1838, d. before June 1848

Third wife: Silvay Major

Sarah Agnes Major
b. Oct. 20, 1843

Ann Eliza Major
b. Sept. 9, 1846

Joseph Major
b. December 1849

Children:

Henry Major (?)

First wife/partner* (unknown)

Thomas Major**
b. ca. 1828
d. between
1840 and 1843

Caroline Major**
b. ca. 1829
d. between
1836 and 1843

Mary Major
b. 1831

Second wife: Ann Major

Sources include the roll of emigrants, the 1843 Liberian census, the letters from Liberia, and other sources.

*Slave marriages were not legally binding, although many enslaved people married in unofficial ceremonies.

**The letters from Liberia imply that Thornton and Washington were Tolbert's children, and that Thomas and Caroline were Austin's children.

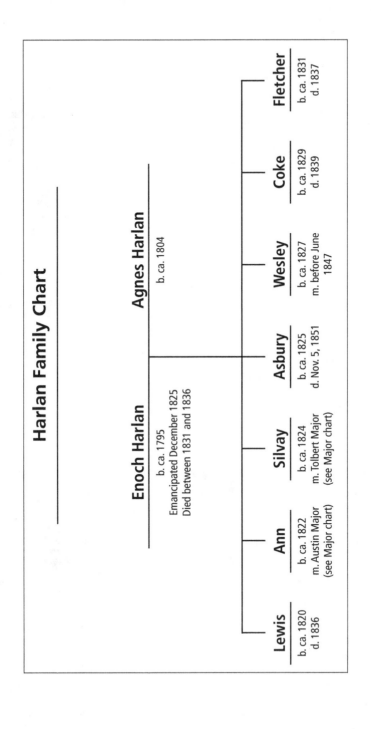

Harlan Family Chart

Enoch Harlan
b. ca. 1795
Emancipated December 1825
Died between 1831 and 1836

Agnes Harlan
b. ca. 1804

Lewis
b. ca. 1820
d. 1836

Ann
b. ca. 1822
m. Austin Major
(see Major chart)

Silvay
b. ca. 1824
m. Tolbert Major
(see Major chart)

Asbury
b. ca. 1825
d. Nov. 5, 1851

Wesley
b. ca. 1827
m. before June
1847

Coke
b. ca. 1829
d. 1839

Fletcher
b. ca. 1831
d. 1837

Ben Major (Former Slave Owner) Family Chart

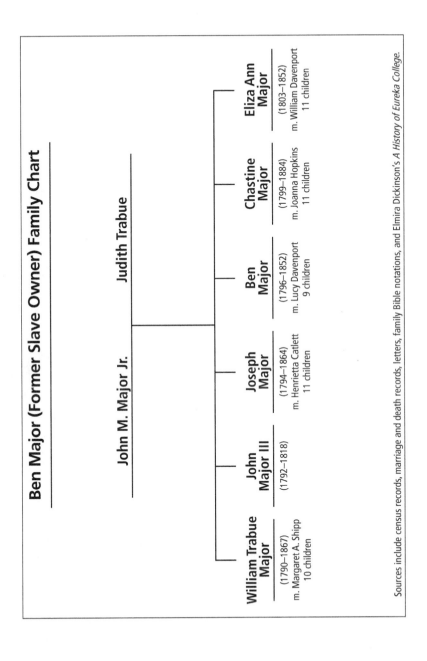

John M. Major Jr.   Judith Trabue

William Trabue Major

(1790–1867)
m. Margaret A. Shipp
10 children

John Major III

(1792–1818)

Joseph Major

(1794–1864)
m. Henrietta Catlett
11 children

Ben Major

(1796–1852)
m. Lucy Davenport
9 children

Chastine Major

(1799–1884)
m. Joanna Hopkins
11 children

Eliza Ann Major

(1803–1852)
m. William Davenport
11 children

Sources include census records, marriage and death records, letters, family Bible notations, and Elmira Dickinson's *A History of Eureka College.*

May I But Safely Reach My Home

Tolbert Major woke at dawn on his last day in America. The sun cast a lavender and peach glow across the cotton curtain in his room at the Staten Island Quarantine Center. Tolbert sat up in his cot and stretched, and then—whispering—woke his sons, Thornton, ten, and Washington, nine. They crept silently across the large room, weaving between the beds of dozens of other sleeping men and boys. They descended the back stairs and headed across the yard to the outhouse. When they finished, Tolbert sent the boys back to wake their uncle and cousins, and he ambled down to the pier.

The brig *Luna* rocked gently at anchor in the bay. Her two masts, wrapped in tightly furled sails and jibs, soared into the pink-tinged sky, and rigging spider-webbed across the vessel. On deck, the crew prepared to set sail for Africa on the afternoon tide.

Tolbert waved to one of men, and then, feeling the need to stretch his legs, he strolled around the quarantine grounds. The walled compound included twenty white frame and brick buildings, wide expanses of grass, a long wooden pier, and a beautiful view. Signs such as "Smallpox House" exposed the center's true purpose, however, and Tolbert did not venture close to the other buildings. None of the formerly enslaved or freeborn black people preparing to board the *Luna* were ill, but New York's mayor had housed them in a vacant building at the quarantine grounds until everyone in their group had arrived.[1]

As Tolbert walked, memories tumbled through his mind: topping tobacco plants in a Kentucky field, the long trip from Hopkinsville to the Northeast, and the smell of the crowds and horses in New York City. He thought, too, of the long voyage ahead of them and the promise of a new life.

By the time Tolbert returned to the building where he had slept, the rest of the emigrants were up. He and his sons carried their gear down to the pier. He spotted his brother, his nephews, and his niece. Agnes Harlan, their former neighbor in Kentucky, her kids, and Tyloa Harlan were already at the pier.

Seventy other people waited with the Majors and Harlans to board the *Luna*. Tolbert saw the Haynes family—John, a free black man from Nicholasville, Kentucky; his wife, Mary; and their children. Rachel and Robert Buchner approached, trailed by their large family. He spotted the Donelsons, formerly enslaved people from a Tennessee plantation just across the state line from the Major farm. Some of them talked and laughed; a few wiped away tears; others stared silently at the water, their thoughts already at sea. They all breathed deeply of the tangy salt air and tried to remain calm.[2]

Tolbert knew that the colonization movement, launched twenty years earlier, was controversial. Some people—black and white—supported the movement and its goals; others stood in fierce opposition. Still, he was convinced that going to Africa was right for him and his family. He recalled a scripture from the book of Micah about sitting quietly under a vine and fig tree; maybe he could find that kind of peace.

He eyed the piles of belongings: clothing, shovels and hammers, pots and pans, a rolled quilt, a straw hat. He, his brother, and their children had more possessions than they had ever owned. Joseph Major, their former owner's brother, had seen to it that each of them had two complete outfits of new clothes, plus the basic supplies they would need. Some of the white ladies from the New York Colonization Society had stitched up even more clothes for the emigrants. The men of the colonization society had collected spades, rakes, hoes, building materials, and crates of books for a library.[3]

G. W. McElroy, the colonization agent who had brought them from Kentucky to New York, had told Tolbert that folks in New York and Pennsylvania had donated four hundred volumes for the settlers. Tolbert knew how to read; he wasn't fast, but maybe now that he wasn't a slave he would have time to finish a whole book.

The previous day—July 4, 1836, America's sixtieth birthday—had been glorious. That morning, Tolbert had watched the steamer *Bolivar* make its way across the bay from Manhattan. When it docked at the quarantine grounds, several well-dressed white ladies and gentlemen, including the managing board and executive committee of the New York Colonization Society, had disembarked. Everyone funneled into one of the large public buildings on the grounds.

At ten o'clock, a send-off ceremony started with a spirited rendition of an old hymn. Those gathered harmonized on the final verse.

> Let cares, like a wild deluge come,
> And storms of sorrow fall!
> May I but safely reach my home,
> My God, my heav'n, my all.[4]

The Methodist Episcopal minister offered an opening prayer and then introduced Dr. Alexander Proudfit of the New York Colonization Society.[5]

"The moment for which you have been anxiously longing has at length arrived," Dr. Proudfit intoned. "You are now embarking for the land which must be dear to you, as it contains the sepulchers and venerated ashes of your forefathers."[6]

Tolbert didn't know what to think about that. Yes, his ancestors were born in Africa, but that was a long time ago. Master Ben Major had told them that Africans led lives very different from their own. What would it be like there?

"We will probably never see you again in the flesh," Dr. Proudfit continued. "We will always rejoice to hear of your prosperity and joy, and be ready to sympathize with you in whatever afflictions you may be called to endure. Recollect at the same time, that your situation is highly and awfully responsible; the results of your future behavior are unspeakably interesting to us, to your colored brethren whom you leave behind, and to the unnumbered millions in Africa."

Tolbert liked Dr. Proudfit. The minister had visited them on Staten Island several times and seemed genuinely interested in their welfare. Still, the man could go on. He exhorted them to work hard, obey the laws of the colony, avoid hard drink, and be strictly upright in all their dealings with the Africans.

"With these few instructions, beloved friends, we bid you an affectionate farewell. Be perfect, be of good comfort, be of one mind, live in peace. May the One whose voice the winds and waves obey protect you on the mighty deep. Amen."

Two other white ministers then stepped up and prayed over the assemblage. Finally, Reverend Amos Herring, a former slave from Virginia, stood. He prayed for safe passage and God's guidance in their new venture before leading the gathering in a closing hymn.[7]

The pomp and ceremony ended, and the building emptied quickly. Most of the white visitors trekked back down the sloping lawns to the pier, the ladies' full skirts sweeping the grass. They boarded the *Bolivar* and, with cheery waves to those on shore, they steamed back home to Manhattan, their families, and afternoon plans.

The black people who had attended the ceremony—the Majors, Harlans, and others who were migrating to Liberia—stayed at the quarantine grounds. They spent the afternoon washing and packing clothes and other supplies. In the evening, they shared a meal. That night, fireworks splashed across the sky, and cannon and musket shots reverberated as New Yorkers celebrated Independence Day. Children, weary from the day's excitement, crawled into the laps of nearby adults and fell asleep.

At mid-morning the next day, Captain Hallet stepped to the *Luna*'s rail and hollered, "Permission to board!" The brig's crew made trip after trip in small boats, ferrying supplies, baggage, and passengers to the waiting ship. As Tolbert and the others stepped aboard, the adults gave their names, ages, occupations, and family information to a colonization society clerk. They stowed their belongings and the children scampered off to explore the ship.[8]

G. W. McElroy and Dr. Proudfit boarded the vessel, too. They chatted with passengers, offered last-minute advice, and checked to make sure all was well. Reverend Herring, the group's de facto leader, boarded the *Luna* with his wife, Leonora, and their little girl, Mary. It wasn't his first trip to Liberia. He had scouted the West African colony three years earlier.[9]

Reverend Herring and Dr. Proudfit cobbled together a makeshift altar on the brig's quarterdeck, led some prayers and hymns, and preached a little more. Tolbert listened impatiently. He had other business to attend to. Finally, the ceremonies ended with a fervent "Amen!" Tolbert glanced across the deck and caught Tyloa's eye. He wove through the crowd of passengers, trailed by his sons. They stepped over and around bundles until they reached her side. Tolbert smiled and took her hand.

They had talked about this the night before, under a dark sky dazzled by fireworks. Now the couple and Tolbert's sons made their way back to the quarterdeck, where Tolbert and Tyloa stood before Dr. Proudfit. The minister, in a simple ceremony, joined the smiling pair in marriage. The other

VIEW OF THE MARINE HOSPITAL AND QUARANTINE GROUNDS, STATEN ISLAND, NEW YORK.

Tolbert and Austin Major, Agnes Harlan, and dozens of other immigrants bound for Liberia were housed at the Staten Island Quarantine Grounds until the entire group was gathered and ready to set sail. (Brown and Quinlin, Library of Congress, Prints and Photographs Division, LC-DIG-pga-00331)

passengers let out a lusty cheer, and even the usually staid Mr. McElroy beamed.[10]

Five o'clock neared, and with it the afternoon tide. Mr. McElroy, Dr. Proudfit, and a few others disembarked the *Luna* by descending a rope ladder and stepped into a smaller craft. They turned, waved to the vessel's passengers, and shouted "Farewell" and "God bless you!"

G. W. McElroy, the colonization society agent, stepped out of the rowboat and back onto the pier at the quarantine grounds. He turned and watched the *Luna's* crew weigh anchor. It was a new beginning for those on board, but an ending of sorts for him. He had labored for months to rescue these men, women, and children from slavery—many of them from his native state of Kentucky.

McElroy thought about all those years he had supported the abolitionist cause. He had become frustrated as years passed with no progress toward ending the wicked practice of slavery and had finally turned to the cause of colonization. It seemed the best compromise, though he would have preferred to see slavery end altogether. He had signed on as an agent for the New York Colonization Society, but before he could put his full support behind the cause, he had wanted to see the colony for himself.

As he watched the *Luna*'s crew, he remembered the day more than a year earlier when he had boarded a similar ship filled with people bound for Liberia. He had spent several months in the colony and concluded that colonization was a holy cause. Even a bout of malaria hadn't dampened his enthusiasm. In a letter to the editor of the *New York Commercial Advertiser*, McElroy wrote, "My zeal for Africa is by no means cooled, nor ever will be, I trust, until my head is buried in the dust . . . for Africa, I hope to live, and labor, and pray."[11]

When McElroy had returned to the United States, he headed to Kentucky to secure passengers for the society's next departing ship. He spoke numerous times throughout the state and met with supporters, free black people, slave owners, and others interested in learning about colonization. He even published a notice in the Louisville newspaper announcing the next planned expedition.[12]

After months of hard work and planning, McElroy secured freedom and a chance to migrate for fifty-six enslaved people. Ben Major and George Harlan of Christian County, Kentucky, and several other Kentucky slave owners freed their people for colonization, as did the estates of Alexander Donelson (Andrew Jackson's brother-in-law) and Peter Fisher of Tennessee.[13]

For enslaved people, being freed through a master's will wasn't a sure thing. The Fisher slaves had had to go to court to secure the freedom promised by their late owner. The Chancery Court of Carthage, Tennessee, ruled that, if freed, the Fisher slaves would not only have to leave the state, they would have to migrate to Liberia.[14]

Finally, in early summer, McElroy and his charges had set off from rural southwestern Kentucky and traveled up the Cumberland River to the Ohio River, then on to Pittsburgh. McElroy was still angry about the disaster that had occurred in Pittsburgh. While he met with members of the city's clergy to solicit supplies, local abolitionists had lured away fourteen of his charges—four of the Fishers and ten of the Donelsons—and convinced them that they would be better off staying in America. A few of the Donelsons changed their minds and later rejoined the group bound for Liberia, but the others had vanished.

The colonization agent was indignant and dismayed. The absconders put him in a bad spot, but it was worse for the estates of the former slave owners. The administrators of Donelson's estate had signed a $5,000 bond to ensure that, if freed, the slaves would go to Liberia. Administrators for Fisher's estate had signed a similar bond for $3,000. The estates now stood to lose that money. The situation could be worse yet for those who had left the party in Pittsburgh. Because they had not met the required conditions, they legally could be returned to slavery if they were caught.

McElroy had chartered a boat to take the group on to Philadelphia from Pittsburgh. From there, they traveled to New York City and finally Staten Island.

He broke from his thoughts and patted his jacket pocket. He still carried an $800 draft for supplies for the Donelsons and a $400 draft for the Fishers, neither of which could be cashed because some of the people for whom the money was intended were not emigrating. He would have to return the uncashed drafts to the executors of the Donelson and Fisher estates. He sighed and wondered how those Donelsons who had boarded the ship would manage without their supply money.

McElroy watched the *Luna*'s crew unfurl thousands of square yards of canvas. The sails snapped and popped in the wind. Soon the brig skimmed a smooth path across the bay and out to sea. By God, it was a handsome craft! It walked the waters like a thing of life.[15]

The Majors, Harlans, and some of the other passengers were experienced river travelers, but their voyage on the *Luna* was their first on the open sea. As the brig glided through the bay, they had only a short time to become accustomed to the feel of the deck moving beneath their feet, the sensation of pitch and sway. The *Luna* broke into open water, and the waves became choppier and deeper—rising, falling, rolling, surging. Before long, the undulating swells triggered almost universal seasickness. One traveler recalled a similar voyage: "Some dropped on deck, some slid below, some groaned, some tried to brave it out with a laugh . . . but all joined in a general regurgitation."[16]

Most of the passengers were not yet thirty; many of the adults were single parents. About a third of the passengers were children, including three babies. The oldest person on board was a woman said to be more than a hundred years old; she was with the Donelsons. A New York reporter had interviewed her on the Fourth of July and asked her about the risk of such a long voyage at her age. She responded, "My children and my grandchildren are going, and I must go, too; and if I die before I get there or after I reach Africa, the road from heaven is as short from there as from here."[17]

Within a day or two, most of the passengers gained their sea legs and settled into a routine that would last for several weeks. Those who had been enslaved were grateful for the luxury of controlling their own time after a life spent doing the bidding of others. Mothers and fathers entertained the children by telling stories and playing games. Those who were literate read the Bible or other books. They shared meals, sewed, and gossiped. In quiet moments, some of the adults prayed, asking God if they had made the right decision. They speculated about what they would find in Africa; more than one of them imagined the horrific voyages their ancestors had taken in the opposite direction.

One morning, the old woman didn't awaken. With tears and prayers, her family slid her body over the rail and consigned her to the sea.[18]

Newlyweds Tolbert and Tyloa tried to steal moments of privacy aboard the crowded vessel. They stood on the deck at night, talking softly and watching the constellations shift as they journeyed across the watery expanse.

Every sunset left behind loved ones and everything else that was familiar. Every sunrise tugged them eastward toward a new life.

2

Slavery and the
Troublesome Question

The story of the Liberian colonists and their long journey to freedom had started decades earlier, as Americans struggled with the thorny issue of slavery. By the early 1800s, slavery was embedded in America's culture and economy. Laws known as slave codes controlled the status and acceptable treatment of enslaved people and the rights of slave owners. Enslaved people could not own property, enter into contracts, testify against white people in court, legally marry, physically defend themselves, or vote. In most southern states, laws prohibited them from learning to read and write. They could not gather unless a white person was present. They could not associate with free black people. Most were not allowed to leave their owner's property without permission.

Former slave and abolitionist Frederick Douglass said, "The condition of a slave is that of the brute beast. . . . he is as much a piece of property as a horse."[1]

Former slave Henry H. Garnett described slavery in more graphic terms:

Brave men . . . are bartered, sold, and mortgaged. Stripped of every sacred right, they are scourged if they affirm that they belong to God. Women . . . are yoked with the cattle to till the soil, and their heartstrings are torn to pieces by cruel separation from their children. Our sisters . . . are unprotected from the lust of tyrants. They have a regard for virtue, and they possess a sense of honor, but there is no respect paid to these jewels of noble character. Driven into unwilling concubinage, their offspring are

sold by their Anglo-Saxon fathers. . . . Our young men are bru-
talized . . . they are called to witness the agonies of the mothers
who bore them, writhing under the lash.[2]

Over the years, northern states had abolished slavery. In 1808, the
United States banned the importation of enslaved people. In the South,
however, slavery continued. Farmers used enslaved people to work cotton, tobacco, hemp, indigo, sugar, and rice crops. Southern state legislatures
had adopted the principle of *partus sequitur ventrum*—any child born to an
enslaved woman was a slave from birth, swelling the number of enslaved
people. The slave trade continued. Ships brought captives from Africa to
Cuba, the Caribbean, Central and South America, and sometimes (ille-
gally) into the United States.

The battle over slavery escalated; emotions ran high; positions became
polarized. Those who supported slavery employed a range of arguments,
including social, cultural, economic, and political arguments. They clutched
Bibles and intoned Old Testament passages and Colossians 3:22: "Servants,
obey in all things your masters." At the bottom of most proslavery arguments lurked culturally embedded racism and a gut-wrenching fear of free
black people.

As enslaved people were freed or bought their own freedom, the number of free black people in the United States increased dramatically, growing to about 230,000 by 1820. Although this number represented less than
3 percent of the total American population, many white men worried that
free black people would cause trouble, incite enslaved people to rebel, take
jobs and houses from poor white people, and—perhaps their deepest fear—
have sex with white women. They ignored the fact that rape and sexual
assault of enslaved people by white men was common.[3]

Those who opposed slavery also used a range of arguments, many of
which had a moral or religious component. Arguments about ending slavery differed in proposed implementation: some people supported a scheme
of gradual emancipation, while others supported immediate abolition of
slavery. Very few white people, though, even zealous abolitionists, supported equal rights for black people. Most of the white population of the
South believed that it was impossible for them to peacefully live side by
side with free black people.

Thomas Jefferson shared those views. "Nothing is more certainly written in the book of fate than that these people are to be free; nor is it less certain that the two races, equally free, cannot live in the same government,"

he wrote in 1821. "Nature, habit, opinion have drawn indelible lines of distinction between them."[4]

Slave owners who concluded that slavery was wrong faced a dilemma—how to divest themselves of enslaved people. Some owners sold their slaves. This relieved the owner of his guilt and his responsibility for them, but, of course, left the slaves in bondage. Other slave owners vowed to keep their enslaved people, treat them fairly, and free them in their wills. Some states outlawed these so-called testamentary manumissions. In some cases, heirs—unwilling to watch their inheritance walk away—challenged such wills in court, resulting in drawn-out legal disputes during which the slaves remained enslaved. Some southern states passed laws making it difficult or even illegal for slave owners to free their people.[5]

And although most enslaved people ached for emancipation, freedom brought its own set of problems. Free black people lived a betwixt-and-between kind of life, laboring as farmers, seamstresses, bakers, barbers, carpenters, and in other semiskilled or unskilled occupations. They faced many of the same restrictions that constrained their enslaved brethren. They could not associate with enslaved people or white people, assemble in groups, testify against white people in court, or vote. Even many northern states passed laws severely restricting the lives of free black people.[6]

"They are not slaves, yet they are not free," said Henry Clay. "The laws, it is true, proclaim them free; but prejudices more powerful than the laws deny them the privileges of free men."[7]

"What to do with the free Negro was a troublesome question in many minds," historian J. Winston Coleman wrote almost a century later. "To turn him loose upon society without means of support was a grave mistake."[8]

Colonization—sending free black people to live elsewhere—was one attempt to address that "troublesome question." In the decades between the Revolutionary War and the Civil War, people across the United States discussed colonization in parlors and on front porches. Newspapers reported regularly on the colonization movement, and editors vigorously debated the pros and cons. Americans discussed colonization in houses of worship and in both houses of Congress. Many prominent men in society and politics supported colonization to varying degrees. They included Thomas Jefferson, Daniel Webster, John Calhoun, James Monroe, James Madison, Francis Scott Key, the Marquis de Lafayette, and Henry Clay.[9]

Slavery was the most divisive issue in American history. For decades before the Civil War, there were calls for dissolution of the Union over slavery. The debate intensified, antislavery and proslavery positions solidified, the number of free black people increased, and colonization became more appealing to many people.[10]

In the last days of 1816, a group of white men, many of them slave owners, met in Washington, D.C., and founded the American Colonization Society. The group was a private venture, not a government agency. Their stated purpose was "to promote and execute a plan for colonizing (with their consent) the free people of color residing in our country, in Africa, or such other places as Congress shall deem most expedient."[11]

Organizers carefully skirted the issues of slavery and its abolition. Henry Clay, who chaired the inaugural meeting, stated, "No attempt was being made to touch or agitate in the slightest degree, a delicate question, connected with another portion of the colored population of this country. It was not proposed to deliberate upon or consider at all, any question of emancipation, or that which was connected with the abolition of slavery."[12]

In Kentucky, many people supported schemes for gradual emancipation, often with the stipulation that the formerly enslaved people leave the state. A Cincinnati newspaper reported on a convention held in May 1835 in Shelbyville, Kentucky. One of the resolutions from the meeting read, in part, "Any scheme of emancipation that will leave the blacks within our borders is more to be deprecated than slavery itself."[13]

Throughout its history, the American Colonization Society emphasized voluntary emigration and did not deport or exile individuals to Liberia. The phrase "with their consent" is part of the organization's founding documents. However, many slave owners and some state and local governments did make emancipation conditional on emigration. The Fishers and Donelsons were bound by such conditions—free only if they left the United States and migrated to Liberia.[14]

Colonization supporters—known as colonizationists—held a range of views on slavery, and they had a mix of motives for sending black people to Africa. Many believed that free black people would become a bad element in American society. Some felt that colonization might redress the sin of slavery and assuage white guilt over having enslaved generations of Africans. Some slave owners welcomed colonization as a means of ridding themselves of enslaved people who were difficult to control or those who had reached the end of their most productive years.

Other colonizationists felt that such a colony would help "civilize" Africans and convert them to Christianity. (Of course, Africa had had large cities and complex civilizations for centuries and Christianity had reached parts of the "dark continent" long before it reached the shores of North

America.) Some colonizationists believed that if black people from America settled on the African coast, their presence would interrupt the slave trade and encourage other channels of trade between America and Africa.

Those white people who supported colonization out of the best intentions believed that black people would be safer and have better opportunities in Africa than they did in the United States—that colonization offered them a fresh start and a new life.

After a colonization society meeting in 1833, John H. Latrobe wrote, "At that meeting it became apparent that Colonization had two sets of friends, who supported it from motives diametrically opposed to each other."[15]

Some enslaved and freeborn black people supported colonization and held a romanticized notion of returning to the land of their ancestors. Many more black people were skeptical of the society's motives and repelled by the notion of colonization. Some opposed it because they believed it undercut attempts at reform within the United States and distracted from the struggle for freedom. Some were concerned that the most educated and financially stable black people would choose to leave, creating what today would be called a brain drain. Others felt that they shouldn't have to leave the country of their birth, particularly since many of them had fought alongside white men during the American Revolution and the War of 1812.

Years later, Frederick Douglass wrote, "I feel that the black man in this land has as much right to stay in this land as the white man. . . . Some of our number have fought and bled for this country. . . . We are *here*, and here we are likely to remain."[16]

Colonization was a compromise—a compromise born of frustration over the seemingly intractable slavery issue and the growing population of free black people. Nevertheless, society agents were dispatched to West Africa to buy land along the coastline for a settlement. The die was cast.

The first colonization ship, the *Elizabeth*, sailed from New York in January 1820 to the colony established at Cape Mesurado. Soon other small settlements were established, and in 1824 the colony was named Liberia, from the Latin for "free."

For ninety-three years, until 1913, the American Colonization Society supported emigration of formerly enslaved people and freeborn black people from the United States to Liberia, ultimately transporting sixteen thousand people across the ocean. It was the largest out-migration in American history.[17]

3

People of Culture and Refinement

Ben Major—the man who had owned and then freed Tolbert, Austin, and their families—had wavy dark hair, thick brows, and expressive eyes. In surviving images of him, his tie is always slightly askew.

By the late summer of 1834, Ben had a wife, a house full of children, a large tobacco farm in Kentucky, several enslaved people, and a tough decision to make. Ben came from a long line of slave owners—at least three generations back—but he wanted to be done with what he called the "curses of slavery." He was ready to renounce it, despite the financial loss and social censure he and his family would face.[1]

Ben was the third son of wealthy farmer John Major Jr. and his wife, Judith Trabue Major. When Ben was born in 1796, the family lived in Kentucky's Bluegrass region, near Frankfort. Farmers in the area raised livestock and grew corn, tobacco, and flax. They wove cloth and sent the surplus, along with other farm products, down the Ohio River to New Orleans. These large farms required a lot of labor and most plantation owners, including John Major, his parents, and his mother-in-law, owned slaves. In addition to field hands, the Majors likely had black household slaves and a "mammy," an enslaved woman who cared for the children.[2]

As part of the plantation class, the Major family led privileged lives. Theirs was a world defined by wealth, acreage, slaveholdings, education, gentility, social position, honor, and connections to power. Private tutors provided Ben and his siblings with an excellent education to prepare them to take their places in that world.[3]

In 1810, Ben's older brother, eighteen-year-old John Major III, started his career in business. He moved to New Orleans to operate a mercantile

Ben Major (1796–1852) was the son of John M. Major Jr. and Judith Trabue. Though descended from a long line of slave owners, Ben decided in his late thirties that he was done with slavery. He freed his enslaved people and they migrated to Liberia. (Major Family Private Collection)

store selling his father's crops and other goods. John likely journeyed to New Orleans by flatboat. River travel was dangerous for many reasons, including the risk of capsized boats, illnesses, and attacks from Native Americans or river pirates. John knew about the dangers. Several years earlier, the Harpe brothers, notorious river pirates and serial murderers, had slaughtered his twelve-year-old cousin John Trabue.[4]

The flatboat, loaded with supplies, the crew, John, and the other passengers would have headed down the Ohio River to where it merged with the Mississippi. They would have floated past Chickasaw Bluffs (the future site of Memphis), past the site of old Fort Nogales, and through land occupied by the Chocktaw, Yazoo, and Natchez. The flatboat likely docked at the port of Natchez-Under-the-Hill to unload and load cargo before continuing to Baton Rouge and then New Orleans, a city of fewer than 18,000 people.[5]

A year later, when Ben was fifteen, he followed John to New Orleans to help run the store. The two brothers operated the business for several years, including during the historic Battle of New Orleans, the final major battle in the War of 1812.

John and Ben sold the goods their father shipped downriver from Kentucky. In 1818, numerous ads in English and French appeared in the *Louisiana State Gazette* for John Major & Co. store.[6] The brothers worked in town and along the wharves daily. They breathed the waterfront stench, heard the babble of dozens of languages, and mingled with buyers, sellers, dockworkers, and visitors from around the world. Livestock, crops, cloth, liquor, furniture, manufactured goods, and more flowed in and out of the Crescent City.

Human beings were one of the commodities bought and sold in New Orleans. The city was the site of the continent's largest slave market. Buyers made their way to the slave pens and auction blocks, where sales surged between November and April. In private showrooms or at public auctions held on Saturday, buyers could purchase field hands, semiskilled or skilled workers, drivers, cooks, maids, seamstresses, mammies to care for children, and "fancy girls" to fulfill men's fantasies. Prospective buyers prodded, stripped, and ogled the men, women, and children offered as merchandise—carefully inspecting "the goods" to drive a hard bargain. Roughly a third of those sold into servitude were children.[7]

In a world defined by race, white society created a special language to indicate degrees of blackness: black, dark-skinned, brown-skinned, mulatto, quadroon, copper, yellow, bright, octoroon. White buyers believed—or pretended to believe—that enslaved people were merely another form of livestock. They coined the word "mulatto" from "mule," the offspring of a horse and a donkey.[8]

It was a particularly brutal side of slavery—one that Ben had likely been protected from on his family farm in Kentucky, but one he would see daily over the next few years.

While the two brothers were far away in Louisiana, their mother died. After Judith's death, her husband, John, moved his other children and his enslaved people about two hundred miles southwest from Frankfort to Christian County, Kentucky. There he built a new home south of the county seat of Hopkinsville. Perhaps John, in his grief, wanted a fresh start, or maybe he embraced the opportunity to purchase acreage not yet exhausted by farming.[9]

John's new home, near the Tennessee state line, was on beautiful, lush land drained by the winding Little River. One local historian wrote, "It is the crookedest stream perhaps in the world, and flows to every point of the compass, sometimes within the distance of a mile."[10]

John's three other sons, William and Joseph, in their twenties, and Chastine, in his late teens, worked alongside him and the family's enslaved people. They built a large, two-story redbrick home, a smokehouse, and

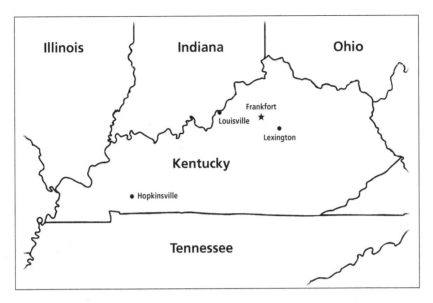

Ben Major was born in Frankfort, Kentucky. He later established a farm in Christian County, just south of Hopkinsville and north of the Tennessee state line.

other outbuildings. They cleared and planted fields, socialized with their neighbors, and settled in, becoming part of the community.

On sultry summer mornings, the enslaved people and early risers in the big house watched wisps of mist drift over the Little River. In the fall, the oak, maple, and hickory trees blazed with brilliant foliage, littering the ground with leaves. Winter brought occasional snowfalls and ice storms, and stark white sycamore trees stretched bony arms skyward. In spring, vivid green leaves burst from the trees, and clouds of white dogwood flowers and rosy redbud brightened the woods.

The Majors took their corn and wheat crops to nearby Lindsey's Mill to be ground into meal and flour. They ate grits, corn bread and biscuits, venison, fish, rabbit, an occasional country ham, sweet potatoes, greens, wild plums, and berries. They grew food crops and a kitchen garden. However, the county's main cash crop was tobacco; successful production was labor-intensive and required many hands.

In the late summer of 1818, a yellow fever epidemic broke out in New Orleans and young John Major fell ill. After battling fever, chills, muscle pain, and jaundice caused by liver damage, he finally succumbed. Ben buried his older brother in New Orleans.

Ben's father, still grieving the loss of his wife and now faced with his son's death, wrote to Ben, pleading, "Return to Kentucky. I wish you to come and live with us; our family is small. Your brothers and sister are anxious, as well as myself, for you to quit New Orleans."[11]

Ben heeded his father's advice and returned to his home state. However, before going to Christian County, he visited his old neighborhood near Frankfort. Maybe he wanted to visit friends and family in the area, or perhaps he already had an eye on eighteen-year-old Lucy Ann Davenport.

Though young, Lucy had already faced several personal tragedies. She was the youngest of five children. Lucy never knew her father, Jonas Davenport; he had died shortly before she was born in 1802. Her three older sisters had died in childhood. When Lucy was twelve, her mother, Alice Redd Davenport, died, leaving Lucy and her brother, William, orphaned. A sympathetic aunt took in the children and raised them.

William Davenport married Ben Major's only sister, sixteen-year-old Eliza Ann, in 1819, and Ben and Lucy married in early 1820 in Christian County. Ben and William became double brothers-in-law and Lucy and Eliza, double sisters-in-law.[12]

Ben and Lucy settled in Christian County. They built a comfortable brick home west of Ben's father's house, started a family, and established a successful farm. But Ben's increasing unease over slavery would ultimately change his life, the lives of his family, and the lives of his enslaved people forever.[13]

4

Serious Doubts on the Slavery Question

By 1820, Ben, his father, and his brothers William and Joseph owned a total of twenty-nine people. When John Major died the following year, his sons inherited his slaves along with land, a home, and family heirlooms. By 1830, Ben, his brothers, and brother-in-law held a total of fifty people in enslavement, far more than the average five or six owned by other individual Kentucky slave owners.[1]

From 1810 to 1860, enslaved people comprised between 20 and 24 percent of Kentucky's population. Most of them lived in the Bluegrass region around Lexington, in the Louisville area, and in southwestern Kentucky. In Christian County, a much higher percentage of the population—almost half—was enslaved. Only in the southwestern part of the state did slavery seem to be an economic necessity because of the need for labor on large tobacco farms.[2]

But Ben harbored strong misgivings about slavery.[3]

"From his childhood, he had serious doubts on the slavery question, and with such doubts, made the subject one continuous study," recalled Elmira Dickinson, a friend of the Majors. "As he reached mature years, these doubts were swept away, and he became convinced that the entire system was radically wrong; and being a man who acted upon his own convictions of what his particular duty was to his God and fellow men, he marked out a course and matured plans."[4]

Ben's experience in New Orleans and his evolving understanding of the underlying brutality inherent in slavery hastened his decision to free his people. His faith was undoubtedly a factor in his decision, too. His parents had raised him in the Baptist church, but he became an early convert to the newly formed Christian Church (Disciples of Christ). Its members believed in inclusion and education. They emphasized the teachings of the New Testament and urged a return to the basics, to a "primitive" form of Christianity. Members were called Disciples.[5] Both of the denomination's founders—Barton W. Stone and Alexander Campbell—opposed slavery. Stone saw no biblical justification for the practice and freed his own enslaved people, saying, "I have emancipated my slaves from a sense of right, choosing poverty with a good conscience, in preference to all the treasures of the world." Alexander Campbell called slavery "that many-headed monster, that Pandora's box, that bitter root, that blighting and blasting curse."[6]

Driven by his own experiences, his values, and his faith, Ben decided that he was done with slavery. He had followed the national conversation about colonization and decided to free all of his enslaved people and help them migrate to Liberia. He would then leave Kentucky and raise his children in the free state of Illinois. Ben paid $30 to become a life member of the American Colonization Society. He pored over the *African Repository*, the organization's publication, and began to put his plans into action.

"He never once hesitated (although at that time it meant almost financial ruin), but determined not only to liberate and colonize his slaves, but at the same time to liberate himself and his immediate family from even a taint of the curse of slavery," Elmira Dickinson recalled.[7]

When slaveholders freed enslaved people, they lost the financial value of those people, the value of their labor, and the value of any children they might have had.

The logistics of freeing enslaved people for colonization were complex. Ben and other emancipators had to gather information about colonization and Liberia, write to the American Colonization Society or one of the state societies, coordinate emancipations with other slave owners so families could stay together, secure funds for passage and supplies, sometimes persuade enslaved people to emigrate, and move the emigrants to the port of departure. On occasion, they had to go to court to fight local emancipation restrictions.[8]

In 1835, one minister wrote to the American Colonization Society, outlining some of the critical questions would-be emigrants had: "I suppose several respectable families in this state of my acquaintance could be induced to emigrate if everything relating to the Society were known here. They wish to know if the Society will transport them *at its own expense*. . . . Where will they take shipping? What will be the provision for them in the Colony? On what conditions will they obtain land? At what season of the year will they emigrate? Will the Society employ an agent to raise a cargo of emigrants from this part of the country?"[9]

People of the time held strong opinions about slavery, abolition, emancipation, and colonization. Family members and neighbors some-times shunned, denounced, threatened, or even harmed those whose views differed from their own. Virginia colonizationist John Hartwell Cocke received "a frightful beating" because of his viewpoints. A mob comprising hundreds of armed men threatened emancipators Isaac Ross and Margaret Reed of Jefferson County, Mississippi.[10]

At a colonization society meeting in early 1835, Reverend Hunt of North Carolina spoke in favor of the movement. The mood of the meet-ing was captured in an eerily prescient passage: "He could not endure the thought of abandoning or breaking up the Colonization Society. It was their last and only hope in the South. If that should fail—a dark cloud would come over them. It would be final as to the hope of a peaceable extinguishment of slavery. Ultimately, it would come to force. . . . there would be, there could be, no compromise. It would be war to the knife, and the knife to the hilt!"[11]

Some of the Disciples of Christ in Christian County supported Ben's decision, but many of his neighbors would have strongly opposed his views. Two of Ben's brothers, William and Chastine, gave up slavery and also made plans to move to Illinois. However, Ben's brother Joseph decided to remain in Kentucky and continued to own people. The Majors were just one of the tens of thousands of southern families divided over slavery.

Undeterred, Ben moved forward. As part of his multi-year plan for emancipation, he taught his enslaved people to read and write, and pre-pared them in other ways to ease their transition to freedom. The Disciples of Christ felt that literacy was important because it enabled people to read the Bible for themselves. Many colonizationists also supported literacy for free black people because they wanted to hear back from Liberia and letters were the only way to keep in touch.[12]

In the spring of 1831, Ben left his farm in the care of Lucy and his enslaved people, mounted his horse, and headed to central Illinois. There he sought land and a new home for his family. He liked what he found in Tazewell County—prairies and forests along the banks of Walnut Creek. He later returned to Illinois and purchased eighty acres.[13]

Ben started to discuss colonization with his enslaved people. He pro-vided information to them about life in Liberia, based on what he had gleaned from the *African Repository*, and he told them that he was planning to free them. What a mix of emotions they must have felt—surely bone-deep joy and relief, but these were likely tempered by doubt and fear. Most enslaved people had learned better than to trust the word of slave owners when it came to talk of freedom.

They no doubt dreamed of being emancipated, but there is no way to know how they felt about going to Liberia. Elmira Dickinson believed that Tolbert, Austin, and the others were initially reluctant to go. She attributed this to their contentment, rather than to any skepticism about the colonization movement or Liberia. "At first, they absolutely refused to entertain a thought of freedom on any grounds. With a kind and considerate master and mistress, and surrounded by all the comforts of which their ignorant minds could conceive, they had no desire for a change."[14]

Historian J. Winston Coleman wrote in 1941, "While enjoying the benevolent features of Kentucky slavery, many black people were averse to accepting freedom with the stipulation that they be deported to far-off Liberia, where conditions were primitive and life hard and uncertain. They were content, in many cases, to remain in bondage under their present masters, to live among their friends and loved ones, and enjoy the happy surroundings of their birthplace."[15]

The words of Dickinson and Coleman reflect attitudes common among white people at the time—characterizing black people as ignorant and dependent, or worse, lazy and degraded, and slave owners as compassionate and caring. Many Kentuckians told themselves that slavery was somehow milder in their state. Still, it is not impossible to believe that some enslaved people, faced with the choice of moving thousands of miles to an unknown land, might consider staying put, even if that meant remaining in bondage.

Ben knew he could not take enslaved people with him to the family's new home in the free state of Illinois. Illinois's Black Law, passed in 1819, required that anyone bringing a slave into the state with the intention of freeing him or her had to post a $1,000 bond. The Black Law placed numerous restrictions on the rights of free black people, too.[16]

Ben was also reluctant to emancipate his enslaved people in Kentucky. The commonwealth required that all free black people carry papers, which required yearly registration and an annual fee. Free black people could not vote, had no legal redress, and were not allowed to physically defend themselves against violence. They were typically paid far less than white people for the same work, and they were often given the dirtiest and most undesirable jobs. The 1830 census lists fewer than a dozen free people of color in

Christian County. In the entire state, free black people comprised less than 1 percent of the population.[17]

Nor could Ben free his people immediately for migration to Africa. The American Colonization Society did not regularly schedule ships for Liberia, but instead waited until they had enough people committed to the trip before chartering a vessel and hiring a crew.

Eager to get on with his new life, Ben made a tough choice. He asked his brother Joseph to care for his enslaved people until they could be freed for colonization.

Many people who emancipated slaves with the intention of sending them to Liberia hired them out beforehand to help offset the cost of passage and supplies. Ben's enslaved people stayed behind in Kentucky and earned their own money working on neighboring plantations and in other businesses.

Joseph carefully tracked their wages and later reported to Ben that his "three boys" had earned $132, one young boy had earned $27, and two women had earned $15.50.[18]

In September 1834, Ben paid $46 to a Hopkinsville wagon maker to build two wagons for the family's move to Illinois. When the wagons were ready, he and Lucy loaded up all of their household goods and, with their five children, journeyed 380 miles north to their new home. The two older children—John, twelve, and Judith, ten—rode horseback. Lucy, more than seven months pregnant, and the three youngest children—William, eight; Benjamin, six; and little Lucy, two—rode in a buggy.[19]

One writer described the journey from Kentucky to Illinois. "Even in the best of weather, the bumpy roads made riding in wagons and carts unpleasant. After a long day of being tossed up and down and to and fro, travelers retired for the evening, fatigued and suffering from sore muscles. Often, the men and boys escaped the rough ride, but were equally as tired and probably as sore from driving hogs and cattle ahead of the wagons."[20]

Day after day on the trail, Lucy arose from a cocoon of blankets and quilts on the ground, prepared breakfast, fed and dressed the youngest children, loaded them into the buggy, then hoisted herself up to the seat to endure endless miles of jostling. She had left behind the small grave of her daughter Ann Eliza, buried on their family farm. She and Ben kept their eyes focused to the north. Every day, Lucy scanned the sky and prayed that the colder weather would hold off until they reached their destination.

The Majors may have been accompanied by other Christian County families. At least ten other local men also disposed of their enslaved people

Ben Major and his family relocated to central Illinois, settling in the small town of Walnut Grove (now Eureka), located roughly between Peoria and Bloomington.

and moved their families to central Illinois at about the same time. Perhaps Lucy had the company of a beloved neighbor or friend, and her children had playmates along the way. One source indicated that two enslaved people accompanied them as far as Carlinville, Illinois, before turning back to Kentucky.[21]

The Majors finally arrived in the small settlement of Walnut Grove on Ben's thirty-eighth birthday, October 31, 1834. Three weeks later, Ben and Lucy welcomed a new baby whom they named Joseph, after Ben's brother who had stayed in Kentucky.

Central Illinois was still a frontier when the Majors arrived. Congress had organized the Illinois Territory in 1809, and it had become a state nine years later. The indigenous people—including the Kickapoo, Chippewa, Ottawa, Potawatomi, Sauk, and Fox—had moved or been moved from their lands between 1819 and 1832. In 1833, the Treaty of Chicago had opened the way for US acquisition and settlement of the last remaining Indian lands in the state. One man remembered the area as "a land of entrancing beauty. The wide prairies, with grassy billows, reached out until, to the human eye, they touched the horizon. The streams of water were skirted with trees . . . charming birds and graceful wild beasts abounded everywhere, untamed and untouched."[22]

The new Illinoisans gradually grew accustomed to the wide flat land, so different from the rolling fields around Hopkinsville. They had always had field hands and house slaves to do the hardest, most onerous work. Now they had to adapt, finding new muscles and earning calluses as they broke sod, downed trees, built homes, erected fences, planted crops, and tended to farm animals, children, and housework. At the end of a hard day, they stood on rough cabin steps or sat astride horses and watched the wind ripple acres of wheat, and the setting sun paint the broad sky in strokes of orange and rose.

Ben's family of eight lived in a two-room log cabin during their first few years in Illinois, quite a change from the elegant plantation homes and large farmhouses of Kentucky. Benjamin J. Radford, who was a child when he came to Walnut Grove from Christian County, described his family's pioneer home. The Major cabin was likely very similar. "On the north were two rooms 16 x 16 with a huge chimney between them, with two wide fireplaces, the one on the west side for heating the family room and the one on the east for cooking, washing, soap-making, lard-rendering, and other sorts of culinary operations. On the south side of these rooms, the roof was extended to cover the girls' bedroom, 8 x 10 feet, opening off the family room, and the boys' bedroom, same size, opening off the kitchen, and a porch between them, 8 x 12 feet."[23] Windows were of oiled paper; floors of rough boards split from trees. Clothing was hung on wooden pegs driven into the walls.[24]

In the spring of 1836, as Ben planted his second year of crops in Illinois, his longtime plan to free his enslaved people finally came to fruition. G. W. McElroy, of the New York Colonization Society, traveled around Kentucky that spring, gathering people for the next planned expedition. McElroy secured the Majors and Harlans for this expedition, along with dozens of other formerly enslaved people from Kentucky and northwestern Tennessee counties.[25]

Perhaps McElroy shared copies of a circular published in 1830 by early Liberian settlers. The publication ensured formerly enslaved and free-born black people that in Liberia:

This small piece of paper, about the size of a check, is a receipt for human beings, the former slaves of Ben Major and his brother Chastine. It was issued to Joseph Major, another brother, by the Christian County Colonization Society. (Major Family Private Collection)

> Our constitution secures to us, so far as our condition allows, all the rights and privileges enjoyed by the citizens of the United States; and these rights and privileges are ours. We are proprietors of the soil we live on, and possess the rights of freeholders. Our suffrages, and what is of more importance, our sentiments and our opinions have their due weight in the government we live under. Our laws are altogether our own; they grew out of our circumstances; are framed for our exclusive benefit, and administered either by officers of our own appointment, or such as possess our confidence. . . . we know nothing of that debasing inferiority, with which our very colour stamped us in America.[26]

The Majors and Harlans were all freed at an unknown date. No emancipation documentation has been discovered; however, perhaps Joseph Major, acting on behalf of his brothers, granted them their liberty. In May 1836, Joseph turned them over to the Christian County Colonization Society, which presumably then signed them over to McElroy. Joseph had provided them with cash and two new sets of clothing per person, for which he billed Ben.[27]

The secretary of the county colonization society handed Joseph a receipt, dated May 20, 1836—a receipt for human beings: "Recd of Joseph Major the emigrants of Benjm Major and Chastine Major in no 11 also one hundred & fifteen dollars for the use of sd emigrants."[28]

This scrap of paper, only eight inches wide and not quite four inches long, launched a new life for the formerly enslaved people.

5

The Scene of Suffering and Misery Is Beyond Description

All was not peaceful in the colony of Liberia.

While Tolbert, Austin, and the others were still enslaved in Kentucky—about a year before the *Luna* sailed—the women of Port Cresson, Liberia, had put their children down to sleep on a quiet June night, then sat with their husbands enjoying the rustle of palm fronds and the sounds of night birds.

Suddenly, shots rang out, feet raced past the small homes, and someone shouted "Fire!" Fathers darted to doorways; mothers roused sleeping children. Outside, warriors set homes ablaze and shot the frightened townspeople as they ran for the woods.

A letter later sent to America captured the sense of chaos: "Scarcely had twilight faded away into the shady indistinctness of a moonlit night, ere dusky wreaths of smoke could be perceived arising from . . . the emigrants' houses, proclaiming that the work of revenge and destruction had commenced. House after house was fired, throwing up for a time a distinct and appalling glare into the midnight sky."[1]

These villagers had arrived in Liberia only seven months earlier, in the fall of 1834. They had settled on land purchased by the New York Colonization Society and the Young Men's Colonization Society of Pennsylvania from local indigenous leader Joe Harris. (Because many of the indigenous leaders interacted with traders from around the world, they often adopted English names.)[2]

One man had described the site for the settlement in an 1834 letter: "There is a beautiful river, the St. John's, which empties into the ocean at that place. On the margin of this sheet of water, there has been a flourishing little town erected during the past year called Edina. . . . The margin of the river and surrounding country is formed of rich, high, and sandy ground. . . . At a distance of twenty or thirty miles in the interior, two large and beautiful mountains of a conical form arise to view . . . the soil is of a sandy texture and is consequently cultivated with great facility."[3]

But the beautiful location had a dark side. The cove and surrounding area had long been a center for slave trafficking, a trade involving most of the indigenous people in the region.

Settlers had christened the new town Port Cresson, in honor of Phila-delphia Quaker and colonization supporter Elliott Cresson. All was peace-ful in the village at first. The town's idealistic residents were committed to principles of peace, temperance, and Christianity, and had outlawed arms and liquor. Within a very short time, their pacifist principles proved fatal.[4]

The attack came on June 10, 1835. Joe Harris—the very man who had sold the land to the colonizationists—led the warriors. The unarmed set-tlers were terrified. They ran for the woods and the river.[5]

Townspeople in nearby Edina heard the shots and saw the night sky light up; "in a state of distressing anxiety and suspense," they waited for dawn. "Next morning, at six a.m., we discovered persons making their way to and assembling on the opposite side of the river . . . the scene of suffer-ing and misery, which this miserable group of beings presented on arrival, is beyond description. Entire families had been cut off, remnants of others [were] naked and wounded. There came the aged and the infirm tottering from the bed of sickness. The husband lamenting the loss of wife, and the mother bewailing, in heartrending sobs the bereavement of her children, whom she had seen murdered."[6]

In a single horrible night, twenty people—three men, four women, and thirteen children, ranging in age from two to ten—were slaughtered. Edward Hankinson, the white vice agent of the colony, and his wife were among those who had survived the terrifying attack. One of the indige-nous people hid them, saving their lives. The Hankinsons decided they were done with Liberia and promptly sailed back to America.[7]

The slave trade was behind the violence. "This murderous act was induced by a slave trader, who, on coming to anchor in the harbor, discovered that a colony of Americans had been planted on the river, and refused to land his goods, alleging that the colonists would interrupt his trade," wrote Samuel Wilkeson, a colonization society agent. "King Joe Harris, finding that the trade in slaves was likely to be thus cut off, resolved on the destruction of the settlement."[8]

Bob Gray, an indigenous leader friendly to the settlers, had tried to warn them of Joe Harris's treachery. The defenselessness of the settlers made them vulnerable. One report noted that "the entire want of the means of military defense among the settlers was at once an inducement to the assault and a cause of its success."[9]

After the attack, a force of 120 settlers from Edina and Port Cresson pursued the warriors and destroyed their towns.[10] In a "palaver" (a parlay) with the settlers, Joe Harris agreed to abandon the slave trade, cede part of his territory to the colonization societies, rebuild the colonists' homes, and reimburse them for stolen and destroyed property. Peace seemed secure.[11]

The colonizationists were reluctant to abandon what they felt was a good site, and they built a new settlement at the mouth of the Saint John River, about three miles from the location of Port Cresson. They named it Bassa Cove. In August 1835, the small population increased with the arrival of twenty-four new colonists aboard the *Indiana*.[12]

American Thomas Buchanan replaced Edward Hankinson as agent. Thomas was a white man and a cousin of James Buchanan, who would later become president of the United States. In December 1835, Buchanan arrived in Bassa Cove aboard the *Independence*, bringing with him provisions, clothing, medicine, and firearms and ammunition.[13]

Upon his arrival in Bassa Cove, he wrote: "It is a paradise. The climate is absolutely good—the soil prolific and various in its productions—the rivers abound in excellent fish and very superior oysters, and the water is pure and wholesome. Our position is somewhat remarkable, having a river at our rear, the ocean in front, and the magnificent St. John sweeping past on our right. The luxuriant and various foliage which overhangs the banks of the river and recedes back into the interminable forests, gives a perpetual freshness to the scene."[14]

Samuel Wilkeson described the new settlement. "The settlers were placed in comfortable homes and busily engaged in clearing and cultivating their farms; public buildings were erected, the necessary officers appointed to administer the laws, a church built, the town plot cleared.... A profitable trade was opened with natives in the interior."[15]

The townspeople also established a two-acre public garden and built a blacksmith's shop, a kiln, and ten more houses to receive another shipload of people from America.[16]

The new people were expected in late summer, aboard the *Luna*.

6

We Have All Landed on the Shores of Africa

Austin Major stood at the bow of the *Luna* and stared at the horizon, impatient to see land again. They had been at sea for more than six weeks, and the excitement and novelty of the voyage had worn off long ago. His children—Mary, Caroline, and Thomas—were weary of being confined aboard a vessel, and the adults were more than ready to begin their new lives. It was August 19, and here, so close to the equator, the sun blazed hot and glared off the waves.[1]

"Land," a sailor shouted. "Land ahead."

Austin gazed intently and saw a hazy bump in the distance. Passengers scrambled to the rail, pointing and chattering. The bump became larger and clearer until the passengers glimpsed the lush beauty of Cape Mesurado, the site of Monrovia, Liberia. The rocky, brush-covered cliff towered eighty feet straight up from the pounding surf.

Several hundred feet from the base of the cliff, Captain Hallet commanded the crew to drop anchor. Austin saw no wharf. He glanced down at the surface of the water, fifteen or twenty feet below, and wondered how on earth they would get to shore.

He spotted a group of African men launching large dugout canoes from a small beach under the cape. The men were powerfully built and naked except for loincloths. As they neared the ship, Austin saw that each man had a blue line tattooed from his forehead to the tip of his nose. Some of them bore additional tattoos on their cheeks. Reverend Herring had told him about the distinctive marks worn by the men of the Kru tribe. Austin had never seen such tattoos, and a shiver traced his spine.[2]

The *Luna*'s crew dropped a rope ladder to the nearest canoe. Ignoring the doubts that nibbled at the edge of his consciousness, Austin clambered down and stepped into the canoe with the barely clothed strangers. The ship rocked; the ladder swayed. He glanced up at Tolbert, who handed down Austin's children and then his own sons. Agnes's oldest boy, Lewis, descended into another canoe and helped his younger brothers—Asbury, Wesley, Coke, and Fletcher—down the rope ladder.[3]

The skirts worn by the women and older girls made descent on the ladder dangerous, but Captain Hallet had an ingenious solution. The crew brought a chair topside and, one at a time, they tied each woman and girl—including Tyloa, Agnes, and her daughters Ann and Silvay—into the seat, then used a hook and tackle to hoist the chair over the rail. Each female dangled for a heart-stopping moment above the waves before being lowered to the waiting canoes.[4]

The Kru men paddled for shore but stopped short of the beach. One of them leaped into chest-deep water and steadied the boat. Another Kru man, tall and strong, slipped into the water, then extended his arms toward Mary, Austin's five-year-old. Before Austin could stop her, Mary smiled and slid into the African's arms. She traced her fingers over the blue lines on his face as he carried her to the beach. Several men and women dressed in clothing more familiar to the passengers had gathered on the shore. One woman took Mary's hand and greeted her in English. The Kru man waded back to the canoe. Tolbert, Austin, and Lewis stepped into the water, too, and carried the other children ashore one by one. Austin helped Agnes, and Lewis piggybacked his sisters to shore.

On his last trip to the canoe, Tolbert lifted out Tyloa and carried her to land. It wasn't quite like carrying her over a threshold or jumping a broom, but it would do.

Austin breathed deeply of Africa; the heavy scent of unfamiliar flowers, dried fish, wood fires, and saltwater mingled in the steamy air. He ran his hands through his hair, stiff with sea spray. Monrovia wasn't their final destination. The captain was delivering mail and cargo, and the crew would take on fresh water and supplies before heading down the coast to Bassa Cove. All of their belongings remained on board, but the captain had encouraged them to explore Monrovia. Mary ran to join Austin, and he swung her up on his shoulders. Caroline and Thomas made their way through the loose sand to their father's side. Some of the Monrovian men directed them toward a trail.

The Majors and Harlans, the Buchners, the Haynes family, the Herrings, and other *Luna* passengers made their way up the half-mile path from the beach, winding up the stony trail to the cliff-top town. Austin felt his calf and thigh muscles tighten as he climbed the hill; it felt good to stretch his legs. They reached the top, and the settlement spread out before them.

Austin saw wide, grassy streets and at least two churches. Houses and businesses were built of wood and stone. Some were utilitarian and little more than shacks. Others were wood-frame houses as handsome as anything he had seen in Kentucky—painted white with neat green shutters and surrounded by tidy vegetable gardens. Mary struggled to get off his shoulders. He set her down, and she ran ahead to catch up with her brother, sister, and cousins.

Austin glanced back at the sea below. The *Luna* and several other ships flying foreign flags waited at anchor. He took one more look at the wide expanse of ocean, stretching forever back to America, then joined his family.

In Monrovia, Austin, Tolbert, and the others found a town not much bigger than Hopkinsville, yet the Liberian settlement felt far more cosmopolitan. It was a crossroads for immigrants, Africans of different backgrounds, and missionaries, traders, and sailors from Europe and Asia.

In 1836, Monrovia (named for colonization supporter and former US president James Monroe) had about two thousand inhabitants, five churches, and several schools. The settlement was a commercial center, trading with indigenous people and international vessels. In a single month the previous year, the marine list for Monrovia recorded seven arrivals of ships and an equal number of departures. From their vantage point atop the promontory, Monrovians had a 180-degree view of the sea; the rain forest encroached at their backs.[5]

A few days later, the *Luna* arrived at the shore of Bassa Cove, about sixty miles down the coastline from Monrovia. Rocky outcroppings here and there interrupted the cove's sandy beaches. Bright hibiscus and bougainvillea bloomed among the greenery. Pelicans, parrots, and gulls crossed the sky. The land was marshy where the green Saint John River flowed into the ocean and leggy mangrove trees waded in the briny water. Beyond the palm-fringed beach rose hills covered with dense forests of mahogany, camwood, cotton trees, and rubber trees.

The settlement had no dock, so passengers again disembarked into Kru canoes. Within minutes, Austin, Tolbert, Agnes, and their families were in their new hometown, far smaller and less developed than Monrovia.

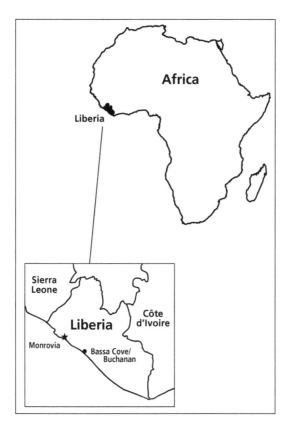

Liberia was established on the Atlantic coast of
Africa between Sierra Leone and the Ivory Coast
(Côte d'Ivoire). Bassa Cove (now Buchanan), where
the *Luna*'s passengers disembarked, is about sixty
miles southeast of the capital, Monrovia.

Three weeks later, Tolbert located some hard-to-find paper and ink
and wrote a letter to his former owner. Tolbert knew that Ben had moved
to central Illinois, but he did not have his new address, so he sent his letter
to Ben's brother Joseph in Kentucky. The letter traveled by ship from Bassa
Cove to Monrovia to New York, where it was postmarked November 8. It
then made its way to Hopkinsville, and Joseph forwarded it to Ben in the
small town of Walnut Grove, Illinois.

Ben slid his finger under the red wax seal and unfolded the letter.[6]

Bassa Cove was a small village when the Majors and Harlans arrived in Liberia in August 1836. (Lehman and Duval, Library of Congress, Prints and Photographs Division, LC-USZ62–22961)

> *Bassa Cove, Western Africa*
> *September 1836*
> *Dear Sir,*
>   *We have all landed on the shores of Africa and got into our houses. We have been here three weeks. So far, I am well pleased to my master in Illinois . . . none of us have been taken with the fever yet. We have a prospect of war with the natives. I hope it will be settled without bloodshed . . .*
>   *It rains here almost every day, more or less. When the rain is over, we come out to over eight gallons, as the soil is sandy. We have not got our farms laid out yet. Each of us will get forty acres, which will be ours when we clear two for every ten . . .*
>   *We have a Sunday school here: three missionary white men, two Baptists and a Methodist.*
>   *As it respects living here, it is altogether different to that in America. Here we have palm oil and rice, sweet potatoes, plantain*

Shortly after arriving in Bassa Cove, Tolbert Major wrote a letter to his former owner, Ben Major: *Dear Sir, We have all landed on the shores of African and got into our houses. We have been here three weeks. . . . none of us have been taken with the fever yet.* (Courtesy of the McLean County Historical Society, Bloomington, Illinois)

and banana, and cassava, a root something like artichoke; it tastes very well when boiled. We have pineapples, limes, etc., though the principal article of food is rice and palm oil.

To W. Woolridge and his family and Ed, my love and compliments. Tell George Major and Henry that it is my desire for them to come to this country. They need not fear the heat. It is not so hot as in America, and we never expect to see frost again. This is now the winter here and the trees are as green as spring. Tell Master Jo Ma-

jor to please to let them come. My love to Mr. Moore in Hopkinsville.
To Gid Overshiner, my respects. To F. Wheatly and his family.
Yours,

Tolbert Major

It had been more than two years since Ben had seen his formerly enslaved people. He must have wondered many times whether they had survived, and if so, how they were doing. A man with Ben's faith would have kept them in his prayers. Perhaps Ben read Tolbert's letter aloud to Lucy and his children or to others who shared his views. He carefully preserved this letter, and as other correspondence arrived from Africa, he tucked it away, too.

Tolbert told Ben that he and his family were settled. The colonization society promised immigrants six months of housing. Many settlers initially lived in round thatched huts similar to those of the indigenous people. They could stay a maximum of six months, but they were then expected to move into their own houses.[7]

Tolbert noted that none of them had been "taken with the fever yet." Malaria, often called emigrants' fever or acclimating fever, was a major concern for colonists. Tolbert's use of the word "yet" implies that he knew that a bout of malaria was nearly inevitable. Some settlers were sick for several days or weeks, then recovered. Others were not so fortunate. On average, the disease killed one of every five immigrants to Liberia within their first year in the country. The youngest and oldest were the most vulnerable.[8]

The Majors and Harlans had arrived during the period known as the "middle dries." This short season of comparatively dry, pleasant weather—in the midst of the rainy season—starts about the third week of July and lasts for three to five weeks. The colony's physician, Dr. J. W. Lugenbeel, wrote, "The sun shines brilliantly and pleasantly all day; and no rain falls at night. The air, however, is always refreshingly cool and agreeable. This is perhaps the most pleasant time in the year."[9]

However, very quickly the middle dries give way to the remainder of the rainy season, which lasts until about October. Pools of standing water provide ample breeding grounds for mosquitoes. In 1836, people didn't know that mosquitoes carry the parasite that causes malaria. Colonization society officials blamed other factors for the disease, including exposure to night air. Dr. Lugenbeel believed the disease was caused by eating too many fruits and vegetables. "From all the observations that I have been able to make, and from all the information I can collect, I am satisfied, that in many cases, sickness in this country may be attributed to imprudence in eating and exposure. The climate is frequently blamed for that which is the result of personal imprudence. There is a great variety of fruits and vegetables in this part of Africa to tempt the appetite, but prudence must be exercised in the use of them, especially by newcomers, or sickness will be the result."[10] (By late 1850, Dr. Lugenbeel had learned that quinine was an effective treatment in the "intermittent form of fever," although he didn't understand why, and he had discovered local herbal teas and botanical treatments. However, he still advocated cupping, blistering, leeches, and other traditional medical treatments for more aggressive forms of malaria. By the late 1850s travelers to Liberia were taking quinine as a preventative.)[11]

All of the Majors and Harlans probably had malaria. Tolbert and Austin later wrote about surviving bouts of fever. Of the *Luna*'s eighty-five passengers, twenty-three died of fever before the year ended—more than one in every four—a higher-than-average mortality rate.[12]

Tolbert also wrote to Ben about the possibility of war. His concern was legitimate. The stretch of West African coastline that became Liberia was not vacant territory awaiting the arrival of settlers from America. Long before the American Colonization Society agents had arrived in Africa, the coast was home to numerous ethnic groups, including the Bassa, Bella, Dei, Gbandi, Gio, Gola, Grebo, Kissi, Kpelle, Krahn, Kru, Loma, Mandingo, Mano, Mende, and Vai.

Their leaders were referred to as kings. Among them were men known to the settlers by their English names: George, Tom, Jimmy, Bob, Willy, and Boatswain. (Boatswain's real name was Sao Baso; he had received his colorful moniker while working on a British ship as a youth.)[13]

The indigenous people were not especially welcoming to the new settlers, whom they identified as 'Merica men or white men or even black-white men. Robert Stockton, an American Colonization Society agent charged with first acquiring land for the settlers, set a poor precedent when he negotiated an agreement with the Dei king by holding a gun to his head and threatening to pull the trigger. The society paid the Dei for their land in tobacco, beads, food, rum, and other items, altogether worth less than $300.[14]

The American Colonization Society claimed that "All the territory of Liberia has been acquired from the native powers under regular treaties and purchases, and paid for by the funds of the Society, aided by special subscriptions entered into for that purpose."[15] However, there may have been misunderstandings between white men who felt they had legitimately acquired land and the indigenous people, who believed that the land was being leased rather than sold, or that it was communal property rather than individual property. There may also have been disputes between indigenous leaders over who had authority to negotiate with the colonization society.

Liberian author C. Patrick Burrowes wrote that there was no individual land ownership in this part of West Africa before the colonists came and that land ownership was dispersed among households and family groups: "One gained access to such land mainly by membership in a lineage which had invested several generations of labor in it."[16]

Anthropologist Warren d'Azevedo believed that at least one ethnic group, the Gola, were concerned that settlers might take control of trade routes along the coast. The Gola, working with the Dei and Vai, had long served as middlemen for groups in the interior who traded with incoming ships, and they did not want colonists to interfere.[17]

The population of Liberia comprised the various indigenous groups, who were not homogenous and who often had conflicts with one another; settlers, who were struggling with culture shock and who often exhibited arrogance toward indigenous people; colonization society officials and employees, who had a range of motives for being there; and slave traders and European merchants motivated by greed. It was a volatile mix that often led to violence.

Indigenous people had attacked settlements in the 1820s and early 1830s. Skirmishes and larger battles continued for decades. In many of the letters sent back to America, colonists mentioned battles and asked for guns and ammunition. Tolbert, Austin, and the others had arrived in a beautiful but very unstable land.

Liberia was very different from southwestern Kentucky. The circular published in 1830 to entice new settlers to Liberia provided this description, written in the flowery language of the time: "Africa furnishes a soil as fertile and produces a vegetation as luxuriant as any in the world. Its boundless forests and beautiful fields are watered by noble rivers and abound in all the productions of tropical climates. . . . Leaving the seaboard, the traveler everywhere, at the distance of a few miles, enters upon a uniform upland country, of moderate elevation, intersected by innumerable rivulets, abounding in springs of unfailing water, and covered with a verdure which knows no other changes except those which refresh and renew its beauties."[18]

Tolbert was a farmer, and much of his September 1836 letter reflected a farmer's concerns—land, weather, soil, and crops. Settlers drew lots for land. Francis Devaney, a Monrovian sheriff visiting the United States in 1830, explained the land distribution system to a congressional committee: "A plat of the town is drawn and laid off in lots, and when new settlers arrive, they employ a lottery to fix their several situations; each being allowed in the town a quarter of an acre, and 15 acres in the neighborhood, which he is at liberty to cultivate for himself. Some who wish to become farmers and to settle at a distance [from town] are allowed small farms of 50 acres."[19]

Tolbert indicated that "each of us" would get forty acres, so perhaps the system differed in settlements outside Monrovia. It is also not clear what Tolbert meant by "each of us"—he could have meant each adult male, each individual, or each family unit.

Under the land allocation system, some settlers received productive plots; others drew title to land that was rocky, sandy, or otherwise difficult to farm. Many of the early settlements, including Bassa Cove, were along the Atlantic coast or rivers, where the land could be swampy or sandy. Inland, thick growth of trees, shrubs, and vines covered the land. Clearing and cultivation was hard work.[20]

Author Catherine Reef described how colonists cleared land for the settlement of Caldwell. "Clearing the land was treacherous work. Tall trees had to be felled with axes, and saplings cut even with the ground. Bushes and vines were cut away using sharp, curved blades known as billhooks. As they labored, the builders of Caldwell had to remain alert for scorpions and insects on the jungle floor and pythons in the branches overhead."[21]

After recovering from their initial bout with fever, Tolbert and the other newcomers had to clear land and build homes. To acquire a fee-simple deed to their land, they had to bring a minimum of two acres under cultivation and build a house within two years. If settlers failed in these tasks, ownership of their land reverted to the American Colonization Society.[22]

In the early years of the settlement, oxen, horses, and mules were rare, and most cultivation was done by hand. Settlers had to bring hoes, shovels, axes, plows, and other basic farming and carpentry tools from America since it was nearly impossible to obtain them in Liberia.

Tolbert noted that the settlement had a Sunday school and missionaries. Many of the settlers mentioned churches and schools in their letters, reflecting a culture that emphasized faith and education. Many historians have noted the strong role that religion and church played in the lives of the settlers. Historian Randall Miller wrote, "The churches provided community life, educational facilities, intellectual sustenance, and an important link with the past. The churches also provided opportunities for assuming leadership positions."[23]

In his letter, Tolbert sent greetings to Ben and Joseph Major and their families. He sent greetings to "W. Woolridge & his family & Ed." These were likely Ben's cousins, William and Edmund Wooldridge (misspelled in the letter).

Tolbert also sent greetings to George Major and Henry and urged Ben to "Tell Master Jo Major to please to let them come." It is not clear what relationship existed between Tolbert, George, and Henry. The 1870 census—the first one after the Civil War—listed a black man named George Major living in Christian County. George would have been between Tolbert and Austin in age, and may have been their brother, and possibly Henry was George's son. It doesn't appear, though, that George and Henry migrated to Liberia. No other Majors appear on the roll of emigrants through 1843, and George and Henry are not mentioned in subsequent letters from Liberia.[24]

When efforts to free family members failed, enslaved people faced a nearly unthinkable decision—continued enslavement to remain close to family, or freedom and colonization in an unknown land, with the near certainty of never seeing family members again. Some chose to go to Liberia with the idea that they would later secure freedom for family members.

For example, Marshall and Rachel Hooper had been enslaved but gained their freedom and sailed to Liberia in 1849. However, Marshall left behind his nineteen enslaved children. He hoped to come back and purchase freedom for his children. In 1852, he returned to the United States determined to negotiate a price for his sixteen-year-old daughter, Emily. He arranged to work as a recruitment agent for the American Colonization Society and earned about $200 of the $600 asking price. Dr. Lugenbeel—who had apparently also traveled from Liberia to America—agreed to pay the remaining balance, essentially purchasing the girl himself. Lugenbeel arranged a payment plan for reimbursement and, in an effort to ensure that father and daughter actually left the United States, told the astonished father that he would transfer title to Emily only after they boarded a ship bound for Liberia.[25]

Tolbert also sent his love to Mr. Moore in Hopkinsville. This was probably James Moore, to whom Tolbert and young Wesley Harlan would later write. He sent his respects, too, to Gid (Gideon) Overshiner, a slave owner in Christian County who owned land along the Little River. Finally,

Tolbert sent his regards to F. Wheatly and his family. Francis Wheatley was a slave owner and Gideon Overshiner's neighbor.[26]

In his letter, Tolbert expressed no ill will against Ben for holding him and his kin in slavery. He wrote, "So far I am well pleased to my master in Illinois."

Some historians who have written about Liberian colonization note that formerly enslaved people may have maintained a cordial, even sub-servient, relationship with their former owners in order to obtain supplies and financial assistance. Tolbert did, in fact, ask Ben for help in later letters. However, the bulk of the letters reveal a relationship that seems genuinely affectionate.

Tolbert's letter to Ben launched a fifteen-year correspondence between the two men.

7

Bowing the Knee to Slavery

Elijah P. Lovejoy was not going to lose another printing press, by God. Those proslavery folks had a right to their beliefs, but he had a right to challenge them. He was a God-fearing citizen—an ordained Presbyterian minister—and he hadn't broken any laws.

A lot of people in St. Louis had objected to his editorials in the *St. Louis Observer*; he had criticized Catholicism and opposed tobacco and liquor. But his editorials against slavery and his calls for immediate and universal emancipation had really stirred people up. He shouldn't have been surprised; Missouri was a slave state and, in 1837, many Missourians were determined to keep it that way. Three times proslavery men had destroyed his printing presses. He had persevered, but the threats of violence against him and his family had been too much. They had finally moved just across the Mississippi River to Alton, Illinois, where he set about establishing the *Alton Observer*.

Elijah greeted the steamboat the day his new printing press arrived. He watched as dock workers offloaded it and stored it in the Godfrey and Gilman warehouse. About twenty of his supporters volunteered to stay with him at the warehouse that night, vigilantly guarding the press until it could be installed at the newspaper office. Though Illinois was a free state, the town of Alton was a center for slave catchers along the Mississippi. There could be trouble.

It wasn't long before a mob gathered at the warehouse. They shouted insults at the men inside, hurled rocks at the windows, and fired guns into the sky. Suddenly, Elijah smelled fire and saw dark smoke drift from the roof across one of the windows. He glanced through a window and spotted a ladder leaning against the outside of the building. He sprinted up the stairs with his friend Royal Weller close on his heels. The two men flung open the roof hatch and crawled out, keeping in the shadows as they made their way toward the ladder. Clumps of smoking pitch had started small fires in a few spots. Elijah and Royal reached the ladder, shoved it over, and crept back into the warehouse.

Downstairs, Elijah exchanged a few quick words with his supporters. They debated what to do: Try to extinguish the fires on the roof? Surrender? Several checked to be sure their guns were loaded. Suddenly they saw the shadow of the ladder cross one of the windows. Elijah and Royal again raced up the stairs and threw open the hatch. A double-barreled shotgun boomed from below.

Elijah was in front of Royal; his body was hit with the shotgun's blast and he died at the warehouse. Royal was badly wounded. Elijah's other supporters surrendered their weapons and the mob surged into the warehouse and destroyed the printing press. Elijah was buried two days later, on his thirty-fifth birthday.[1]

Even as some freeborn blacks and formerly enslaved people from America were settling in Liberia, the rift over slavery deepened within the United States. The Society of Friends (Quakers) and many others had opposed slavery since before the American Revolution. The first abolitionist organization—the ponderously named Society for the Relief of Free Negroes Unlawfully Held in Bondage—had formed in 1775. Abolitionist sentiments increased during the Second Great Awakening, and the American Anti-Slavery Society was formed in 1833. But the louder the voices of the abolitionists, the more stubbornly slave owners in the South clung to slavery.

As a result of the "Charleston Mail Crisis," in which the Charleston post office resisted delivering abolitionist materials in South Carolina, US Postmaster General Amos Kendall, a supporter of Andrew Jackson, blocked delivery of such mail in slaveholding states in 1835. (Kendall had once been editor-in-chief of the *Argus of Western America*, published in Frankfort, Kentucky, Ben Major's hometown. Kendall had also once tutored Henry Clay's children. He was only seven years older than Ben and it is possible the two men knew one another.)

Slave owners who once thought of slavery as a necessary evil now declared it a good thing: a means by which to civilize black people, a Christian duty to care for those whom they characterized as unable to care for themselves, and an institution vital to the economy.[2]

In an attempt to silence antislavery voices, the US House of Representatives passed a gag rule in late May 1836. The effort was led by legislators from the South, including Committee Chair Henry L. Pickney and Representative James Hammond of South Carolina and Speaker of the House James Polk of Tennessee.

The resolution read:

> Resolved, that Congress possesses no constitutional authority
> to interfere in any way with the institution of Slavery in any of
> the States of the Union; Resolved, that Congress ought not to
> interfere in any way with Slavery in the District of Columbia;
> Resolved, that all petitions, memorials, resolutions, propositions,
> or papers, relating in any way or to any extent whatever to the
> subject of slavery, or the abolition of slavery, shall, without being
> either printed or referred, be laid upon the table, and that no
> further action whatever shall be had thereon.[3]

The resolution—an astonishing bit of obstructionism—automatically tabled action on all antislavery petitions without hearing them. Southern newspapers celebrated the gag rule. An article published in the *Weekly Standard* of Raleigh claimed, "The abolition question was the grand contrivance which was to breed an incurable schism between the northern and southern democracy . . . Congress will not suffer the abominable topic to be touched."[4]

Many people in the North were horrified. The *Pittsburgh Gazette* quoted Pennsylvania governor John Ritner: "And last, but worst of all, come the base bowing of the knee to the dark spirit of slavery." In the same article, the journalist wrote of the resolution, "It yields up the right of petition, the right of discussion, and the right of legislation. It is a virtual enactment of Gag Law upon the press, and a refusal to hear the people on the subject."[5]

Even stricter versions of the gag rule were passed in succeeding sessions of Congress. The rules remained in place for more than eight years, until Representative John Quincy Adams finally succeeded in repealing them in 1844, claiming that they violated the First Amendment right to petition the government for a redress of grievances.[6]

Although the furious national debate over slavery could no longer be heard in the House of Representatives, it continued unabated in meeting halls, churches, country stores, front parlors, and in newspapers. Antislavery activists portrayed Elijah Lovejoy as a martyr, and accounts of his murder filled abolitionist newspapers. Ben Major likely read about Lovejoy's murder in his own state.

The gag rule and violence against the antislavery movement drove positions on slavery even further apart. For enslaved and free black people in the United States, things were getting worse.

8

We Are All Needy

Shots rang out and panicked townspeople raced past Tolbert. The Fishmen were attacking the village again. Tolbert frantically glanced around, trying to locate Thornton and Washington. Suddenly he heard a familiar voice cry out in pain. He spun around and saw twelve-year-old Washington sprawled on the ground. Blood poured from his shoulder.

> *Bassa Cove, May 20th, 1839*
> *My Dear Master,*
>> *It is a long time since I have seen you. I have seen very many things since I have seen you. Some are new & interesting in the highest degree & some again are too horrible to mention, but the Lord has carried us through them, blessed be his name. He does all things well . . .*

The Majors and Harlans had lived in Liberia for two years and nine months when Tolbert wrote his second letter. Since their arrival, the settlers had familiarized themselves with their new home, learning about the different plants, animals, and local people, exploring the shoreline, and perhaps venturing up the Saint John River. They had grown accustomed to the chatter of monkeys in the treetops and the chirp of crickets in the bush. They fell asleep to the constant buzz of mosquitoes, the sound of the surf, and the wind in the palms.[1]

Bassa Cove was a beautiful setting, but it was certainly different from Kentucky. Did they miss the change of seasons—the bright daffodils, fragrant honeysuckle, fields of broad tobacco leaves, and colorful fall leaves? In his first letter, Tolbert had written that they would never see frost again. The average temperature in Liberia ranged between 78 and 85 degrees Fahrenheit, with humidity from 65 to 80 percent, comparable to average summers in Hopkinsville. However, in Liberia, the heat and humidity lasted all year and temperatures exceeded 90 degrees in the dry season. Did Tolbert and the others sometimes yearn for a crisp, frosty morning?

At least two more ships had brought passengers to Bassa Cove since the 1836 arrival of the *Luna*. The *Charlotte Harper* arrived in August 1837. She brought supplies for the colonists and several passengers, including the Reverend John J. Matthias, the new white governor of the Bassa Cove colony, and his wife, as well as two doctors, a millwright, two teachers, and four new settlers.[2]

Few white people were allowed in the colony—only missionaries and colonization society employees. Laws barred white people from participating in trade or owning a business.

As the colonization movement matured, societies started sending out black professionals, especially teachers and a few people with medical training. Many white people were convinced that black people were more suited to the African climate and less vulnerable to "emigrant fever." G. W. McElroy wrote to Ralph Gurley in 1836, "Southern blacks . . . are as healthy and healthier in Liberia than in Mississippi. A fact on this point: A Mr. Moore, a colored man from Mississippi, told me that during the five months he had been in Africa, both he and his family, and all who came out in the same expedition, had enjoyed better health than they usually experienced in their native state; that not one had died or even been sick, with what was termed an African fever."[3]

What appears to be a racist notion was proven partially correct more than a century later. Certain genetic anomalies in hemoglobin result in a higher resistance to malaria. However, if a child receives the anomaly from both parents, it results in sickle cell anemia.[4]

A few months after his arrival, Governor Matthias wrote, "The climate, with the exception of the acclimating process, is the finest imaginable. There is scarcely any variation in the temperature. It is now the 24th of December; the birds are singing; a greater variety of song or plumage I never heard or saw; and nature, the year round, wears the livery of freshness and life. Our colony (Bassa Cove) is gradually assuming the state and consequence of an organized government."[5]

By 1838 Bassa Cove had a harbor, and early that year a group of seventy-two emigrants from North Carolina arrived aboard the *Marine*. One of the passengers was Louis Sheridan. He was of mixed ancestry, but was listed as white in the 1810, 1820, and 1830 censuses for Bladen County, North Carolina. Sheridan was a well-educated and successful business-man, worth $15,000 to $20,000 by the mid-1830s. He also owned sixteen enslaved people. His relationship with them is not known. Free black peo-ple sometimes purchased their enslaved relatives or friends to keep them from being sold away.[6]

Sheridan had felt restricted in North Carolina by the anti-free-black laws and decided to try his luck in Liberia. American Colonization Society officials had, in fact, approached Sheridan about leading the group of set-tlers aboard the *Luna*, but he declined and instead joined the later group aboard the *Marine*.[7]

He was initially unimpressed with Liberia, writing that he and his shipmates "were expected to stay in pens of thatch and bamboo, to eat rotten cornmeal, and to relocate to Bexley, a newly established settlement six miles up the Saint John's River." Angered at the primitive state of the settlement and a reception that he felt was not in line with his status, he fired off an angry letter to a New York abolitionist, detailing the problems he had found. The colonization society could not easily refute his allega-tions; however, they offered him a concession. They allowed Sheridan to lease six hundred acres of land in Bexley for a plantation, which eventually employed one hundred men.[8]

Perhaps one of the incidents that Tolbert found too horrible to men-tion was the murder of Reverend Josiah F. C. Finley, governor of the Mis-sissippi colony at Sinoe River, south of Bassa Cove. The governor was traveling north on his way to Monrovia in September 1838, accompa-nied by some men whom the settlers routinely referred to as "Fishmen." Near Bassa Cove, these men robbed and killed him. Governor Finley was rumored to have been in league with the notorious slave trader Captain Theodore Canot, and he was carrying Spanish doubloons when he was attacked.[9]

Tolbert's letter continued: "I have . . . the honor of being married to a very worthy woman & we have been blessed with a boy. We are all well, thank God for his goodness; he is good & his kind care is over all his work."

Tolbert Major and Tyloa Harlan had been married aboard the *Luna* before it left New York, according to a contemporary newspaper account. However, no other documentation about Tyloa has surfaced. Her name does not appear on the official colonization society roll of emigrants or on a later census of Liberia. Tolbert never mentioned her by name in any of his letters, nor did any of the other people who corresponded with Ben. The basic facts of her life, her relationships, and her death remain unknown.[10]

Her last name implies that Tyloa was owned by George Harlan or one of his relatives. Tolbert likely became acquainted with her while they were still in Kentucky, working on neighboring plantations. Tyloa survived the voyage to Liberia, but she was deceased by 1843 when someone else is listed as Tolbert's spouse. In this 1839 letter, Tolbert is likely referring to Tyloa.

Ben was probably pleased to hear about the couple's new baby. He and his wife, Lucy, had also welcomed another child in 1836—a little girl they named Anna Elizabeth. However, Tolbert never mentioned his little boy again; he likely died at a young age.

> *We were all getting along very well; that is, Tho Austin Wa &*
> *Thorton and Myself. Old aunt Hanah is dead; she died & both of*
> *her sons. Why sir, your endowed family was all doing well. We had*
> *learned how to be our own Masters [illegible], but we have had war*
> *& that has distressed all very much. Indeed, we have had the most of*
> *[our] things destroyed. Washington was shot in the war; he was shot*
> *in the back near his left shoulder. The ball is not out yet & he is not*
> *able to do anything.*

The Fishmen warriors had attacked Bassa Cove in May 1839, the same month Tolbert penned this letter. It was not the first or last time this group attacked the community. In April of that year, Fishmen Black Will and Grando had joined other kings and leaders in Grand Bassa in signing a treaty with the settlers—a treaty the Fishmen violated within weeks.[11]

Peyton Skipwith, a stonemason, wrote to his former owner, "We have continual wars amongst the natives arround us . . . the fisherman [sic] at Grand Bassa Cove like to have taken that settlement . . . the natives are very savage when they think they have the advantage."[12]

In Tolbert's letter, "Tho Austin Wa & Thorton" were Thomas, Austin, Washington, and Thornton. When Tolbert wrote this letter, Thomas was about eleven; Washington, twelve; and Thornton, thirteen. Tolbert also referred to "old aunt Hanah." No older female named Hanah or Hannah appears in the colony's roll of emigrants.

By April 1839, the colony of Bassa Cove had united with Monrovia and several other settlements into the Commonwealth of Liberia. Thomas Buchanan was appointed governor. About five weeks before Tolbert wrote his letter to Ben, the governor visited Bassa Cove and nearby Edina to share the new commonwealth's constitution with the residents. He wrote a letter to the colonization society telling of his arrival at the cove. "Men, women and children crowded around the boat as it struck the beach, and for a time, I was literally overwhelmed with kindness and affection. . . . I called a public meeting of the citizens of both settlements, and laid before them the new Constitution, and the addresses of your Board and the Boards of New York and Pennsylvania. The Constitution was listened to with evident pleasure and adopted unanimously."[13]

Governor Buchanan had arrived in Liberia in January 1836, replacing Edward Hankinson as agent for the colonization society. He was only twenty-eight when he arrived. He was a popular man and known for heading his own troops when defense of the colony was required. In an 1840 letter, one man wrote of Buchanan: "He is an intelligent man and is in every respect qualified for the station he holds. He is mild, but firm and determined—understands well the kind of people he has to govern. He has frequently exposed himself in conflicts with the natives, and they all respect and fear him: as he always heads his troops they call him the war Governor—say his name is Big Cannon (Buchanan) and that he obtained that name by being so great a warrior in his own country."[14]

Tolbert concluded:

We are all needy & should be glad if you would send us out some things, if you please. We are trying to get along again. Tell all of your family howdy. Dear Sir, I am in haste & must bid you goodbye. Your humble servant,

Tolbert Major

Tolbert's letter reflected two recurring themes in the letters from Liberian settlers: a desire to succeed independently in their new life and the reluctant admission that continued help from America was necessary, at least initially.

The colonists, though of African descent, were not African. They had been born in America, as had their parents and very likely their grandparents, great-grandparents, and perhaps more distant generations. They had landed on the shores of a country wholly unfamiliar to them. They did not speak the languages and did not know the land, the plants, or the animals. The country's proximity to the equator meant that even the night skies, the seasons, the tides, and length of day were all unfamiliar.[15]

Despite any possible romantic notions about returning to an ancestral homeland, the reality was that they knew little or nothing about Africa or its inhabitants and carried with them the attitudes and biases of the American South. Notions about shared kinship often vanished when the settlers were faced with the reality of life along the West African coast. This was reflected in letters to America, such as the one written by Peyton Skipwith: "It is something strange to think that these people of Africa are calld [sic] our ancestors." Another settler, Simon Harrison, wrote, "I am here in the land of Naked people."[16]

When immigrants first arrived, the promised six months of shelter often consisted of thatched huts, as Lewis Sheridan had discovered to his dismay. These were built of reeds and plastered on the exterior with mud. Matting lined the interior walls. Cooking was done in outdoor kitchens, where okra and peppers were hung up to dry. In later years, the American Colonization Society sent to Liberia prefabricated structures known as "receptacles" to house newly arrived settlers. These dormitory-style buildings were two stories high, ninety-six feet long, and thirty-six feet wide.[17]

Sometimes, however, because of lack of funds or inefficiency, the society failed to follow through on the promise of shelter and provisions, leaving settlers to survive on their own in a strange land. When settlers asked for supplies from their former masters and others in America, they weren't making frivolous requests.[18]

Tolbert often asked Ben for supplies, but not in a subservient manner. He offered reciprocity to the extent that he could do so. He never asked for luxuries and rarely requested anything beyond bare necessities.

Many settlers complained that food rations were inadequate. Author Marie Tyler-McGraw told of a letter sent by the Bullock family in 1827 in which the family listed their weekly rations: a pint each of rice and meal, a half pint of palm oil, a half-pound of meat, and a few other items to be used in trade.[19]

After a discouraging and publicly damaging 1843 census of the colony, the American Colonization Society officials made a more concerted effort to urge would-be emigrants to bring necessary supplies with them. Still, in 1849, settler Henry B. Stewart complained about the six-month ration, noting that it fell short three months after their arrival.[20]

The *African Repository* published an article, "Things Which Every Emigrant to Liberia Ought to Know," that listed nine guidelines for emigrants, including "They should understand they are going to a new country" and emphasized self-reliance, hard work, personal responsibility, and the importance of education. The article included a lengthy list of recommended supplies: "1 grubbing hoe, 1 weeding hoe, 1 light axe, 1 chopping and nail hatchet, 1 drawing knife, 1 spade, one 1 inch auger, two nail gimlets . . . a hand saw, straw or shuck mattresses and bedding, tin cups and spoons, saucepans, plates and bowls, cups and saucers, knives and forks, a two-gallon pot, a Dutch oven, a tea kettle, a teapot, a coffee pot, a coffee mill, and other little conveniences. . . ."[21]

Ben had paid for clothing, supplies, and implements for his formerly enslaved people to take to Liberia. However, in subsequent letters Tolbert and Austin revealed that everything they owned had been stolen, so even settlers who brought supplies with them often were unable to retain them. These thefts continued for some time. In 1845, Joseph Jenkins Roberts wrote of frequent robberies by indigenous people:

> In some instances, they have been guilty of depredations of the most aggravated character—entering the houses of defenceless widows, robbing them of every article of value, leaving whole families in a miserable state of destitution and want. . . . After long watching, it was ascertained that the marauders belonged to the towns of Bob Gray and his son Young Bob. Application for redress was promptly made to those chiefs, who expressed great concern and sympathy for the sufferers, promising to deliver over to the colonial authorities the offenders, and make immediate reparation for the wrong committed. These promises, though made again and again, have never been complied with.[22]

The American Colonization Society, in addressing the colonists' concerns, cited the difficulty of settling any new land, and compared the settlement of Liberia to early colonies in America. An annual report from the society's board of managers noted, "Nearly one half the first Plymouth emigrants died in the course of four months. The first three attempts to plant a colony in Virginia totally failed. In six months, ninety of the one hundred settlers who landed at Jamestown died." These statistics probably provided stark comfort to Liberian settlers struggling to stay alive.[23]

During their first few years in Liberia, the Majors and Harlans may have thought about the early settlement of Kentucky. They were probably descended from enslaved people brought into Kentucky in the late 1700s and perhaps had heard tales of pioneering times. The early Kentucky settlers—black and white—had also faced hunger, deprivation, disease, wild animals, grueling work, and wars with indigenous people. Perhaps these memories gave the Liberian settlers courage and hope when life was hard.

Despite their hardships, Tolbert closed his letter with a cheery greeting—"Tell all of your family howdy."

9

We Have Had War with the Natives

Lewis Harlan moaned in his sleep. His mother, Agnes, hurried across the dirt floor of the hut and knelt beside his simple wooden bed. She dipped a cloth in a bowl of water, wrung it out, folded it, and laid it across his feverish brow.

Lord! He had lost so much weight in just days. He had been a good-sized boy—big for sixteen, nearly a man—when they arrived in Bassa Cove. Now he looked frail, diminished, weak.

Back in Kentucky, Master George had warned them about emigrant's fever. He wanted them to be prepared, to know what they might face. But Agnes had thought her family could avoid the disease. They were all strong and healthy. She was determined to emigrate, to find a new home for herself and her children. Kentucky was no place for them. Her husband, Enoch Harlan, had been enslaved but then freed, but even free black people had a rough time of it in America.

She vividly remembered the day he had been emancipated. Enoch woke up early, slid out of the warm bed they shared, silently slipped into his clothes, and stepped out the cabin door. The sun was just coming up over the fields, green with new growth. He had sat on a wooden chair on their small porch, filled his pipe with tobacco he had helped grow and harvest, and watched the sun creep over the horizon on his last day of enslavement. Later that morning, George and Silas Harlan, two of the brothers who co-owned him, mounted their horses and headed to Hopkinsville for court day. There they submitted a document freeing Enoch and a man named Nat. The document was duly recorded in the court order book and—with the bang of a gavel—Enoch was a free man. But Agnes and the children were still enslaved, and Enoch stayed on at George Harlan's farm and worked the soil until the day he died.[1]

When Master Harlan had offered Agnes the opportunity to migrate to Liberia, she quickly consented, craving freedom and a fresh start for herself and her children. Lewis, her oldest, could help her clear land, plant crops, and care for his younger siblings.

But within weeks after the *Luna* landed, folks started to fall sick. First came the headaches and fevers, then achy joints and bad chills. Some of the sick recovered; many did not. Rachel and Robert Buchner had come over on the *Luna* with their seven children. Agnes had heard that both of them were sick. They had already buried one child, and several others in their family were ill. Their daughter Harriet, in her early twenties, was caring for the entire family.

The day before, one of the settlers who had been in the colony for a while had brought dried plant material to Agnes and showed her how to brew tea for Lewis. The concoction was bitter and Lewis didn't like it, but Agnes made him drink it. It hadn't helped. Until yesterday, Lewis had at least responded when she called his name, but now he was slipping away a little each hour. He had had the shakes the night before and had moaned so much that he kept the other children awake. She finally sent them over to the nearby huts the Majors shared. They had been there all day, and now it was twilight again.

Agnes slid the cloth from her son's forehead and mopped the sweat from his face, his arms and hands, rinsing the cloth each time. She held his hand and told him she loved him. Already on her knees, she clasped her hands together, clenched her eyes, and begged God—begged him—to spare her son. She prayed harder than she had ever prayed in her life.

She stood, wiped tears from her eyes and cheeks, picked up the bowl, and stepped out into the evening air. She walked to the bucket of water Tolbert had fetched for her and refilled the bowl. She stretched a little to ease the stiffness in her knees and back, took a deep breath, swatted a mosquito on her arm, and then stepped again into the gloom of the hut.

She knelt beside Lewis, looked at his face in repose, and knew he was gone.

A short note from Tolbert to another Christian County man was included in his letter of May 1839. In his salutation, Tolbert started to write "Hopkinsville," then crossed it out and wrote "Mr. More." The recipient was likely a man named James Moore in Hopkinsville. The letter has a two-by-three-inch hole in it, and the bottom of the letter is torn.[2]

> *Bassa Cove, May 20th, 1839*
> *Dear Mr. ~~Hopkins~~ More,*
> *I take this opportunity*
> *to write you a few lines to inform [you]*
> *that I & my wife's health is well. Please tell*
> *Mr. George   that Agnes Harlin*
> *& her daug   ell but her two*
> *sons are   died first he*
> *Died soon [illegible]   here & Henry*
> *has been de   six months he*
> *died in the cou   ect that he had a*
> *good deal of   his mother was none*
> *off better for it. For he was alone among*
> *the country people.*

The hole in the note is unfortunate, for Tolbert was trying to convey important news. He seemed to be saying that Agnes Harlan and her daughters were well, but that two of Agnes's sons had died. Lewis was the first; he succumbed to malaria within a few weeks after their arrival.[3]

Malaria symptoms include high fever, headache, fatigue, joint and muscle pain, chills, sweating, dry cough, nausea, and vomiting. The disease can be debilitating or fatal. Those who survive take weeks or even months to fully recover; some never recover their previous vitality. Survivors often battle reoccurrences of the disease months or years later.

There are hundreds of ways to die in West Africa. In addition to malaria, the settlers risked tuberculosis, dysentery, leprosy, typhoid fever, hepatitis, and countless other viral and bacterial diseases. They faced danger from leopards, baboons, crocodiles, and snakes. They faced drought, dust storms, and tropical heat and humidity. Cockroaches, spiders, termites, rats, fire ants, driver ants, fleas, flies, and parasites—including the insidious guinea worm—plagued the colonists. But malaria was the leading cause of death, causing more than 40 percent of deaths among Liberian settlers from 1820 to 1842.

Historian Eric Burin called the colony a death trap and noted that malaria and diseases killed 29 percent of the people who arrived in Liberia between 1820 and 1830. Fresh graves, grieving families, widows, widowers, and orphans were all too common in Bassa Cove.[4] Within only four months of the *Luna*'s arrival, Lewis Harlan, six of the nine Buchners, and several other of the brig's passengers had died of the disease.[5]

But people in America in the 1830s faced many of the same and similar threats. Malaria was common in the southern United States and even as far north as Illinois. Tuberculosis, yellow fever, typhoid, measles, and cholera took countless lives each year in the United States. Hurricanes ravaged coastal areas; tornadoes destroyed towns and farms farther inland. Those who moved west often faced dangerous animals, including bears, wolves, panthers, and rattlesnakes.

Women born between 1800 and 1819 in the south-central United States had a life expectancy of only thirty-three years. They died of diseases, in accidents, and—all too frequently—of complications from childbirth. Mothers and fathers made the sad but often accurate assumption that half of their offspring would not survive childhood.[6]

Even those immigrants to Liberia who fully understood the odds may have decided that it was a risk worth taking.

Tolbert noted that Henry had been dead six months and that he may have died in the country—the interior of the settlement. No one named Henry Harlan appears on the roll of emigrants. However, a seven-year-old boy named Coke Harlan is listed, along with the notation that he died in 1839 of pleurisy. Perhaps this is the boy to whom Tolbert referred. Formerly enslaved people sometimes changed their names after obtaining freedom. (One family changed their surname to Liberty; another family used Hope.) Tolbert noted that "he was alone among the country people"—the settlers' term for the indigenous people. It is unclear, however, why the boy was with them.

Long before the colonists arrived on the west coast of Africa, many indigenous people practiced a custom known as "pawning"—trading the labor of their children to pay debts or obtain property. The practice was similar to indentured servitude, a system long practiced in America. Many Liberian colonists took local children into their homes as pawns or household help; they supported the practice by arguing that it helped "civilize" and Christianize the African children. There may have also been some element of cultural exchange or building of alliances between the settlers and indigenous people. For indigenous people involved in foreign trade, having a child in their family learn English and American customs would have been highly advantageous, but it was a system vulnerable to abuse.[7]

It is possible that the boy to whom Tolbert referred had been sent to live with an indigenous family—either to work off a debt or in exchange for

their child living in Agnes's household. Tolbert wrote that Agnes was grieving the loss of her children; she was "none off better for it."

He continued: "Agnes says that she wishes that her good Master Harlin please to send her some necessarys, for she is needy, for we have had war
with the natives & and they destroyed . . ." The letter is torn here.

George Harlan, Agnes's former owner, was the oldest of seven sons
of Elijah Harlan and Mary Porterfield of Berkley County, Virginia (now
West Virginia). His father died when George was only thirteen, leaving his
mother to care for her large brood by herself.[8] George was born in 1776,
only a few months before the American colonists declared their independence from Great Britain. In 1812, he fought on the American side when
the United States again went to war against England. Sometime before
the war, Mary moved her family to Kentucky, where she and her sons co-
owned land and other property.[9]

In May 1825, George and his brothers submitted an agreement to the
court in Christian County to free two enslaved people: one of them was
Enoch, Agnes's late husband. He was described as "about thirty years old,
is six feet and ⅝ inches high, a dark mulatto, has a scar above the left eye,
also on his right foot."[10]

Enoch and Agnes had been together for a few years by the time he
was freed. The couple had three children by 1825, and Agnes had another
baby the year that Enoch was emancipated.

Although he had participated in freeing the two men, George Harlan
had not abandoned slavery. By 1830, he owned ten enslaved people; census records did not list them by name, only by gender and age range. Four
of George's enslaved people match the ages and genders for Agnes and
three of her sons. He also owned one other female slave, who may have
been Tyloa. The census lists one free person of color in his household, likely
Enoch.[11]

George, a farmer and blacksmith, had poor luck with wives. After the
deaths of his first two wives, Sarah and Susanna, he married Margaret King
in June 1824. Margaret inherited four stepchildren from her predecessor
wives, and the couple had six children of their own.[12]

About ten years later, George decided to give up slavery and move his
family to Illinois. There they purchased a large tract of government land in
Macoupin County and built a new life. However, before he left Kentucky,
George—apparently working with Ben Major—freed Agnes and her children to go to Liberia. Their value was equivalent to $65,000 to $75,000 in
2017 dollars.[13]

What motivated George, who owned many enslaved people and hundreds of acres of Kentucky land, to give up slavery and move to another state? No letters, journals, or other documents have been discovered that reveal his motivations.

Tolbert also wrote of a recent war. The settlers and indigenous people engaged in numerous skirmishes; most were over trade, including the slave trade. Just as the institution of slavery was deeply entrenched in the American South and elsewhere, the practice of selling people into slavery was entrenched in many of the indigenous cultures along the western coast of Africa. "For over three centuries, the widespread and injurious trade deeply scarred the societies along this coast," wrote Liberian author C. Patrick Burrowes. "On the one hand, the common people (especially in the interior) were victimized by the trade. On the other hand, rulers (particularly along the coast) grew dependent on it for the guns and jewelry that ensured their prestige."[14]

However, the practice of slavery varied among African cultures. It was often very different from the western institution of chattel slavery for life.

The Major collection of letters, now housed at the McLean County Museum of History in Bloomington, Illinois, includes a folder with two fragments of a letter. Folds in the two fragments align. On the bottom of one fragment are James Moore's name (spelled "More") and "Hopkinsville." Just to the right of Moore's name are Tolbert's name and "Bassa Cove." These fragments seem to be part of the May 20 letter. If so, the final sentence of the letter—"for we have had war with the natives and they destroyed . . ."—concludes: "everything I had & I find it very hard to get along, for my two small boys [illegible] able to help me, for I have to help them. Tell my uncle [illegible] Harlin that I want him to please to send me out some things, for I am very needy at this time. The war has destroyed us so that we do not know what to do. I like the place very much indeed & . . ."

The left side of the second fragment is missing where the first three lines would have been, and the whole right side of the fragment is missing. The words that remain are: "the war has not [illegible] . . . we should have been very . . . Give my love to all of my fa . . . tell them that I want to see th . . . very much indeed."

These fragments provide intriguing clues about family relationships. Three young boys with the last name Major arrived on the *Luna:* Thomas, Washington, and Thornton. In his letter, Tolbert links "Tho" with Austin's name, and "Wa" and "Thorton" with himself, implying that Thomas was Austin's son, and Washington and Thornton were Tolbert's sons. In this fragment of the letter, he refers to "my two small boys." He also refers to an uncle with the last name Harlin. Maybe Tolbert was related to the Harlans, or perhaps this was a term of affection for an older, unrelated man.

It is curious that this letter to James Moore remained with the letters sent to Ben Major. Since the letter to Moore starts on the bottom of the letter to Ben, perhaps Ben copied the note to Moore and mailed it to him in Christian County, retaining the original.

Ben kept this and all of the other letters he received from Africa and closely followed the colonization movement his entire life.

10

My Heart Yet Bleeds

Spring was in full bloom in Augusta, Georgia, but Emily Thomas Tubman wasn't paying attention to the sunshine or the cheerful azaleas. She was preoccupied by a promise she had made to her husband on his deathbed—that she would find a way to free the family's enslaved people. She sat at her desk, opened a bottle of ink, and picked up her pen. It was the day before her forty-second birthday.

Emily was born in Virginia in 1794; she grew up in Franklin County, Kentucky. After her father died, Henry Clay, the "Great Compromiser," became her guardian. (A local attorney, John Allen, later assumed guardianship of the Thomas children.)[1]

In 1818, on a trip to Georgia, Emily met and married Richard Tubman, an Englishman who was twenty-eight years her senior. The couple lived most of the year in Augusta, where Richard owned several plantations. Each summer they traveled to Kentucky so Emily could visit friends and family, and so the couple could avoid the yellow fever that plagued the Deep South. On their trip north in 1836, Richard fell gravely ill in the mountains of North Carolina. He died in his wife's arms, and Emily and some of their slaves buried him alongside the road. His last wish was that Emily free their enslaved people.[2]

Georgia lawmakers had prohibited so-called domestic emancipations—those that allowed formerly enslaved people to remain in the state. Richard was aware of the law when he prepared his will. He named Emily executor and left a gift of $5,000 to the University of Georgia, on the condition that the legislature allow the emancipation. Legislators, however, declined his offer.[3]

Emily remained undaunted. She had been taking what amounted to a crash course in business from her brother, an attorney and Yale graduate. She was both determined and confident in her own intelligence and her understanding of the law. Anxious to get the matter resolved, she wrote to Henry Clay, who was then president of the American Colonization Society, a position he held from 1836 to 1849. She also traveled to Washington to discuss colonization with Clay and other society officials. Emily returned home and offered her enslaved people a choice. She would free them and pay for their passage to Liberia, or they could remain enslaved and stay with her.

She apparently was expecting a visit from Reverend Ralph Gurley of the colonization society so she could obtain more details about emigration to Liberia. When he failed to appear in Augusta, she sat at her writing desk and drafted a letter to him.[4]

Augusta, March 20, 1837
Dear Sir,

Your letter of the 14th February came in due time, and I have been waiting with the hope of having a personal interview with you that I might obtain some information with respect to Liberia from you that I desire to have, should my servants determine to go there—the season is now so far advanced I fear you have declined coming, and therefore must apply by letter.

My late husband desires me in his will to emancipate 48 of our slaves and remove them to one of the U States in which I deem the Laws calculated to give them most protection and liberty—I have thought it not departing from the spirit of the will (the happiness and comfort of these people) to lay before them such information with regard to Liberia as I could collect, and let them choose a home for themselves. They now have the subject under consideration and I expect to know their decision on Saturday.

I am inclined to think they will divide on going to Africa, and as you have long been known to the Country as an active friend of Colonization, and perhaps better acquainted with the subject, both from personal observation of that Country and other sources of information, than any other person in our Country, I have taken the liberty of requesting your opinion and advice, as to which of the settlements I had better send my people. Health is of paramount importance, next to that, the greatest prospect of comfort and success in business—specify what outfit would be necessary for their comfort, be minute on this subject if you please and what the probable expense of their passage—also at what time they may probably sail. I am anxious for them to go as soon as possible—two or three of the number declined to be liberated, having preferred to remain as they are, desiring no greater burden than they now have—they may, however, think differently when they see the others starting.

This family I think will be quite an acquisition to Liberia. They have been liberated for their great fidelity and good conduct. They have been brought up [illegible]. The older ones skilled in the business—they are honest, industrious, and not an intemperate one among them. You will oblige me very much by answering this by express mail immediately.

Yours Respectfully,

Emily Tho. Tubman

Emily eventually lost patience with the American Colonization Society and worked instead with the Maryland Colonization Society. The Tubman settlers arrived in Liberia in the summer of 1837 aboard the *Baltimore* and settled in the Maryland colony southeast of Bassa Cove. The colonization society received a $10,000 bequest from Richard Tubman's estate for their emigration and settlement.[5]

Two of the enslaved people Emily freed were a married couple, Sylvia and William Shadrach Tubman. Their grandson William Tubman would become president of Liberia in 1944.

Those who chose to stay in Georgia were, of course, still enslaved. However, Emily provided individual parcels of land for them, equipped them to be independent farmers, and paid them wages.

After making these arrangements, Emily started a new life. She opened a textile mill and became a major shareholder in a railroad and several banks. She ultimately more than doubled her inheritance. She provided funds to build several Disciples of Christ churches in Georgia, rebuilt the Frankfort (Kentucky) Christian Church after a fire, gave generously to church-sponsored colleges, and donated $30,000 to the Foreign Christian Missionary Society. She also founded a public high school for girls and built low-cost housing for women who were widowed during the Civil War. Emily died at the age of ninety-one and is buried in Frankfort. A statue of her was erected in front of the Augusta First Christian Church to honor her life and legacy.

Emily Tubman was only two years older than Ben Major, and they had grown up in the same county and same social strata. Like Ben, Emily was a Disciple of Christ, was committed to supporting churches and schools, and chose to colonize her formerly enslaved people in Liberia. Her guardian, Henry Clay, was related to Ben by marriage. Emily was also a friend of Disciples of Christ founder Alexander Campbell, who knew Ben. With so much in common, it is likely that they knew of one another and perhaps were directly acquainted.

Published history of the 1800s focuses on the accomplishments and experiences of white men. White males were usually the ones writing history, so it is far easier to find documentation for them. However, it would be negligent to discuss the colonization of Liberia without including the contributions of women—both black and white—who supported the movement.

Wives of slave owners were in a unique position. In theory, they were models of purity and perfection placed on a pedestal; in reality, they were as completely under the control of the master as his enslaved people. They had few legal rights and lacked both independence and a political voice.

Catherine Clinton conducted extensive research for her book *The Plantation Mistress* and concluded that the image of the genteel, pampered southern lady depicted in novels and films is more fable than fact. These women carried out critical and complex functions that contributed greatly to the financial and social success of their husbands. Although Clinton's research focused on Virginia, the Carolinas, Georgia, Alabama, Mississippi, and Louisiana, her findings likely apply—at least in part—to plantation mistresses in Kentucky.[6]

The responsibilities of plantation mistresses included oversight of food production (including gardens, orchards, dairies, and smokehouses), housekeeping, quilting, sewing, weaving, making pillows and featherbeds, production of candles and soap, preserving meats and vegetables, providing hospitality to visitors, brewing home remedies, caring for the sick and injured, attending deathbeds, handling family correspondence and household finances, and—when their husbands traveled—providing oversight of the plantation and crops. Having enslaved people did not relieve them of hands-on work. They were also isolated on rural properties and discouraged from involvement in politics and current events. They were not allowed to travel without chaperones, which limited their mobility and increased their isolation.

They were expected to have and raise large families. For example, Lucy Major (Ben's wife) had nine children. Henrietta Major (Joseph's wife), Joanna Major (Chastine's wife), and Ben's sister, Eliza Ann Davenport, each had eleven children. Margaret Major (William's wife) had ten children. Families were also expected to take in orphaned kin and unmarried female relatives.

Then there was the issue Mary Boykin Chesnut alluded to in her diary. "God forgive us, but ours is a monstrous system, a wrong, and an iniquity. . . . Like the patriarchs of old, our men live all in one house with their wives and their concubines, and the mulattoes one sees in every family exactly resemble the white children—and every lady tells you who is the father of all the mulatto children in everybody's household, but those in her own she seems to think drop from the clouds."[7]

Many plantation mistresses were exposed daily to indisputable evidence that their husbands or sons were sexually assaulting black women. There was little they could do to alter the situation, although some tried.

Plantation mistresses had limited experiences and perspectives, myriad responsibilities, little free time, and almost no control or power to make important decisions, although, of course, the constraints and restrictions on their lives cannot be compared to those borne by enslaved people.

Although only about 10 percent of all slave owners were women, 21 percent of slave owners who emancipated and colonized enslaved people were female. Women were also more likely to engage in multiple acts of manumission and typically freed a greater proportion of their enslaved people.[8]

For example, the *Liberian Packet*, which sailed in January 1850, carried nine formerly enslaved people freed by sisters Isabella and Dorcas Doak; nine emancipated by Margaret See; nine by Fanny Bernard; and four by Dorothea Bratton. The thirty-one formerly enslaved people freed by these five women accounted for more than a quarter of the ship's passengers.[9]

The *African Repository* frequently listed women among those donating to the organization. Their donations ranged widely: Miss Elizabeth B. Morris, $25; Mrs. White, 50 cents; Miss Lorrain, $5; and Miss Hollingshead and Mrs. Wm. Dimock, $1 each. Mrs. E. H. Peabody of Springfield, Massachusetts, donated $125, the proceeds of a fundraising fair. Eliza B. Morris of Wilmington, Delaware, sent in $200 "from the fruits of her industry." Elizabeth Davis, of Montgomery County, Maryland, left a bequest of $2,000. Elizabeth Cole of Erie, Pennsylvania, left a $1,000 bequest.[10]

In May 1835, the editor of the *New York Commercial Advertiser* received a box containing a lace counterpane. Mary C. Frost, "a young lady of New York," had made the bedspread, which had been exhibited at a fair and was valued at $500. In her letter to the editor, she asked that it be sold and half the proceeds of the sale be donated to the colonization society.[11]

Prominent white southern women colonizationists included Ann Randolph Page, Mary Blackford, Margaret Mercer, and Mary Lee Custis. Ann Randolph Page, who was related to the Washington, Lee, and Custis families, sent twenty-four people to Liberia. Mary Blackford of Fredericksburg, Virginia, was characterized as "a firm and long-tried friend of colonization." Working closely with her mother, Lucy Minor, she founded two auxiliary colonization societies for women. Her mother freed a dozen of her enslaved people for migration to Liberia.[12] Margaret Mercer was one of the most prominent women in the colonization movement. She taught all of her enslaved people to read and paid for a medical education for one of her formerly enslaved people. Her many efforts on behalf of the cause were acknowledged when the American Colonization Society named one of their ships for her.[13] And Mary ("Molly") Lee Custis was part of a historic American family. Her husband was Martha Washington's grandson, George Washington Parke Custis, and her son-in-law was Robert E. Lee. Molly was an Episcopal lay leader and heavily involved in the colonization movement. She and her daughter, Mary Anna Randolph Custis Lee, engaged in a steady campaign of letter writing and promotion of the colonization cause.

These women and others took private actions and often made public statements in support of colonization. Some of them were related to or married to men who were involved in colonization; others defied male relatives to support the movement. Their efforts, while welcomed by the national and auxiliary colonization societies, were not always embraced by people closer to them.

John Hartwell Cocke, a stalwart advocate of colonization who had been beaten by his neighbors for his views, still objected when his second wife, Louisa Maxwell Holmes, became involved in the cause. He wrote to a friend, "[We] must put down the petticoats—at least as far as their claim to take the platform of public debate and enter into all the rough and tumble of the war of words."[14]

However big the sacrifices and however strenuous the efforts of white women for the colonization cause, freeborn and freed black women were ultimately the ones who had to step aboard the Liberian-bound ships and build new lives on foreign soil.

Women who were enslaved lived hard lives, working from before dawn to past dusk. Historian Elizabeth Fox-Genovese outlined typical responsibilities: "Slaves worked in the kitchens and smokehouses . . . to produce three meals a day, except perhaps on Sunday, and to hang and smoke innumerable pounds of pork. Slaves waited on table. Slaves washed and ironed, took up and put down carpets; carried the huge steaming pots for the preservation of fruits; lifted the barrels in which cucumbers soaked in brine; pried open the barrels of flour; swept the floors and dusted furniture; hoed and weeded gardens; collected eggs from poultry . . . spun and wove and sewed household linens and 'negro clothes.'"[15]

In the first two decades of colonization, 45 percent of the emancipated emigrants were female, and many of them were widows or single mothers with small children. They welcomed the broader rights afforded to them in Liberia, and even though they likely knew settling in a new land would be hard work, they would at least be working for themselves and their families. In Liberia, single women were eligible for land grants, and the 1847 constitution protected women's property from their husbands' creditors. However, they still could not vote and only by an act of the legislature could a couple divorce.[16]

In Liberia, women fulfilled traditional roles but also did whatever else was needed to care for their families. Agnes Harlan was typical. She no doubt labored hard under the African sun to feed and clothe her family and to try to keep them alive despite malaria, other diseases, and injuries from battle.

Other female settlers from America worked equally hard to establish new lives in Africa. Martha Harris Ricks came to Liberia with her husband, Sion Harris (sometimes called Zion). In 1840, when the mission station where they were living was attacked, Martha was in the thick of things, reloading weapons for her husband and other defenders. In 1848, when the new republic's president, his wife, and other members of his family traveled to America, Martha and Sion went with them. After Sion was killed (struck by a bolt of lightning), Martha married a man named Henry Ricks. She farmed and raised turkeys, ducks, and sheep. She particularly admired Queen Victoria and spent twenty-five years making her an appliquéd quilt that depicted the Liberian coffee tree in full bloom. On a trip to England in 1892, she was able to gain an audience with the queen at Windsor Castle and present the quilt to her in person.[17]

Another Liberian settler, the widowed Amelia Roberts, brought her family to Liberia in 1829 aboard the *Harriet*. She nursed all six of her children through malaria. Her son Joseph Jenkins Roberts became Liberia's first president.[18]

Diana McKay Sheridan came to Liberia without her husband, Alfred Miller, who remained enslaved in America. Diana had six children and arrived in Cape Mount, Liberia, in 1857. She and her children built a cabin on her lot, cleared land, and planted crops. Looking ahead, Diana saved corn to use as seed the following season and grew numerous other crops. She persevered and built a new life for herself and her children.[19]

Harriet Waring, a freeborn woman, migrated in 1824 from Virginia to Liberia aboard the *Cyrus* with her husband, Colston, and their six children. Colston Waring was a free black man, a merchant, and a Baptist preacher. He had traveled to Liberia in 1823 and returned to America to report favorably on conditions in the colony, leading the couple to decide to migrate. By 1835, Colston and some of the Waring children had died.[20]

Harriet wrote to Reverend Ralph Gurley of the American Colonization Society, telling him of her family's plight and asking for help with their business.[21]

Monrovia, Liberia, 5th March 1835
Rev. R. R. Gurley
Dear Sir,
You have heard ere this of the death of my husband, Mr. Waring. He died the 12 August last, and while I communicated to you the mournful tidings, my heart yet bleeds. Yes, sir, I am a widow with four small children. I do not, however, mourn as one without hope. My dear husband's end was peace[ful]. And I feel thankful to God who has declared himself a father of the fatherless and the widow's stay that he has supported me in all my heavy afflictions and trials. My family are as well as could be expected, circumstances considered.
I received a letter from you since the death of my husband. My son-in-law Mr. [John] Lewis carries on the business in part that Mr. Waring conducted. And any interference on your part in our favor will be very thankfully received. Business in the Colony is not as flourishing as has it been some times past. My love and respects to Mrs. Gurley and family.

I remain yours,
respectfully,

Harriet G. Waring

Harriet remarried in 1839. Her new husband, Nathaniel Brander, had been an agent for the American Colonization Society and later served as a Liberian Supreme Court justice and then vice president of Liberia. One of Harriet's daughters, Jane Rose Waring, married Joseph Jenkins Roberts and became Liberia's first First Lady. Another daughter, Susanna, was married to John N. Lewis, the associate editor of the *Liberian Herald*, and she played a key role in the ceremony marking Liberia's transition to a republic.[22]

Though stories of these particular women and some others survived, most female migrants to Liberia lived, labored, and died in obscurity. Succeeding in a new country was hard and was especially difficult for women without partners, but who often had large families. Sometimes, by dint of hard work and luck, they survived and built new lives. Often they and their children lived in poverty and died without leaving a trace of their existence.

We Stand in Great Need of Seed

On a late December day in 1840, Ben Major saddled his horse for a ride from Walnut Grove to nearby Washington, Illinois. As Ben pulled up his coat collar to ward off the cold, he glanced at his recently completed frame house. He was glad the family had settled into the snug new home and were out of the old log cabin before winter started.

Ben set out, and as he covered the eight miles between the two towns, he composed a mental list of the supplies he needed and reminded himself to pick up the mail.

Tolbert had received a letter from Ben in August 1840 and responded in October. His letter was postmarked December 10, nearly two months after it was written. (Outgoing mail from Liberia was handed over to ships' captains and postmarked only after it arrived at a US port.) The letter was addressed to Ben in Washington, Tazewell County, Illinois. Washington was a small town west of Walnut Grove and the site of the local post office.

> *Bassa Cove, October the 17th, 1840*
> *Dear father,*
>   *I was very happy to hear from you and the more to . . . see the much regard you have for me. I received your letter [of] Aug. the 8th, 1840. I am well & family. I have married since I arrived here and [am] happy to say that I have a very good industrious wife and one that may be depended on, and if she had a chance, she could do much more with such as wheels, cards, looms and their utensils notwithstanding.*

Tolbert addressed Ben as "dear father." Some slave owners fathered children with their enslaved women; however, Ben was only seven years older than Tolbert and was not his biological father.

Tolbert again wrote of his wife, noting that she was industrious, but could do much more with spinning wheels and other tools to produce cloth from raw cotton. (Cards are tools used to comb debris from wool and cotton and to align the fibers.) The colonists frequently mentioned the shortage of cloth and thread. They likely would have learned how to make cloth while living in Kentucky.

Author Alice Dunnigan wrote of enslaved people in Kentucky, "Most of the cloth from which they made clothing was homespun on their own plantations. Old slaves who were unable to work in the field were assigned the task of carding wool, spinning cotton, weaving and dyeing. . . . weaving and making garments were common practices in Kentucky, as well as in other slave states."[1]

Tolbert continued:

> *Since I left you, I have met with a great misfortune. When I arrived here, I was put in a thatch house, where I was taken down with the fever and the natives broke in upon me and [have] taken everything I had in this world. I like this country very well, although one cannot raise as much here as they can in the States on account of the rough [?] & since I was robbed, I have been obliged to take up all of my time in working for people to support myself & family.*

Tolbert seemed to have assumed the role of family patriarch, and his letters to Ben implied something of a relationship between peers—between the leader of one family and the leader of another—rather than the relationship between a slave and owner.

> *We have rice for bread & cassavas & yams & potatos. We use palm oil for lard. Meat is very scarce here. The palm tree which I have just mentioned is, I believe, the greatest in this country & I think any other. First, it [provides] the oil. Second, it gives wine. Thirdly, it gives cabbages that is as good if not better than those with you. In fact, I believe its match is not to be found on the globe, at least not in this county. The fig & bananas is very good, three of the plan-*

tain species, which is also very good and plenty in these parts. This plant never bears but once, but yet always has another scion ready to take its place.[2]

Tolbert clearly remained a farmer at heart, listing the country's various crops and offering praise for the many uses of the palm tree. Settlers harvested the local fruit—bananas, oranges, grapefruits, mangos, pawpaws, and soursops, a tart and spiny fruit. They also grew food crops, including rice, cassava, sweet potatoes, yams, greens, melons, lima beans, tomatoes, okra, and peanuts (also known as groundnuts or groundpeas) in Liberia's reddish soil. The Majors and Harlans would have been familiar with some of these vegetables and fruits from their gardens in southwest Kentucky, but many were new and exotic to them.

Cassava, also known as manioc, was a particularly important plant for those living in Liberia. Cassava was imported to West Africa by traders in the 1700s. The shrubs grow from four to eight feet tall, and have white fleshy roots, which are harvested when they are six to eighteen inches long. The roots are peeled and boiled, and the resulting dish tastes much like fresh chestnuts. The roots can also be pounded in mortars and made into flour.[3]

Settlers also grew cash crops, such as coffee or sugar, that they could sell or barter; however, their efforts to farm were stymied by a lack of equipment and expertise. Two months after Tolbert wrote this letter, Governor Buchanan sent a plea for farm animals and equipment.

> We suffer very much still from the want of draft animals, and we can never hope to succeed in our agricultural operations until the Colony is well provided in this respect. All the jacks [male donkeys] brought out last year by myself are dead. The fine large cattle of the interior suffer so much from the effects of the climate on the coast that it is impossible to work them … oxen are always dying before they are accustomed to the yoke.… Would it not be advisable to send a small steam engine of six or eight horse power for the sugar mill? The same fire that raises the steam might also boil the sugar, and thus the expense of carrying on the work would be actually less than by animal power. If the engine was a little larger, a shingle machine and even a sawmill might be connected with the sugar mill. What do you think of it?[4]

Tolbert wrote of the scarcity of meat, but Liberia didn't lack meat; the country had plenty of fish and wild game, locally referred to as bush meat. Bush meat included monkeys, antelope, deer, and "small meat"—squirrels, mongoose, rats, and bats. The Saint John River had an abundance of catfish, tilapia, and huge Nile perch. The ocean provided all sorts of fish, as well as oysters and turtles. But the settlers wanted the type of meat they were used to eating in America.

> *I was very much obliged to you for the things which you sent me, or rather us, but whether we received all that you sent us or not, I cannot tell. I received five pieces of cloth, namely one of mixed cotton; one of calico, thirty-four yards; three pieces of bleached cotton; three rolls of raw cotton, containing about a pound each. I also received 125 skeins of white [?] thread. I would be very glad, sir, if you would tell us how much you sent us and the definite amount with their names & their numbers. The box we received was broke open when we received it.*

Settlers struggled constantly to obtain supplies. No well-stocked stores or reliable distribution channels existed in the country. Immigrants and indigenous people had to either grow or make what they needed, or buy or trade for supplies that came to Bassa Cove by the occasional ship. A bill of lading for the *May Wilkes*, which sailed from New Orleans to Monrovia in 1847, provides a glimpse into the type of supplies the society sent to Liberia: lard, beef (dried or salted), pork, beans, vinegar, flour, mackerel, tobacco, shingles, and lumber. Other shipments included molasses, cornmeal, rice, raisins, herring, writing paper, candles, soap, hand tools, cloth, and spices.[5]

The box Ben had sent to Tolbert was broken open when they received it. Accusations of pilfering were sometimes leveled against others, including ship crews and agents of the American Colonization Society. Settlers often indicated in their correspondence that they did not receive expected parcels and letters. Sometimes supplies sent to Liberia were lost or damaged during shipping.[6]

The society, which perpetually struggled for funds, had to simultaneously supply the settlers and generate money for the colony's operation. In Liberia, Governor Buchanan juggled twin challenges in meeting the needs of the settlers while remaining accountable to the society board. In the fall of 1839, he wrote to the board and informed them that he had employed a man named Joseph Jenkins Roberts as the superintendent of public works and as a storekeeper in Monrovia; he had appointed Louis Sheridan to fulfill similar roles at Bassa Cove. (Sheridan, the ambitious entrepreneur who had arrived in Bassa Cove in 1838, had mended fences with the society by then.)[7]

Buchanan wrote:

> With the aid of these two agents at the extremities of the Colony, in charge of the great business interests, we shall ensure prompt and efficient action in every department; and your commercial views can be satisfactorily carried out. . . . My plan is this: to make the stores here [in Monrovia] and at Bassa Cove great centres of mercantile operations, filling them with goods of every kind suitable for the market, by which we can supply the merchants, to the exclusion of foreign traders, and afford to the people all they require of foreign goods at reasonable prices. In this way, we can easily in a short time secure all the business of this part of the coast for the Colonists, and keep your ships supplied with freight in oil, camwood, &c., &c.[8]

In his role as storekeeper at Bassa Cove, Sheridan replaced a man named Stephen A. Benson. Sheridan died in about 1843, but Joseph Jenkins Roberts and Stephen Benson were to become well-known men in the colony.[9]

Buchanan's plan to operate a retail store at Bassa Cove did not last long. About a year later, he ceased selling items on a retail basis, citing the many demands for store credit from people who had, or believed they had, a claim on the society for assistance. He instead appointed Sheridan to manage retail business for the colony on a commission basis. The Bassa Cove store did, however, continue to supply society workers and newcomers with goods and provisions.[10]

Tolbert concluded:

> *Please try to help us all you can: tobacco, cloth, large wash basins is great [to] sell in this country. We stand in great need of seed, such as cabbage seed, onion, mustard & buckwheat seed. If you should send us anything, do send us your son John to bring it or put it in very strict hands.*
>
> *I am, sir, yours,*
>
> *Tolbert Major*

Tolbert and Austin likely used the much-requested tobacco and other items for trade rather than for personal use. At the time, the principal articles of trade imported to Liberia were tobacco, rum, gunpowder, muskets, cotton and silk fabric, hardware, crockery and glassware, and beads. Principal exports were palm oil and camwood.[11]

Tolbert asked that Ben have his son accompany any shipments to Liberia. There's no indication that young John Major ever did so. He then closed with a postscript: "P.S. Friends is very scarce. Since [we] had our misfortune, no one hath ever been so good as to give us the worth of a pin. It appears that the people here strives to eat each other instead of striving to help each other. I [am] happy to tell you that for Christ's sake, [I have] committed my soul."

Tolbert's postscript is poignant. All of the settlers struggled and probably had little to share. However, Tolbert may have been referring to indigenous groups when he wrote "the people here strives to eat each other." Acts of ritual cannibalism were not unheard of, and violence between ethnic groups and between those groups and settlers was common.

A few months before Tolbert wrote this letter, two groups of indigenous people with opposing views had been at war near Bassa Cove. On one side were King Bob Gray and King Joe Harris (who had finally solidified his position as an ally of the settlers), and on the other side were some of the troublesome Fishmen and several inhabitants of New Cesters. New Cesters was located along the coast, between Bassa Cove and the Maryland settlement at Sinoe River.[12]

Governor Buchanan wrote, "It appears that the New Cesters people, who have for years driven a profitable business as factors for the slavers, accused Bob and Joe some time since of being inimical to the country, because of their having sold land to the Americans and countenanced the establishment of the settlement, thereby throwing obstacles in the way of the Slave Trade."[13]

Buchanan referred to the same group in an August 1839 letter. "Things at Bassa Cove remain in status quo. The Fishmen are still in their old place and will doubtless remain until we apply force to expel them."[14]

Six months later, Buchanan reported that slave trader Theodore Canot of New Cesters had agreed to surrender 103 enslaved people to a British naval lieutenant and abandon the slave trade. In the same letter, Buchanan noted that the slave factories at Gallinas (north of Monrovia) had been attacked by the British. He expressed hope that perhaps the settlers could acquire the land, thus ending the slave trade for good, but his hopes were dashed when a ship captained by a Spaniard landed there in June 1841 to purchase enslaved people.[15]

By 1842, a Dr. Hall reported:

> The very establishment of the colonies has absolutely broken up the slavers within their boundaries. The location of the first colony was on an island that had, from time immemorial, been occupied by slave factories. The first severe war in which this colony was engaged was on the question of the slave trade. The slave factories of Trade Town and New Cesters was broken up by [Rev. Jehudi] Ashmun early in the history of the colony. Subsequently two factories have at different times been destroyed by the colonists at Little Bassa, and that, too, through hard fighting. Grand Bassa was always a slave mart—the last slaves were shipped . . . in March 1832.[16]

Dr. Hall's assessment of the situation was optimistic. In a June 1842 letter to the American Colonization Society, Joseph Jenkins Roberts reported spotting in Bassa Cove "a long, black suspicious-looking schooner." The next day, he met a stranger in Bassa Cove, "a white man who spoke good English." Roberts discovered that the man was the "supercargo" for the anchored schooner, the man responsible for the ship's commercial concerns. Roberts asked him his objective in visiting the coastline of Africa. The stranger responded that he had come for palm oil and camwood. Roberts challenged him.

> I said to him at once, you have come to purchase slaves, to which he made no reply. . . . I told him I knew him to be a slaver, and as such, he must leave the settlement immediately. He departed forthwith . . . the fourth day the vessel got underway and stood up the coast: she sailed very fast. I got information from the Fishmen at the Cove that she would return in a few days to take a cargo of slaves. . . . She did return in about ten or fifteen days, took in a cargo of 250 slaves, and put to sea—all done in about 12 hours.[17]

Affectionately, Your Friend and Brother

At nearly the same time that Tolbert, Austin, Agnes, and their families were starting over in Liberia, Ben and his family were settling in Illinois. All of the families had left behind relatives, friends, and other loved ones.

Ben had three living brothers and one brother-in-law. In 1835, Ben's oldest brother, former slave owner William T. Major, moved his family from Kentucky to Bloomington, Illinois, about thirty miles from Ben's new home.[1]

Ben's youngest brother, Chastine, had owned seven people in 1830. Some accounts indicate he sold them to the highest bidder before leaving Kentucky. However, the receipt from the Christian County Colonization Society acknowledges delivery of "emigrants" from both Ben and Chastine. It is likely Chastine freed and colonized one or more of his enslaved people so that they could accompany their family members to Liberia. He then relocated with his wife and children to Danvers Township in Illinois.[2]

William Davenport, Ben's brother-in-law, was a lawyer and a Disciples of Christ preacher in Christian County, where he founded the Hopkinsville Christian Church. Perhaps influenced by the Majors or driven by his own beliefs, Davenport decided to divest himself of his bondsmen, and he used multiple methods to do so. He freed some of his enslaved people—some went to Liberia and others stayed in Kentucky—and sold the remainder to local people who owned their family members. He moved to Tazewell County, Illinois, in 1834.[3]

It would be logical to think that Ben was closer to and had more in common with his brothers in Illinois, who had divested themselves of enslaved people, than he did with his brother Joseph, who stayed in Kentucky and continued to own slaves. Yet Ben's surviving records seem to indicate otherwise. Chastine and William did not live far from Ben, but apparently visited and wrote infrequently. Ben kept no letters from Chastine and only a couple notes from William, but he retained more than two dozen letters from Joseph. Ben and Joseph were only two years apart in age; there seems to have been a strong bond between them.

Although Joseph purchased land in Illinois and toyed with the idea of moving there, he ultimately remained in Kentucky. Ben took care of Joseph's land and interests in Illinois; in turn, Joseph took care of Ben's remaining Christian County business. Joseph wrote often to Ben about business matters—conveying news or seeking advice. He wrote about his family, friends, and neighbors in Christian County, and sent church news. He also asked how Ben's formerly enslaved people were faring in Africa.[4]

Joseph's letters to Ben were affectionate and warm. A few days before Christmas 1844, he opened a letter to Ben by writing, "I am surrounded tonight by a house full of company, yet notwithstanding, must devote a short time in writing to you." He opened another letter by saying he had designated part of his day to "writing to my best friends, and commence with this, which I write especially for you." He ended the letter with "I ever remain your best friend and brother."

Joseph also evidently shared with Ben a strong faith. He closed one New Year's Eve letter to Ben with "May you all, together with us, be guided, protected, and at last received by our Lord and Savior Jesus Christ."[5]

Joseph did not appear to be as close to William or Chastine. He mentioned a visit from William and his wife in an 1837 letter, but in 1850 wrote to Ben, "I scarcely ever hear from brothers William and Chastine."[6]

Of the five Major siblings—William, Joseph, Ben, Chastine, and Eliza Ann—only Joseph continued to own slaves, and his holdings increased over time. He owned eight in 1820, ten in 1830, nine in 1840, seventeen in 1850, and twenty-two in 1860. He owned other humans until his death about a year before the end of the Civil War.[7]

Although Joseph frequently mentioned his desire to relocate to Illinois, such a move would have required him to abandon slavery, something he seemed unable to do. In an 1840 letter, Ben wrote to Joseph, encouraging him to move to Illinois. "From the tenor of your letter, I discover still a lurking in your breast to cultivate your fields adjoining the walnut grove with your own hand and those of your children . . . how can I cherish this feeling?"[8]

However, in the same letter, Ben revealed that the actions of his oldest brother, William, may not have been quite what they seemed, which may help explain the distance between them.

> I do seriously regret the course that our Dear Brother Wm has taken. I have not seen him since he returned but am told he has brought another negro with him—this makes two, a boy and a girl, and if I am not mistaken to the signs of the times, Isaac and Jincy are to soon follow, then he will have four negroes working for him as slaves in a free country under the false name of being free. This too is in opposition to the Constitution and Laws of this state and [he] subjects himself to severe penalties should anyone feel proper to prosecute him, but there are several others around Bloomington that have done the same and I suppose they conclude if it is sanctioned in one instance they cannot condemn it in another, and so they who disregard the laws of the land go unpunished again. He is a teacher of the religion of Christ and exhorts his brethren to "be in subjugation to the powers that be" . . . when he was in Ky the laws and constitution secured to him the right to do as he pleased with his slaves but as soon as he became a Citizen of Illinois, he is, as it were, sworn to support the Constitution and Laws of Illinois.[9]

Ben wrote these words in a draft letter to Joseph. There is no way to ascertain if he ever mailed a final version of the letter. Nor is there any way to determine if what he wrote about William was accurate. Some sources indicate that William brought a few of his formerly enslaved people with him to Illinois; however, they could have been working in the household as paid servants.

In the final paragraph of this letter, Ben wrote, "You are well apprised of the sacrifices I made to secure myself and my family from the Curses of Slavery, but should they be permitted to be brought to our country by those of the Slave States . . . I will have failed in the grand object that brought me to Illinois."[10]

Ben's words left no doubt as to how he felt about slavery or why he left Kentucky.

The Dark Clouds Begin to Disappear

Austin Major hefted a shovelful of the heavy soil onto the growing pile of dirt. He jammed the shovel blade into the mound and straightened up. Glancing at the hot sun, he wiped sweat from his brow and tears from his cheeks.

He was weary of burying children. He had buried Agnes's younger sons, Fletcher and Coke. He had been too sick to help bury her oldest when he died. He felt bad for Agnes; she was a good woman and didn't deserve such grief. Then again, none of them did.

He tried to help the other settlers when he could. He had offered today to bury the child of another widow in town. She had no man to help her, and she was laid low with grief.

Austin sighed deeply; the heavy air smelled of rotting vegetation and animal dung. He picked up the shovel again. He knew his brother was writing a letter today, and he wanted to finish with the grave in time to add a note of his own.

October the 17th, 1840, B. Cove
Dear father,

I embrace this opportunity to write you these few lines which will inform you of my health, which is good at the present. In compliance with your request, I now give you a statement of my condition. Soon after I arrived here, I was put in a thatch house, where I was taken down sick with the fever and when helpless, the natives came in and took everything that I possessed in this world . . . they came again

in about two years and burned my house with all that I had . . . my
sickness held me at least two years.

I have suffered much since I come here, but the dark clouds begin
to disappear again if you can send us some few articles of trade, such
as tobacco, cloth, pipes, beads such as china beads; it will be a profit to
both of us. I can buy palm oil, camwood, ivory . . . that is, if you can
make it convenient to send these things as goods is so dear here I can-
not buy them and make any profit at all. Do try to send these articles,
for which you shall not lose . . . if you do send these things, do try to
send them by some very particular person.

Austin was considering trading to support his family. He proposed a
business deal to Ben and promised him "it will be a profit to both of us"
and "you shall not lose." Many settlers, battling repeated bouts of malaria,
unfamiliar with the soils and plants of Africa, and often without farming
tools or draft animals, decided that trading would provide a more stable
livelihood.

Farming is hard work, especially for people weakened by malaria. The
Liberian settlers faced other obstacles as well. Historian Randall Miller
wrote, "The dense forest growth yielded grudgingly to the ax. Much of the
arable land on the flat coastal plain was engrossed by early arrivals in the
colony. Heavy West African rains washed out crops, strange and terrifying crop pests ravaged the fields and drove the farmers to perplexity, and
American crops and farming practices were inappropriate to conditions in
West Africa."[1]

There may have been other reasons the settlers avoided farming. Historian Claude Clegg noted, "While some immigrants defined freedom as
the opportunity to own land, a sizable number of people who had come
to Liberia conceived of freedom as liberty from the often demeaning field
labor that they had known so well in America. . . . there were those who
found the appeal of trading irresistible and who devoted much more time
to these transactions than to agriculture."[2]

Austin's letter continued: "I am happy to inform you of the goodness
of God to my soul. Since I come here, the Lord have spoke peace to both
of our souls or all of our souls. If I never see you in this life, I thirst to meet
you in bright glory . . . I do intend to strive to live as much aboveboard as
possible."

Ben and his formerly enslaved people shared an abiding faith in God;

it motivated Ben to free his enslaved people, and helped the settlers persevere in the face of endless challenges and almost overwhelming losses. The Majors, Harlans, and other settlers often expressed gratitude to God and wrote of an enduring faith in providence and a strong belief in the hereafter. "These misfortunes which I have told you of have caused us to labor hard to support our families, but after Christmas, we expect to clear farmland and commence trying to do something for ourselves," Austin wrote.

This remark and Tolbert's request for seeds indicated that they had not totally abandoned the idea of farming. Many of the settlers, under the right conditions, did succeed in agriculture.

In the month before Austin and Tolbert wrote their letters, Governor Buchanan noted in a dispatch, "I have had several applications from the older settlers of Edina and Bassa Cove for farms at that place, which I am disposed to grant, on my next visit there. Our progress in the agricultural department, though not rapid, is steady. . . . There have been twenty-three thousand coffee trees planted at Bexley, Bassa Cove and Edina: of that number, nearly 19,000 were planted this year." By 1843, the settlers had planted a total of 21,197 coffee trees.[3]

Like his older brother, Austin added a postscript: "P.S. You will please to write George Harlin to write to my mother-in-law, Enoch Harlin's wife . . . She have met with a great misfortune. She have lost three of her sons. This is four letters I have sent, I received one. Excuse the very [bad] handwriting . . ."

The Majors and Harlans had struggled in their first four years in Liberia. Agnes had lost three sons: sixteen-year-old Lewis in 1836; six-year-old Fletcher in 1837, and ten-year-old Coke in 1839. They were buried in the soil of a land still unfamiliar to her.

Young Washington Major had been shot. Tolbert, Austin, and probably most of the others had survived the fever. In addition to these woes, Austin's house had been burned. All they had accumulated had been stolen. Children dead, houses burned, property stolen—Austin and Tolbert must have often thought of the biblical story of Job. Did they ever lament to God or lose faith?

Buried in the postscript is a hint of good news. Austin refers to Agnes as his mother-in-law. At some point after arriving in Liberia, Austin married Ann, Agnes's daughter. She would have been eighteen at the time Austin wrote this letter.[4]

14

I Cannot Banish the Horrid Picture

Governor Thomas Buchanan stepped aboard the schooner in Sierra Leone. It wasn't big, maybe 120 tons or so. The stench hit him immediately: sweat, vomit, putrefying wounds, human waste, and the unmistakable smell of corpses. Even the brisk sea breeze couldn't sweep it away. The governor of Sierra Leone, northwest of Liberia, had told Buchanan that there were 427 enslaved people aboard the ship when it was captured off the coast of West Africa and brought to port in his country.

On every available space, above and below decks, Africans were sitting, lying, holding one another—many of them fearfully watched Buchanan walk past. A few glared at him in defiance. Others had the vacant stares of those in shock or without hope.

Governor Buchanan, who had learned that the captain of the slave ship was an American, unleashed his anger in a letter to the American Colonization Society. "The Governor [of Sierra Leone], at my insistence, promised to send him down here and deliver him up to me, to be sent to the United States. Is there any hope that our Government will hang him?"[1]

He continued. "There are about two thousand slaves now at New Cesters and Gallinas. The whole country, for five hundred miles to the right and left of us, has been devastated with wars caused entirely by the Slave Trade, throughout the whole summer; God only knows where it is to end."[2]

In 1845, W. B. Hoyt reported that the US *Yorktown* had captured a different slave ship, the *Pons,* en route to Rio de Janeiro. Hoyt boarded the vessel, which originally had 900 enslaved people on board; more than 140 of them were dead just two weeks later when the ship arrived in Monrovia, Liberia.

It is utterly impossible for language to convey an appropriate idea of the suffering of that wretched company. The decks were literally crowded with poor abject beings. The living and the dying were huddled together with less care than is bestowed upon the brute creation . . . as I came on the crowded deck, I saw directly in front of me one emaciated and worn down by long suffering to a mere skeleton. I looked over into the steerage. The hot, mephitic air almost overpowered me. At the foot of the ladder lay two of the most miserable beings I had ever beheld. They were reduced, as the one above named, so that their bones almost protruded from their flesh. Large sores had been worn upon their sides and limbs, as they had been compelled to lay upon the hard plank composing the deck of the vessel . . . I cannot banish the horrid picture.[3]

Despite the laws, good intentions, and concerted efforts to halt the slave trade, it continued along the west coast of Africa for decades after the first colonists arrived.

15

I Will Send You Some Coffee

Ben Major glanced around the front parlor. Lucy and nineteen-year-old Judith had spent the previous day tidying the house for company. A small pitcher filled with bluebells brightened the front hall table. It was early May in Walnut Grove; the days had warmed enough that there was no need for a fire in the parlor fireplace.

Ben had seen many of their anticipated guests that morning at church. He had scheduled the colonization meeting in the early afternoon, after his neighbors and friends had returned home and finished their Sunday dinners. He heard the creak of wagon wheels and laughter and calls of "Good afternoon" as the townspeople greeted one another. He stepped to the door.

Soon colonization supporters from Walnut Grove and nearby towns occupied every chair in the parlor. Ben's sons brought in more chairs until the room was filled, and some of the men stood against the back wall.

Lucy and Judith moved among their guests, handing them china cups and saucers and pouring fresh coffee from a silver coffeepot that had been in Ben's family for generations.

Ben spotted his brother-in-law, William Davenport, and young Sue Grant, a local teacher, among the guests. He stepped to the front of the room and welcomed everyone. He asked if they would allow him to share a letter he had received from Africa months earlier. He pulled a piece of paper from his breast pocket and unfolded it. Bits of red sealing wax clung to the paper.

Ben cleared his throat and began to read aloud.

Bassa Cove
August the 7, 1843
My dear much-beloved father,

  It is with pleasure that I take this opportunity of writing you this letter to inform you that we are all well, and I sincerely hope, Father, these few lines may find you and your much-beloved family in the same, as well as under the blessing of God.

  But I am sorry to inform you that Washington and Thomas is both dead. Washington died with a bleeding; it was thought that some of his blood vessels broke from the wound he received in the war two or three years ago. Thomas died with a long, lingering disease. But nevertheless, the Lord works all things for the best.

  Another thing I am sorry to inform you of and that is this: I had the misfortune to get my house burned into ashes about two months ago. My loss was great and had it not have been for my plantation, I do not know what I would have done. But I do not feel no ways discouraged at all, for as long as life lasts and my health is good, I do not feel discouraged.

Ben paused, cleared his throat, then continued.

  I would send you some of the produce of this country, but I have no one to send it by and another thing, I do not know where to send them so you can get them. But if you will send me word where to send I will send you some coffee and other things if it will be acceptable with you, and some groundnuts and many other things.

  We are well satisfied in this country, and I will say, this is the place for the man of color, even if we cannot get as much of the benefits of this country as you do in yours or as we did in the country that gave us birth. But, you may know, in all new countries, how it is, and as this is the commencement of things, we will do all that we can do and leave the balance for the rising generation and God our father. . . . Our wives send their love to all your women.

Ben looked up. In a voice thick with emotion, he told his listeners that Tolbert had followed through on his promise, shipping coffee from his own plantation all the way to Walnut Grove. Ben gestured at the cups his guests held and, with tears in his eyes, said, "Brethren, that coffee will drink sweet without any sugar."[1]

Tolbert Major established a coffee plantation and sent Ben Major coffee from his trees. (Jean de La Roque, 1716, Library of Congress Rare Book and Special Collections Division, https://lccn.loc.gov/96518498)

This letter—signed by both Tolbert and Austin, but likely written by Tolbert—seemed to mark a turning point. Despite the rocky start and setbacks, Tolbert was at last an established farmer, and although his house had been burned to ashes, he still had his coffee plantation.

The *coffea liberica* plant is native to Liberia. The trees produce a bean similar in flavor to *robusta* coffee and grow in the plains and forest of the country. The leaves and berries are larger than those of the *arabica* trees, and the large, white blooms are as fragrant as jasmine. Coffee farmers top the trees to keep them shorter and bushier, making the job of harvesting the ripe berries easier.

CENSUS—Continued.

Names.	Age.	No. in family.	Date.	Where born.	Connexions in the colony.	Profession.	Extent of education.	Health.
Mary Ann Haws	31	–	April, 1836	–	–	Washerwoman	None	Good.
Sarah Johnson	12	–	do	–	Mary's daughter	–	At school	do.
Charles Johnson	8	3	do	–	Mary's son	–	do	do.
Austin Major	35	–	do	–	–	Laborer	None	do.
Ann Major	21	–	do	–	Austin Major's wife	–	do	do.
Mary Major	12	–	do	–	Austin Major's daughter	–	At school	do.
Talbert Major	40	–	do	–	–	Laborer	None	do.
Silvy Major	19	–	do	–	Talbert Major's wife	–	do	do.
Agnes Hubbard	39	–	do	–	Ann's mother	–	do	do.
Asbury Hubbard	18	–	do	–	Agnes Hubbard's son	Laborer	do	do.
Wesley Hubbard	16	8	do	–	do do	–	do	do.
John Dunn	50	–	do	–	–	Farmer	do	Decline.
Susan Dunn	20	–	do	–	John Dunn's wife	–	do	Good.
Polly Barns	8	–	March, 1840	–	Orphan	–	At school	do.
Elizabeth Barns	3	–	–	In the colony	Daughter of J. and S.	–	–	do.
John Donaldson	46	–	March, 1840	–	–	Farmer	None	do.
Keziah Donaldson	30	–	do	–	John Donaldson's wife	do	do	do.
Mary Donaldson	15	7	–	–	Keziah Donaldson's sister	–	do	do.
Emanuel Nutter	35	–	Jan., 1833	–	–	Carpenter	do	do.
Susan Nutter	40	–	–	–	Emanuel Nutter's wife	–	do	do.
Ann Nutter	14	–	Jan., 1833	–	Emanuel Nutter's daughter	–	Reads and writes	do.
Henry Toliver	18	–	Dec., 1834	–	Son of Esther Toliver	–	None	do.
David Madison	25	–	do	–	–	–	Reads	do.
Charlotte Madison	50	6	July, 1827	–	David Madison's wife	Cook	None	Feeble.
Esther Toliver	45	–	Dec., 1834	–	–	do	do	do.
Maria Toliver	13	2	do	–	Esther Toliver's daughter	–	At school	Good.
Henry J. Roberts	22	–	March, 1829	–	Son of Amelia	Trader	Reads and writes	do.
Isaiah Hollster	18	2	Feb., 1833	–	Orphan	Apprentice	do	do.
Edward Lyles	30	–	Feb., 1838	–	–	Carpenter	do	do.
Judy Lyles	20	–	Dec., 1834	–	Edward Lyles's wife	–	None	do.
Margaret Lyles	12	–	Feb., 1838	–	Edward Lyles's daughter	–	At school	do.
Benjamin Lyles	7	–	do	–	Edward Lyles's son	–	do	do.

Seven years after the *Luna* brought the Majors and Harlans to Liberia, the colony conducted a census. Five Majors and three Harlans (listed under the name Hubbard) are shown living in Bassa Cave in 1843. (American Colonization Society, "Census of the Colony of Liberia," in *Tables Showing the Number of Emigrants and Recaptured Africans Sent to the Colony of Liberia . . . Together with A Census of the Colony* [Washington, D.C.: American Colonization Society, 1845])

After the tropical sun had ripened the coffee berries to a deep red, Tolbert and his family would have harvested them, and then extracted and roasted the beans before shipping them to Ben.

Tolbert's letter also relayed bad news: the deaths of Washington and Thomas. Washington would have been about fifteen years old when he died, and Thomas about fourteen. The Majors and Harlans had two new graves to tend.[2]

By 1843, half of the Major and Harlan settlers had died. This death rate was not unusual. In September 1843, only a month after this letter was written, the American Colonization Society conducted a census. The results were discouraging.[3]

Since 1820, the society had sent 4,454 people to Liberia. By 1843, only 1,736 remained. More than five hundred people had migrated out of the colony; many went to Sierra Leone or to the Maryland colony at Cape Palmas (which later became part of Liberia). More than one hundred had returned to the United States. Almost 50 percent had died.[4]

Of the *Luna*'s eighty-five passengers, forty-eight (56 percent) were dead by the time of the 1843 census, only seven years after the ship arrived in Liberia. Others had moved to Sierra Leone or Cape Palmas; one had returned to the United States. Besides the Harlans and Majors, only two other passengers from that voyage—John Dunn and his daughter, Susan—were still living in Bassa Cove in 1843.

In all of the Liberian settlements (excluding Maryland), the population was about 30,000, including indigenous people and "recaptives"—people rescued from slave ships and returned to Africa.[5] Bassa Cove, like most Liberian towns, was small. The census listed only 124 people—including children and babies—living in the settlement eight years after it was established. Monrovia, the largest town, had 912 people in 1843; other relatively large towns were Caldwell (311) and New Georgia (264), a town established by recaptives.

The 1843 census revealed something else. Tolbert had remarried; his new wife was Silvay Major, Agnes's younger daughter.

Despite his losses and the grim official status of the colony, Tolbert told Ben in his letter, "I do not feel discouraged . . . I will say this is the place for the man of color."

Other Liberian settlers expressed similar sentiments in their letters to America. James C. Minor wrote in an 1833 letter to his former owner, "Ho! All ye that are by the pale faces' laws oppressed, come over to the above mentioned destiny." In an 1846 letter, Abraham Blackford wrote, "Africa is the very country for the colored man," a sentiment echoed in 1860 by James Skipwith, who wrote that Liberia "is the Best Country for the Black man that is to Be found on the face of the Earth." Although these sentiments were common, they weren't universal.[6]

Wesley Harlan, the younger of Agnes's two surviving sons, turned sixteen in 1843. He had lived in Liberia since he was nine years old. At his mother's urging, he had written several times to George Harlan, the family's former owner, but had never received a reply.

Wesley thought Ben Major might have information about the Harlans or know how to reach them. He added a note to Tolbert's letter.

Mr. Magers
Dear Sir,
    It [is] with pleasure that your humble servant attempts to inform you that he is well, and it is my honest desire to have this to find you,

*sir, and [your] family in the same. All of my people is well and are
doing as well as can be expected in a new country.*

*I myself have had many downfalls like others, but with ambition
it is that I overcome them all, and if there is anyone delights in this
country, it surely is me.*

*But I want you to have the goodness to condescend so much as to
write me, if you please, where Mr. George Harlan is or his family, as
I have sent and sent a short letter, but no answer. Do, dear sir, do me
this favor.*

I remain yours, with due respect,

Wesley Harland

In this and subsequent letters, Wesley emerged as a thoughtful young
man, eager to learn and to correspond with those he knew in America. He
alluded to the many difficulties all the settlers, including children, routinely
faced. However, his words—"with ambition it is that I overcome them
all"—reflected what seems to have been his natural optimism.

Although the settlers faced dangers in Liberia, the colony was also a
place of great beauty and potential. Bassa Cove was on the south side of
the Saint John, one of Liberia's largest rivers, near where it empties into the
Atlantic Ocean. The town's settlers had expansive views of tall palm trees
swaying in tropical breezes, sandy beaches, endless ocean, and spectacular
sunsets. Farther inland lay rolling plains, foothills, rain forests, and finally
mountains. The soil, once cleared, was productive, and settlers were able to
grow a range of crops.

William C. Burke, a former slave, wrote, "It is a Land of Cooling
Brooks and Sunny plains where the melody of Birds are sweet and where
the Leaves are always green, a Land that will abundantly satisfy the Hus-
bandman for his toils."[7]

British writer Graham Greene summarized his impressions of the
Liberian forest: "the lovely swooping flight of the small bright rice-birds,
the fragile yellow cotton flowers growing with no stalk directly out of the
canes, something like a wild rose, transparent primrose petals with a small
red centre and a black stamen; butterflies, palms, goats and rocks and great
straight silver cotton trees, and through the canes, the graceful walking
women with baskets on their heads."[8]

The camwood trees (sometimes called barwood or sandalwood)
brightened the understory of the forest with their small glossy leaves; dye

could be extracted from the heavy, dark red wood. The rubber trees and palms soared above the camwood trees. The cotton trees were particularly exotic. The trees were massive in girth and height, towering above the other trees and covered in pale gray bark. But most striking were the wide, flat roots flowing from their trunks—they looked like giant rippled ribbons perched on edge.

Wesley was perhaps like most teenagers living in small towns: restless, bored, and eager to see the bigger world. He added a postscript for Ben: "P.S. I want to come over to see you all. Write me if you think [it] best to come and remain a few months with you or not."

Wesley's postscript was only the first time he suggested coming to America for a visit. Many settlers quit the colony altogether or left for temporary visits elsewhere. Some returned to America to work as agents for the colonization society, encouraging people to emigrate; some returned and told harrowing tales of Africa, discouraging would-be settlers; and some came back to secure the liberty of family members.[9]

Emily Hooper, the young woman whose parents had worked so diligently to bring her to Liberia, decided seven years later that she wanted to go back to America. She wrote to her former mistress asking if she could return to North Carolina as a slave. As it was no longer legal to import enslaved people into the United States, the North Carolina legislature accommodated her by passing a special bill. The legislation stipulated that "Emily Hooper, a negro and a citizen of Liberia, be and she is hereby permitted, voluntarily, to return to the state of slavery, as the slave of her former owner, Miss Sally Mallet of Chapel Hill."[10]

It is unclear why Emily wanted to return. Newspaper articles of the day reflect differing biases about colonization in the North and South. The *Detroit Free Press* indicated that Emily's father had "held a station of consequence in the republic of Liberia" and that both of her parents were dead, precipitating her decision to return to America. The *American Advocate*, published in Kingston, North Carolina, made no mention of her father's position or her parents' deaths, but indicated that Emily "is sick of free negro colony, is sick of freedom, and prefers living with her mistress . . . than to being fleeced by abolition friends (?) in Liberia." (The parenthetical question mark appears in the original article.)[11]

Eight months later, Wesley would send a much longer letter to Ben.

16

This Accursed Thing Slavery

Wesley, born into slavery in America and living in freedom in Liberia, penned one of the most moving passages in the Major collection of letters from Africa.[1]

> *Bassa Cove, West Africa, Liberia*
> *April the 4–1844*
> *Dear friend,*
>   *I am happy that I have this opportunity of writing you a few lines. This leaves me well and I do hope you are in good health and all your family. Dear sir, there is nothing very strange that I have to relate to you at this time. It would be a pleasure to me to have a regular communication with you so that we would be able to have information from one continent to the other. Not that I am so much concerned about the affairs in the U States, but it would be some satisfaction to me indeed to know the state of things.*
>   *I hope the United States are almost giving up the habit of slave-holding, and I think if they would, God would bless them more . . . it is time that Christendom would let her light shine & lay aside such darkness and abominations and crimes . . . I am ashamed of the U States or that part that indulges in this accursed thing slavery, and I do not know why they do indulge in it . . . it seems as it is almost impossible for so many colored people to live there in slavery; however, it is always the best to stand still and see the salvation of God as the Israelites did when they . . . had the tyrannical yoke of bondage on. I hope God will offer the people eyes that they may see, as they are blind . . .*

One objective of colonization was to interrupt the slave trade on the west coast of Africa. Although importation of enslaved people into many countries had been prohibited by then and the slave trade labeled piracy, it continued. Slave traders' agents worked with local men who captured people from the interior of the country or purchased them from others who had captured them and transported them to the coast. There the slave traders housed the captives in the notorious slave factories or temporary pens known as barracoons until they had collected enough for a shipload. More than a quarter of Africans captured for slavery were children.[2]

A statement from an Englishman who helped capture a Brazilian slave ship in the early 1830s gives a sense of the horrors of these vessels:

> [The ship] had taken in on the coast of Africa 336 males and
> 226 females, making in all 562, and had been out 17 days, dur-
> ing which she had thrown overboard 55! The slaves were all
> enclosed under grated hatchways, between decks. The space was
> so low that they sat between each other's legs ... there was no
> possibility of their lying down or at all changing their position
> night or day ... [they were] packed up and wedged together as
> tight as they could cram, in low cells, three feet high, the greater
> part of which, except that immediately under the guarded
> hatchways, was shut out from light or air.[3]

Men, women, and children were regularly sold into bondage in and around Bassa Cove. Governor Buchanan, previous governors, and the settlers had all attempted to halt the trade.

A missionary living in Edina (just across the river from Bassa Cove) wrote in 1836: "Two or three weeks ago, a little boy, about eight years old, who was frequently following me about and jabbering in the country language, was carried off to be a slave.... He was carried to the seashore, but the slave vessel had just gone; so they brought him back, much to the joy of the boy, who said he cried all the way to the sea."[4]

In September 1839, Governor Buchanan reported sending a company of volunteers to close down a barracoon near Little Bassa.

> The expedition was completely successful; the barracoon was
> captured with the discharge of a gun, the principal of the
> concern having fled with his slaves on the approach of our men.
> While quietly in possession, however, and awaiting the arrival of

vessels which were to bring off the goods, the party was furiously assaulted by a large body of natives. They were received with steady bravery. . . . Throughout that and the following day, the fight was again and again renewed, but always the result was the same. As often as the natives attacked the barracoon, they were repulsed. . . . The destruction of this large and well-protected slaver's establishment will, without doubt, produce a lasting and salutatory effect upon the natives and those civilized savages from other lands, who have so long cursed this coast with their presence.[5]

Although this particular expedition was successful, the slave trade continued along the Liberian coast. American, English, and French cruisers patrolled the coastline, trying to capture slave ships and rescue captives, with mixed results. In the 1840s, more than six hundred ships suspected to be involved in the slave trade were captured. When these slave ships were intercepted, the people rescued from them—recaptives—were taken to Liberia.[6]

The rest of Wesley's 1844 letter was something of a schoolboy's report on his country.

> *The next thing that comes under our notice is to give you a brief account of this commonwealth. In all the settlements, there are between 4 & 5 thousand (4000 or 5000) in inhabitants on plantations . . . [and] the settlements. The most popular ones are on the seaboard; we have some settlement up the river.*
> *The commonwealth is about 20 or 23 years old. It is governed by, or it is, a Republican government. We send 10 counselors annually to legislate for us and make laws.*

Liberia was never a state-sponsored colonial territory. The American Colonization Society—a private organization supported by membership dues, donations, and subscriptions—governed Liberia for most of the first twenty years of the colony's existence. The society acquired land, organized settlements, appointed a hierarchy of resident officials, established rules, and provided military training and weapons for defense.[7]

In 1839, the board of directors pulled together the various settlements into the Commonwealth of Liberia. (The settlement known as Maryland in Africa did not join the Republic of Liberia until 1857.) The new commonwealth's constitution established an executive branch, headed by the governor, a judicial branch, and a legislative branch made up of representatives from the various settlements. A council of residents advised the governor. The constitution established two counties: Montserrado County, which included Monrovia, and Grand Bassa County, which included Bassa Cove and Edina. The constitution also specifically outlawed slavery and the slave trade in Liberia.[8]

In 1841, Joseph Jenkins Roberts, a freeborn man of mixed ancestry, became governor. It had been only two years since the white governor, Thomas Buchanan, had appointed Roberts storekeeper and public works superintendent in Monrovia. After Buchanan died of fever in September 1841 at the age of thirty-two, Roberts became the first non-white governor of Liberia. White men would never again govern the colony.[9]

Wesley's letter, a long one, continued with information about currency, crops, and farming in Liberia:

> The next thing, the currency of this commonwealth is not acknowledged by foreign countries. The currency is paper money formed on camwood. There are no gold nor silver in circulation. Camwood may be had in large quantities if men have goods suitable for the market of wood. But there are no wood on the seaboard; it is all in the interior of this country and merchants buy it from the natives. But the settlers never goes there, owing to so many difficulties that they would have to contend with.
>
> Palm oil—this is a thing that are made on a very large scale. The natives makes a great deal of it and a man, for 25 leaves of tobacco, may buy 2 gallons . . . these are [some] of the best things that we have here for the market of this country, as there is not tobacco made here.
>
> The next thing that we will notice is farming. This may be common here, but it is one thing to have a farm and another thing to make that farm make money . . . farming in this country is not like farming there. It is 2 years all after a man comes to this country before he can learn the art of farming and then it is five years before he can make anything on that farm that will be worth a brass cent. Coffee can be made in that time and there is nothing else that will be of any [illegible] to him without he wants it for his own family . . . he may make a living at the business, but not a very good one. Rice, yams, potatoes, cassavas or the breadfruits, soursops, guavas,

plantains, bananas, pawpaws, oranges, limes, lemons . . . there is no
necessity or it is not worthwhile for me to tell you what the produce
of this country is, as you know all about all the zones and that, more
than I can tell you. The land is terrible good back from the seashores
about 20 or 36 miles, good enough to make anything.

Young Wesley had watched Tolbert, Austin, and the others struggle to make a living from the land. His comment—"It is one thing to have a farm and another thing to make that farm make money"—surely resonates with farmers everywhere.

Settlers who wanted to farm in Liberia faced many challenges: dense vegetation, lack of farm animals to pull plows, few farming tools and seeds, sparse knowledge about crops and seasons in a new country, and—depending on the luck of the draw for lots—poor soil. Wild animals were sometimes a problem, too. One settler wrote to his former owner, "I have been visited by a leopard since my settlement on my farm. He took of[f] two Goats and one hog."[10]

Many of those who wished to farm struggled because of malaria. The course of the disease often left survivors weak for months after the initial bout and susceptible to future occurrences. Skirmishes and larger battles with indigenous people also interfered with farming, as did intertribal warfare that had nothing to do with the settlers. Only a few weeks after Wesley penned this letter, a settler in Monrovia wrote, "To tell you the truth, the whole of the country amongst the different tribes are at war to this day."[11]

Wesley closed his letter by noting the importance of coming to Liberia with money and supplies in order to succeed:

I imagine the men that have been in this country 15 or 16 years
lives as well as any man in the U States, that is, if he is a industrious
man and better than many. But if a man comes to this country, if he
has not any money nor goods, he never will get up . . . if this sheet of
paper would hold all, I would tell you about it. He has to work hard
all day if he hopes for [illegible] ℔s of tobacco and then sometimes it
is so bad that he cannot sell it. . . . Work a whole day and glad to get
work. At this rate, it is a hard thing for a poor man to make enough
for his family to live off or by in this country. When he first come, the
first 6 months, he is sick and he . . . [gets] in debt for things for the
support of his family. Some 2 or 3 hundred dollars and it [is] five
or 6 years before he is able to pay this and then it is five or six more

before he can do anything for hisself. Would say more, but not room. Am yours respectfully,

Wesley Harlan

Wesley wasn't done. He scribbled notes in the margins of the letter.

Will you be so good as to see where George Harlan's family is and write to them for me; also, any of the Harlans, as I do not know where they is. Also John J. Grifon of Kentucky of Christian County, also the Bradsawes family—see if Shebay Bradshaw has anything of John J. Grifon and his family . . . so write me and tell me all about everything that I would like to know. Do[n't] forget G. Harlan family.

US census records for 1830 and 1840 do not list a John Grifon or Griffin in Christian County. An Edward Bradshaw is listed on the 1830 census on the same page as Joseph Major, indicating that the men lived near one another. If the Shebay Bradshaw that Wesley mentioned was a slave, she or he would not have been listed by name on the census.

At least seven times, Wesley, Tolbert, and Austin asked Ben for information on George Harlan and his family. No evidence has been found that George ever corresponded with his formerly enslaved people.

Wesley wrote an additional note in very tiny script on the address panel of the letter. To read the note, the letter has to be folded in the manner in which it was sealed.

By me writing in this way, I hope you will not let it get in the slave stalls, for it may be the means of making some slaves disobedient to their masters. I hope that I will be able to see you before long, as I am coming to America before long or next spring or summer if I had silver money enough after I got to New York [illegible] if you will ask Mr. Harlan [illegible] write to them [to ask] if they could enclose a draft one way or the other of about 50 dollars in cash and will settle for it; if they do and send me the draft in a letter and when I arrives in New York, I will draw the money and come on. Not that I am dependent on this money forever or dependent on them, but I mainly want to borrow after I gets to New York, as well. Send no silver. WH

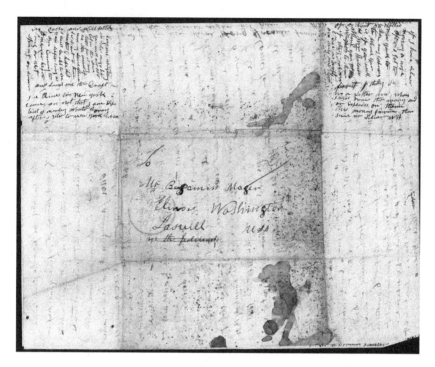

Paper and ink were often difficult to obtain. In this 1844 letter to Ben Major, Wesley Harlan added a note in very tiny script on the address panel of the letter. To read the note, the letter has to be folded in the manner in which it was sealed. (Courtesy of the McLean County Historical Society, Bloomington, Illinois)

This little note is remarkable for several reasons. First, it reinforced Wesley's strong desire to visit America. This seems to have been the common wanderlust of a young man trapped in a small town. Not only was Bassa Cove tiny, it was sixty miles from any sizeable town, isolated by the sea on one side and forests on the other sides.

In this note, Wesley asked Ben to contact George Harlan to arrange a draft of $50, apparently for expenses. This seems a bold request from a young man who had had no contact with his former owner for six years. Wesley expressed the same wish to come to America in his next two letters, so he apparently was unsuccessful in getting the loan.

He also wrote a cautionary note about his own letter: "I hope you will not let it get in the slave stalls, for it may be the means of making some slaves disobedient to their masters." Wesley knew that slavery continued in the United States, but he didn't seem to understand that slavery was illegal in Ben's new home state of Illinois. In theory, at least, no enslaved people or slave quarters existed in Illinois. But the note also implies that Wesley, once enslaved himself, still believed (or at least wanted to convince Ben that he believed) that enslaved people should be obedient to their masters and that hearing about life in Liberia might entice enslaved people to rebel.

17

Decidedly Antislavery

Ben was not the only Christian County man who abandoned slavery and migrated to Illinois. Several of his relatives, friends, and neighbors took similar actions. Their opposition to slavery seems to have emerged from their commitment to the principles of the Christian Church (Disciples of Christ), their friendships with the fellowship's antislavery founders, and their personal convictions.

Ben, William, and Chastine had joined the Disciples church in the late 1820s. By the early 1830s they had all adopted antislavery views (although, as Ben noted, William's convictions may have been wobbly). Their sister, Eliza Ann, and her husband, William Davenport, also came to oppose slavery.[1]

Other Christian County men who moved to central Illinois in 1834 and 1835 included James Alfred Lindsey, a Disciples preacher who had been Ben's friend and neighbor in Christian County; Elijah Dickinson (Elmira Dickinson's father); brothers Mordecai and Thomas Bullock (who were related to the Majors); Benjamin Johnson Radford; and another Disciples preacher, James Robeson. The men had much in common: all of them had once owned other humans; all came to oppose slavery; all divested themselves of their enslaved people; and all were Disciples of Christ. These men coordinated their moves to Illinois, working together both in Kentucky to prepare for their departure and in their new state to get established.[2]

The father of Mordecai and Thomas Bullock, also named Thomas, owned twenty-three people in 1830. In early 1834, Thomas wrote in his will:

My wish is that all my slaves that have arrived at the age of 21 years at my death shall have the privilege of going to Liberia or some place of freedom out of the bounds of these United States; if they accept the offer, then in that case, they are to be hired out for the purpose of raising funds to carry them thither; all those under that age shall have the same privilege when they come of age. . . . My wish is that all offspring of my slaves be taught to read the Scriptures and raised with the expectation of being free at the age of 21 years, provided they go to Liberia or some place of freedom out of the bounds of the U.S.[3]

Church historian Nathaniel Haynes specifically mentioned Ben and William T. Major in a list of "representative Disciples of Christ who were active in their antislavery views." In a speech Haynes delivered in 1913, he mentioned the Disciples who came into Illinois from the 1830s through the 1850s and noted that "most of these immigrants came because of their aversion to the 'peculiar institution.'" He cited Ben as an example and wrote, "The attitude of the Disciples of Christ during those years throughout this portion of the state was decidedly antislavery."[4]

These men made moral decisions and then acted upon their beliefs. It took courage for them to differ with family and friends in Kentucky over the contentious issue of slavery. Their abandonment of slavery came at a personal cost: disruption to the lives of their families, opposition from friends and neighbors who continued to support the enslavement of human beings, and often great financial loss.

The average enslaved person sold for between $600 and $700 at auction; skilled people could sell for up to $1,500. The value of the slaves Ben freed was equivalent to about $108,000 in 2017 dollars.[5]

Ben and some of the other Christian County men who came to Illinois were both antislavery and pro-colonization. Some abolitionists—frustrated by decades of activism without an end to slavery—supported colonization. However, many prominent abolitionists opposed it, preferring to continue the fight for emancipation and equality in America. In 1832, William Lloyd Garrison published a series of anti-colonization essays in his newspaper, the *Liberator*. Samuel Cornish's abolitionist newspaper, the *Colored American*, also attacked the colonization movement. Some of these abolitionists changed their positions on colonization, first supporting it, then opposing it, or vice versa. Attitudes shifted as violence between antislavery and proslavery forces increased and positions became rigid. White abolitionist Gerrit Smith first supported colonization, donating thousands of dollars to the American Colonization Society and serving as a vice president of the New York society in the mid-1830s, before reversing course. Both Frederick Douglass and Martin R. Delaney initially denounced colonization, but later softened their views as proslavery positions solidified and more anti-free-black laws passed.[6]

The objectives of the colonization movement shifted over time as well. Although founders of the American Colonization Society originally intended it as a means to help freeborn black people migrate to Africa, increasing numbers of formerly enslaved people departed for Liberia, too. Some were freed by their owners, others purchased their own freedom with money they had earned by hiring out their labor, and still others borrowed money to purchase their freedom, with promises of repayment from future wages.

Occasionally enslaved people contacted the American Colonization Society directly for assistance. In May 1848, the society received a letter signed by James Wrial (James Rial Starkey) of Newburn, North Carolina.

> You no doubt will be somewhat astonished at first to learn that the humble writer of this communication is a slave, belonging to a gentleman of this place, who does not consider himself able to manumit me without some compensation. I am now about 25 years of age, the greater portion of my life has been spent as a house servant, where I learned the art of reading and writing. I have been anxious for the last three or four years to go to Liberia, and am the more so now since she has proclaimed her independence. But sir, I wish to act honest in getting there, and as I cannot get the means to pay for my time so I can go, I can see no way to accomplish the long desired object unless I could induce someone to advance the required amount.[7]

Because one of the society's objectives was to end the slave trade, the organization did not purchase enslaved people, even to free them. However, this young man's letter and a subsequent one were published in the *African Repository* with an appeal to readers for assistance. It took a while and a second published appeal, but by late 1850, through his own efforts and donations, James had secured adequate funds to go to Liberia. There were even some surplus funds to be applied to purchasing freedom for his wife and two young children.[8]

18

I Have Been in the Legislature

Wesley strolled along the streets of Monrovia. At the edge of town, he peered down the steep cliff of Cape Mesurado; he could see where the Saint Paul River met the Atlantic Ocean. He had first glimpsed Africa down on that beach. The canoes, the Kru men, the trip ashore, the welcome they had received—he remembered it vividly.

The town had grown and changed in ten years. There were dozens more buildings now and more people, too. He wandered through the market where people sold bush meat, spices, peppers, fruit, and the striped cloth the Loma people made. Over small charcoal fires, women cooked jollof rice, and *fufu* and *dumboy*—Wesley liked the dumplings and decided to buy some later for dinner. A dozen languages and accents swirled around him, from natives dressed and undressed in a variety of ways, to Americans, Englishmen, and others. He thought he heard a scrap of French, a word or two of Portuguese. Back home in Bassa Cove, he had frequented the waterfront, picking up odd jobs and odd bits of languages.

When he had earned enough money for passage on the *Packet* to Monrovia, he had told Ma that he was going. She didn't like it, but he was nineteen. He wanted to see a little of the world. Finally, she consented when he asked to go to the Methodist Episcopal Annual Conference in Monrovia. He was going early so he could watch the legislature in action, too.

He remembered how Governor Buchanan used to talk with the folks of Bassa Cove about how things worked, and how excited everyone had been when Mr. Roberts became governor. Reverend Herring had told him that soon Liberia would be a republic and there would be a new constitution. If they were to run things themselves—and he intended to be a part of that—then he needed to understand it all.

Wesley took a final glance around the bustling market, then stopped a man and asked for directions to the capitol.

Bassa Cove
Jan. 18, 1846

This leaves me well, and I hope you are the same. I was very glad to hear from you indeed, and more especial because that was the first letter that I received from you since my arrival in this country. It seems to me that the people have forgot me altogether. I hope we will be able to keep up a regular correspondence with each other hereafter.

About a year and a half after his previous letter to Ben, Wesley again sent letters to America, this time to James Moore of Christian County. The 1830 US census records four men named James Moore living in the county; the man to whom Wesley wrote was likely James W. Moore, born in 1806 in Virginia. Moore was a planter and owner of a home called "The Cedars" on Clarksville Pike in Christian County.[1]

In this letter and his next one to Moore, Wesley sketched out a picture of the colony, reporting on the land, produce, crime, religion, and the various settlements. James Moore forwarded Wesley's letters to the American Colonization Society, which published them in the *African Repository* in September 1847, spelling Wesley's last name as Horland.[2]

James Moore had initiated the correspondence, and Wesley was very grateful. He wrote, "It seems to me that the people have forgot me altogether."

Colonization was difficult for everyone, but adults usually had some choice in the matter. Wesley was only nine when he boarded the *Luna*. He had left behind the only home he had ever known. Some of his family members were with him in Liberia, but he clearly missed many of the people who had stayed in Kentucky.[3]

It is unclear what relationship existed between Moore and Wesley or why Moore wrote to the young man. Perhaps the Harlans had lived near or worked on Moore's property in the months before emigrating. Tolbert had also written to Moore, so clearly the families knew him well.

Someone with the last name Moore had signed the receipt obtained by Joseph Major from the Christian County Colonization Society; however, the preceding initials are illegible. If James Moore was involved with the society, he may have been close to the Majors and Harlans in the last few days before they left Kentucky.

Wesley wrote:

> *The first thing that I will consider, is the condition of the colony. From the information that I have received since my arrival, I am happy to say this is a very good country; and any man may make a living in this country if he will.*
>
> *Let us notice the land. The land is good. The land in one mile of the ocean is good enough to raise anything most on it; and the farther you go back, the better the land is. The land is not very large timber, but very good. I have [seen] some timber in this country four feet in diameter. But I do not think that is as large as timber in the U. States, therefore, I say it is not very large. The land is very well timbered—that is, there is plenty of it.*
>
> *Hilly Land. —The land is not very hilly—it is as level as any country, or as any part of the U. States I have seen. There is a chain of mountains that runs from the northern extremity of Africa to the Cape of Good Hope. These are very large mountains. This I have from modern travelers.*
>
> *Produce of Africa. —There is palm oil, rice, cassavas, yams, potatoes, coffee, cabbage, watermelon, and many other things that I might name, sugar cane, &c., &c. Cattle, sheep, hogs, goats, and fouls of various kinds, &c.*
>
> *Crimes. —There is indeed some crimes in this country of a very bad nature, but not a great many of them.*
>
> *Religion. —This people is a religious people, there is no question about that. They are a church-going people. They go to meeting every Sabbath. I had the pleasure of being at the last Annual Conference at Monrovia, on the 9th instant [the ninth of January], and I remained there for some days, and was very much gratified, having [heard] some very able ministers.*

Eight years earlier, the *Colonization Herald* had reported, "The state of morals in the colonies is emphatically of a high order. Sabbath breaking, drunkenness, profanity, and quarreling are vices almost unknown in Liberia. A temperance society formed in 1834 numbered in a few weeks after its organization 500 members, at that time more than one-fifth of the whole population. At Bassa Cove and Cape Palmas, the sale and use of ardent

As a teenager, Wesley Harlan yearned to visit the broader world. In 1846, he traveled about sixty miles from Bassa Cove to Monrovia, the capital of Liberia, where he watched the legislature in action. ("Liberian Senate," by Robert K. Griffin, circa 1856, Library of Congress, Prints and Photographs Division, LC-USZC4–4908)

spirits are forbidden by law." In 1844, an article in the *African Repository* reported that there had been nine convictions for murder, eleven for kidnapping, seventeen for burglary, and 291 for grand and petty larceny.[4]

The colonists had established churches soon after arriving in Africa, and subsequent waves of settlers seemed every bit as faithful as the original colonists. American newspapers closely followed the colonization effort and kept readers apprised of progress. An 1838 *Boston Recorder* article reported, "The frame of a Presbyterian church has been raised at Bassa Cove, and the Baptists were erecting a house for their worship at Edina, under a large tree, beneath which human sacrifices were once offered to the devil."[5]

By 1843, Bassa Cove had two churches—Baptist and Methodist—with ninety-three members altogether. The Methodists had a slight edge. Only 124 people lived in Bassa Cove then, so fully three-quarters of the population belonged to a religious congregation.[6]

The number of settlements. —There are ten or fifteen settlements, but Monrovia is the largest—that also is the seat of government. We have legislature every year, commencing on the 5th of this month. The business is managed very well, indeed; this I am a witness to. I have been in the legislature and seen them myself.

Myself and my mother's family—my mother is well, and my sister and two brothers; Asbury and mother. The people that came to this country with us, the Majors, there is three men and two women alive; Hopkins, two alive; Alexander Horland, mother and two of his sisters—he is dead, the most of his people did not die with the fever. Some of them was shot in the last war with the natives. As for the people, they are all employed in doing something. There is not any of the very lazy; by this, do not understand me to say there is no lazy ones among us, for there is.

Wesley's letter included valuable information about the Harlans and Majors, although some of it is confusing. Ann and Silvay, both still living, were Agnes's daughters and, therefore, Wesley's sisters. So why does Wesley mention only one sister in this letter? The most likely explanations are that Wesley intended to say "sisters," and left off the *s,* or that the editor of the *African Repository* made a mistake in transcribing the letter.[7]

Wesley's mention of two surviving brothers is confusing, too. Of the five Harlan boys who had immigrated to Liberia, only Asbury and Wesley were alive by 1843. Perhaps Wesley meant that Agnes had two sons still alive; or possibly, instead of "my sister and two brothers," he meant to write "my two sisters and brother." He also wrote that three of the Major men and two women were still alive. These numbers don't tally with other documentation either. He mentioned two other families: the Hopkins and Horlands. These surnames are not on the *Luna's* list of passengers or in the 1843 census for Bassa Cove.

Earlier in the letter, Wesley had written about people working for a living in Liberia. Colonization officials and others had written to America about the need to send hard-working people to Liberia. Only three months after Wesley wrote this letter, Governor Roberts wrote to Reverend A. M. Cowan of the Kentucky Colonization Society to confirm that a shipload of immigrants had arrived. Roberts wrote, "It must be remembered that in Liberia as in every other country, it requires some exertions for men to place themselves in easy circumstances. Do send us some of your enterprising men from Kentucky."[8]

Stephen A. Benson (later vice president and president of Liberia) wrote of Bassa Cove in an 1846 letter:

We have one of the finest countries in Liberia, as regards health, fertility, and natural resources, it is not excelled; all we want is good industrious immigrants that will go cheerfully to work on their arrival, and in a few years, they will be independent . . . in Bassa Cove a number wish to move out on their farms, but as yet our number is too small to be divided, as our surrounding natives are not as effectually subdued as they are in our sister country.[9]

For the colony of Liberia to succeed there had to be sufficient numbers of settlers to work the land and fend off attacks from indigenous people, and the colonists had to be well equipped, well prepared emotionally and physically, and ready to work hard in relative isolation. There also had to be enough newly arriving settlers or new babies to offset the population losses caused by disease. These were the same criteria for success in the early days of America and, in fact, in any attempt at colonization.

Wesley concluded, again indicating that he wanted to visit America: "I expect to come to the U. States before long, if you think it advisable. I am doing a little of most everything." The very next day, Wesley wrote a second letter to Moore. In it, he provided an extensive overview of the settlements in the country, including his hometown of Bassa Cove.

Bassa Cove
Jan. 19, 1846
I told you that I would say something more in my next [letter] that would afford you more satisfaction as it regards this country. The next thing that I will notice is the situation of the settlements. Monrovia is the capital of the Colony of Liberia. The population of Monrovia is about one thousand men, women and children. This settlement is on a cape extending in the Atlantic Ocean, and it is a very elevated place. It is bound on the north by the ocean, on the east by the Saint Paul's river, and on the west by the ocean. The buildings is made of wood, stone and bricks; the people that live here is those that follows merchandising. The revenue is somewhere between eight and ten thousand dollars a year. There is mechanics also in the place,

of almost every kind, so there is not much need of me naming the different employments.

There is also three or four settlements up the Saint Paul's river. There, people are farmers, so they live without having anything to do with trading; these settlements is about 18 miles [from] the farthest settlement; there is some missionary stations the other side of the settlements.

Wesley then listed and described the various towns along the coast in sequence from northwest to southeast—including Marshall on the Junk River, Edina (named for Edinburgh, Scotland, whose people had been supportive of colonization), and Bexley—before writing about Bassa Cove.[10]

Bassa Cove.—This little place has had more to contend with than the most of the settlements. It has been consumed by fire by natives, but we have nothing to dread at this time. This settlement is the capital of the country of Grand Bassa. This is a very fine settlement and the best that I have seen since I have been in this country. This settlement is one mile south of Edina, situated on the south side of the St. John's river, bound on the east by the Benson river, on the west by the ocean.

Bassa Cove had indeed experienced more than its share of misery. This included repeated attacks from the Fishmen, as well as antagonism from British seamen.

Some of the contention between indigenous people and the settlers sprang from general distrust and growing apprehension as the settlements became more populated and the settlers acquired land, interrupted the slave trade, sought to evangelize local people, and killed game. Many of the settlers looked down on the indigenous people, which created more tension. Some of the indigenous groups who had been involved in the slave trade looked with disdain upon the settlers, considering them merely liberated slaves.[11] The settlers and indigenous people did not understand one another's cultures or traditions and lacked a common language with which to communicate.

However, by the late 1840s, when Wesley penned this letter, the settlers had come to know a little more about the indigenous people. James S. Payne was a Bassa Cove schoolteacher who had migrated to Liberia when he was eleven. In a speech, Payne characterized the indigenous people as shrewd and intelligent, and he said they were known to drive hard bargains: "As you advance in the interior, you find they are generally excellent artisans. They raise their own cotton; spin and manufacture it into wearing apparel. They tan leather most beautifully and make from it various articles of utility. Iron ore, also, is found in some great abundance, and by means of their rude furnaces and forges dug down in the earth, they turn out a variety of implements, such as knives, spears, and many excellent things."[12]

The different ethnic groups had their own artistic and musical traditions, judicial and administrative structures, poetry and stories, secret societies, belief systems, oral histories, and spiritual traditions. Many were Muslim; others were animists and believed that all creatures, objects, and places had spirits; still others practiced ancestor worship. Various groups had expertise in seafaring, basket making, weaving, iron making, farming, fishing, and hunting. The Mandingo had a reputation as excellent traders. The Kru were known as experienced mariners. (One historian wrote, "Everything in Liberia, trade good or human, passed through the hands of the Krumen.")[13]

Edward Wilmot Blyden, known as the father of Pan-Africanism, identified several key elements of African culture. These included a focus on the family, the practice of polygamy, cooperation and mutual aid within the community, a lack of individualistic competition, different notions of wealth, a willingness to turn work into play, communion with nature, and a sense of spirituality.[14] Some of the settlers were beginning to understand and respect these indigenous cultural elements.

Wesley next described the settlements of Sinoe and Cape Palmas, south of Bassa Cove. He noted the populations of the various settlements: Monrovia (without the upper settlements), 1,000; Marshall, 80; Edina, 75 to 120; Bexley and Bassa Cove, about 150 each; Cape Palmas, 100 to 150. He then concluded:

> As for myself, I am endeavoring, by the assistance of God, to do the best I can. I am endeavoring to preach the Gospel of Christ, and this I think nothing less than my duty. I am a member of the Methodist Church.
>
> I have not been sick two weeks since I have been in this country, and if the Lord is willing, I intend to see your face once more. I do hope you will advise me what to do in this respect. I would like to come there very well; but I do not know the law that you have

among you as yet. I would be glad if you would write me all the news. Write to my people for me. This leaves me well.

Wesley was tempering his wish to come to America by seeking more information about the laws. Of those Liberian colonists who returned to the United States, very few came only to visit, especially after passage of the Fugitive Slave Act of 1850. Though cautious, Wesley seemed determined to visit the United States, telling Moore, "I intend to see your face once more."

19

I Am Nothing but
a Plain Christian

Ben sat in his reading chair in the library. When he and Lucy had sketched out plans for the new house, he had included this room and furnished it with a proper desk and chair, a well-cushioned armchair, good lamps, and as many bookcases as the room could hold. Here, for years, he had done his farm accounts, written his correspondence, and read. He had long subscribed to publications that reflected his interests in colonization, botanical medicine, and his church. His books were all neatly shelved, but the periodicals didn't fit as well in the bookcases and were more troublesome to store.

Lucy had been after him to do something with the stacks of *Christian Preacher*, *Millennial Harbinger*, *Thomsonian Recorder*, *Botanico-Medical Recorder*, and the *African Repository*. This morning, she had handed him a ball of twine and a pair of scissors and had given him a gentle push toward the door of his library.

Ben leaned from his chair and picked up a copy of the *African Repository* that lay near the top of the stack. He thumbed through the journal until he found the page with his letter on it.[1]

Washington, Tazewell Co., March 29, 1846
Rev. W. McLean,
   Sir . . . In one of the no. of the Repository for '45 I see this notice. "Letters for the citizens of Liberia should be forwarded, post paid; care of Rev. W. McLean, Colonization Rooms Washington City." I therefore take the liberty to enclose you this letter hoping you will give it a speedy and safe conveyance.

Measles.—Give repeated doses of salts, nitre powders, and bleed freely.

Putrid Sore Throat.—Bleed freely in all cases, blister, give antimonial powders, and calomel.

St. Anthony's Fire.—A pint of blood should be taken at a time, and often repeated; purge with salts, and wash the parts affected with lead water.

Nettle Rash.—Purge with sulphur, cream of tartar and mercury.

Inflammation of the Brain.—Bleed—20 ounces should be taken from a good large orifice, apply leeches, cup &c.; physic with jalap, nitre, calomel and tartar. When the patient can bear no more bleeding, a large blister should be applied to the back of the neck.

Apoplexy.—Take at least one quart of blood instantly, and repeat it in less quantities; a blister of a large size should be applied to the back of the neck. Give a strong purge of calomel, jalap and aloes. If the patient is unable to swallow, it should be injected down his throat with a long flexible tube.

Inflammation of the Eyes.—Bleed, give repeated doses of salts, nitre and jalap. Blister behind the ears; apply a wash to the eyes made of white vitriol—sometimes an ointment of calomel, and sometimes a wash of corrosive sublimate.

Quinsy.—Bleed freely, purge freely with salts, apply a large blister to the back of the neck, make incisions in the palate, lance the tonsils.

Mumps.—Lax diet, purge with salts or oil, and sometimes bleed.

Earache.—The patient should be bled, purged with salts, and have a blister applied to the neck.

Toothache.—Purge with salts, give salt petre, apply a blister near the affected part, and use opium.

Bleeding at the Nose.—Purge with salts and alum; and, if these and other means do not effect a cure, apply blisters and bleed.

Pleurisy.—Take a pint of blood at a time from a large orifice, without delay, repeat it in six hours, or after a blister is drawn. A large dose of salts should be given the first day, and often repeated the same day in smaller doses. This treatment should be followed till bad symptoms disappear.

Spitting of Blood.—Bleed, give a dose of salts, blue vitriol, alum &c.

Consumption.—Bleed, blister, and give mercury, salts and anodynes.

Asthma.—Bleed, blister, give ipecacuanha, Dover's powders, squills, nitre and garlics, and smoke tobacco.

Whooping Cough.—Bleed, apply leeches over the breast, purge and blister. Give opium, antimony, and Fowler's solution of arsenic.

Catarrh.—Bleed, blister on the breast, purge with salts every forty eight hours; give nitre, antimony and opium.

Influenza.—Give emetics, purge with salts; bleed and blister, give calomel and peregoric.

Dropsy.—Bleed repeatedly, purge with salts, antimony, nitre and fox glove. Give steel and calomel.

Rheumatism.—Bleed freely three or four times, purge, sweat, give colchicum, Dover's powders, and wash the parts affected with cold lead water.

Palsy.—Bleed and purge and blister repeatedly. Give mercury freely.

Gout.—Bleed freely, and purge often with salts and calomel.

Inflammation of the Bowels.—Bleed, blister and purge.

Inflammation of the Stomach.—Bleed, blister and purge.

Dysentery.—Bleed, give salts, oil and cal omel.

Colic.—Bleed, give oil, calomel, jalap, salts, peppermint, ether and opium.

Liver Complaint.—Bleed moderately and repeatedly, blister and apply tartar plasters, purge with salts.

Jaundice.—Put a blister over the region of the liver, purge with aloes and calomel for ten or twelve days.

Strangury.—Bleed, blister and purge.

Hysterics.—Bleed, purge briskly, and give calomel.

Crooked-Backed Children.—Put in issues, each side of the spine, of poisonous substances.

Fevers.—Bleed, puke, purge and blister, give calomel, antimony, opium, &c. &c.

Thus we might proceed till we had reckoned some thirteen hundred different diseases, as the old faculty calls them, and the words, *bleed, blister and purge; salts, antimony, nitre, opium and calomel,* would still be seen, expressive of what was necessary to restore the sick to health; yet every one of these words signify what is directly opposed to the laws of the animal economy, called the laws of physiology. Notwithstanding this, the professors of this ridiculous and deadly practice, have the impudence to reproach the Botanic Physicians for doctoring, as they suppose, all diseases alike.—*Thomsonian Spy.*

One ounce of calomel or quicksilver, beat up with the white of two eggs, is the most effectual "do up" for bed-bugs yet known.—What a striking analogy in its effects upon vermin and the human body.—*Buchan.*

Ben Major followed the Thomsonian system of medicine and subscribed to several publications advocating botanical treatments. This page, from one of Ben's copies of the *Botanico-Medical Recorder,* lists traditional remedies for several ailments, followed by a scathing rebuke (lower right column) from "Thomsonian Spy," labeling such treatment "ridiculous and deadly." (Photograph by Susan E. Lindsey, Major Family Private Collection)

In 1834, I emigrated from Ky. to this state, leaving behind some ten slaves to be shipped to Liberia, by the first conveyance (by the Hopkinsville Aux. Col. Soc.) and I think on the 4th of July they all embarked on the brig Luner from the port of N York for the place of destination. They arrived safe and were settled in Bassa Cove. Owing to the disturbance of the natives they suffered much loss by fire, their houses being burned up with all their plunder, one of the men received a wound in the shoulder from a shot, from which he never recovered though lived an invalid a year or two; during their distress, I sent once and again to them necessities & when I last heard from them they had measurably repaired their losses.

I have written them through the mails, but received no answer, which is my apology for troubling you with this. The family sent out by me consisted of four men, all under the age of 25; two women, one 40, the other 20; & 4 children. The old woman and one of the children died in the acclimating fever, the remainder were well Aug. '44.

On the back of the Repository you address me (Rev.) which I wish you to drop in future, as [I] am nothing but a plain Christian.

Respectfully,

Ben Major

Ben was a man of deep faith. The last line of his letter reflected his humility but belied his lifelong involvement in the work of his church. While still in Kentucky, Ben and James Alfred Lindsey had converted the Baptist Church in Noah Springs (on land that is now part of Fort Campbell) to a Disciples of Christ congregation.

When Ben and his family moved to Walnut Grove, they found a church already established; the first meetinghouse was a log building. Ben immediately became very involved in the leadership of the local church. He was elected an elder in 1836 and participated in statewide conventions of the church and fundraising efforts.

Ben subscribed to and read church publications, including *Christian Baptist, Christian Disciple, Christian Preacher,* and Alexander Campbell's *Millennial Harbinger.* In fact, Campbell had appointed Ben to solicit other subscribers for church publications.[2]

Ben Major left the state of Kentucky and migrated to central Illinois in the fall of 1834, settling in the small town of Walnut Grove, later renamed Eureka. There he established this prosperous farm. The barn was built after Ben's death. (Major Family Private Collection)

Many of Ben's friends and relatives were equally involved in the church. William Davenport founded the First Christian Church of Hopkinsville in 1832, became a well-known preacher in Illinois, and was active in church politics. William T. Major founded the First Christian Church of Bloomington, Illinois. James Alfred Lindsey founded twenty or thirty churches in central Illinois, and three of his six sons became Disciples preachers.[3]

These men all knew the denomination's founder, Alexander Campbell. In 1846, Campbell had visited the group of Kentuckians who had moved to Illinois. He later recalled the journey in the *Millennial Harbinger*: "We progressed to the centre of Walnut Grove, [to] the pleasant residence of brother Ben Major. There we found a host of old Kentuckian soldiers whom I knew many years ago, amongst whom were brethren Lindsey, Davenport, Palmer, &c. Brother J. T. Jones, who had conducted me from Winchester here in his carriage, addressed the audience assembled at brother Major's, whom I followed with a few words. Next day we set out for Bloomington, where we safely arrived that same evening, and found ourselves at home at the hospitable mansion of brother W. Major."[4] Perhaps that evening at Ben Major's home, after the others had left, Ben and Alexander Campbell sat in front of the fire and talked about slavery and colonization, as well as their deep and abiding faith. Maybe Ben shared with Campbell his stash of letters from Africa.

In 1846, the same year Ben penned the published letter, he donated a building site for the new meetinghouse of the Christian church in Walnut Grove. He was active in church affairs his entire life and served occasionally as a lay preacher. Many people referred to him as "Reverend."[5]

Ben's letter to William McLain (which Ben misspelled as McLean) confirms many details found in other documents, but also raises questions. The numbers and ages of people Ben says he sent to Liberia don't neatly align with the *Luna* passenger list, the 1843 Liberian census, and other documentation. There could be several reasons for this. Ages of enslaved people were not carefully tracked, and Ben wrote this letter ten years after he had freed his people. He may have remembered their ages incorrectly. Also, many people who had been enslaved changed their names once they were freed, discarding the legacy of bondage but making them hard to track. Finally, some of the people listed on the roll of emigrants are listed by only their first names.

The receipt from the Christian County Colonization Society was for the "emigrants of Benjm Major and Chastine Major in no 11." G. W. McElroy, the colonization society agent who accompanied the group from Kentucky to New York, recorded that he had received eleven from Ben Major; presumably, that number includes any formerly enslaved people once held by Chastine.[6]

It has been more than 180 years since Ben freed his enslaved people. It is possible that no documentation survives that can resolve these contradictions.

20

I Want to See You and Your Wife and Children Very Bad

Tolbert sat outside his small home and watched his daughter Sarah scamper in the dappled sunlight. She would be five in a few months. Silvay was cooking and taking care of the baby. His kids were Africans—it was hard to believe.

It had been almost eleven years since the *Luna* had sailed from New York. So much had happened since then. They had all worked hard. Shed a lot of tears, too. But he tried not to look back; he focused on the future. His children were born into freedom. That counted for a lot.

Sometimes, though, he still thought about Kentucky and the folks he had left behind. He wondered how the Majors were doing in Illinois.

Africa, Grand Bassa County, June 26th, 1847
Dear father,

I write you these few lines to inform you of my health, which is good at this time present & I hope these few lines may find you and your family in good health.

The sheep in this country affords no wool; they have straight hair like a dog.

When I lived with you, I was used to eating meat 3 times a day, but if I get it once a week here, I think that I am doing very well indeed, for I have to pay 37½ cents a pound of meat. Flour is $300 a barrel.

I did think once that I would come home, but I have declined coming until I make one or 2 good crops, so that I can have some-thing to bring with me.

The women would do more than what they do, but they have no looms to weave cloth and all the cloth that we get, we pay from 75 to 50 & 25 cents a yard for it.

I want to see you and your wife and children very bad. I forgot one thing and that is this: my children talks about you and mother very much. Please to have the profile of you and your wife drawn and send it to me for my children to look at when I am dead.

Tolbert's Liberian-born children had never met Ben. His request for a portrait of Ben and Lucy implied that he frequently spoke of the Major family to his children. Perhaps he told them stories of Kentucky, too, and his trip to New York and his long voyage to Africa.

The relationships between enslaved people, owners, and the owners' families were complex. Many slave owners were physically, emotionally, or sexually abusive to enslaved people—beating or whipping them, depriving them of food, separating them from family members, and constantly threatening to sell them down the river. House slaves were exposed daily to a standard of living they could never attain. Field hands lived in substandard cabins or quarters. Slave owners literally held the power of life and death over their enslaved people. They could treat them with compassion and kindness, or beat them, rape them, kill them, sell them, change their names, or force them into sexual relationships—all with relative impunity.

Yet it appears that—in at least some cases—slave owners and enslaved people achieved a level of genuine caring for one another, something approaching a familial connection. They lived in close quarters and interacted daily with one another. Enslaved people observed private moments between members of the owner's family and overheard arguments, disagreements, flirtations, and affectionate whispers. They cared for young, sick, or elderly white family members and saw them at their most vulnerable. Black people took care of the physical needs of the white families, cooking, cleaning, helping to raise children, and working the land. Black women often served as wet nurses, literally providing sustenance to white babies. White families—to a greater or lesser extent—sustained their enslaved people by providing food, clothing, shelter, religious instruction, and medical care.

Historian Lindsey Apple described Henry Clay's household. "The lives of family members and their servants were closely linked. Clay children played with the children of black servants. They listened to the stories of the women in the kitchens, absorbing lessons of biblical morality and common decency.... Though paternalistic, the relationship between family and servants was anything but segregated. It reflects the complexity of race in the American South, and perhaps in the nation."[1]

Historian Randall Miller came to a similar conclusion. "The lives of black and white—slave and master—were inexorably bound up with one another in that peculiar symbiosis that was the antebellum South. By proximity and necessity, they worked together, they sometimes prayed together, they sometimes played together, and they even slept together. Violently, yet even lovingly, their lives intersected in countless complex ways."[2]

Enslaved people sometimes did form strong connections to the white families they served. This may well have been true for Ben and his formerly enslaved people. Ben's attempt to send a letter to Liberia via the American Colonization Society after not hearing from Tolbert or Austin for a time indicates that he was genuinely concerned about their well-being.

But however congenial the relationship, it was never a relationship of equals. Enslaved people were constantly aware of their place in the household. It was a matter of survival to know and follow the rules. They may have pretended greater affection for owners as a means of getting along or exhibited subservient behavior to survive—they almost certainly would not have complained to their owners. It is likely that the slaves knew their owners' families far better than the families knew the slaves. To survive, enslaved people had to be able to gauge the moods and desires of the owner's family.

Tolbert continued:

> My oldest daughter, Sarah, is about 5 years old and she can read a little. She is considered to be a very sensible child by the people [for] her age . . . my mother-in-law, Enoch Harlan's wife, inquires very much about you and should like to hear from you at all times, her and her children. She told me to write a few lines for her. She still remains a widow. She is about 50 years old and she looks to be about 26 years old and her hair is as black as ever it was. She still is a striving to serve the Lord yet. She has got 4 children living. Wesley is married.
>
> She says that she wants you to inquire for George Harlan's family and write her about them. She says that she has wrote so often to them and never got any answer. She wants you to write to her about them.

Tolbert was obviously proud that Sarah was learning to read. The settlers valued education. Early in the colonization of Liberia, schools and even a library were established in Monrovia. Most of the smaller settlements were slower to set up schools and, at least initially, settlers constantly struggled to obtain supplies and retain teachers.

The American Colonization Society board of managers considered the universal education of children a priority and mandated that schools be established in the major settlements. They proposed that permanent schoolhouses be built, and the society committed $100 toward each. They also proposed that parents or guardians of the children pay tuition.[3]

By September 1843, the Missionary Society of the Methodist Episcopal Church had established a school in the Edina-Bassa Cove area. James S. Payne (a future president of Liberia) was the teacher. He had eighteen pupils: fourteen children of settlers and four indigenous children.[4]

Other teachers included Ann Wilkins, a white woman who came to Liberia in 1838 to establish a school for girls, the Millsburg Academy; she taught there for nineteen years. Lavinia Johnson, a black missionary and teacher, arrived in Liberia in 1846, and Laura Brush, a white woman, arrived in 1847 to teach school.

Some of the adult settlers also attended school, catching up on an education previously denied them. "You may be somewhat surprised to Learn by this Letter that I have become a schoolboy in my middle time of Lief [life]," William C. Burke wrote.[5]

Tolbert noted that Agnes still looked about twenty-six. If the ages listed in the emigrant roll for Agnes and Tolbert are correct, she was forty-six and Tolbert was forty-seven. Although Enoch had died long before, Agnes remained a widow.

There were many widows in Liberia. Some had lost their husbands before migrating; others lost their spouses after they arrived—from diseases or accidents or in battle. Many widows chose not to remarry, even though plenty of marriageable men lived in the colony. Another husband often meant more children for younger women who remarried. Agnes was only thirty-two when she arrived in Liberia, yet she was the matriarch of a large family that included seven children and teenagers. It is unlikely she wanted more children. Or perhaps Agnes chose to remain a widow out of loyalty or love for her deceased husband.

Widows who chose to stay single often relied heavily on male relatives for help. Women could earn a living in Liberia in only a few ways—selling produce, taking in laundry, working as seamstresses—and the wages they could earn on their own were meager and often failed to provide adequately for their children.

Matilda Lomax wrote to her former owner about her husband's death by drowning, saying he had left her "with three small Children to provid for, in this New Country Where Every thinge is hard for a widow without sofficient means to take care of them." In another letter, Matilda noted that she could earn only 25 cents a day while a man working as a stonemason (as her father had) could earn six times as much.[6]

Tolbert again asked Ben, on Agnes's behalf, about George Harlan. For years, Agnes and her family had persisted in seeking information about George Harlan and his family. She obviously felt a close connection with the white Harlans, much as Tolbert and Austin felt for the white Major family.

Tolbert added a final bit of family news. Wesley, about twenty years old, had married. Tolbert didn't provide the name of Wesley's new wife.

Tolbert also never directly told Ben that he had married Silvay Major, who was twenty-one years younger than he was. However, in this letter he mentions that Agnes is his mother-in-law.

Tolbert concluded:

> *Please to remember me and brother Austin Major. We want to write to you 2 times a year, but we have no paper. Please to send me some paper.*
> *Yours truly,*
>
> *Tolbert Major*

Tolbert's closing request indicated why he had not written more frequently. Paper was scarce, expensive, and quickly fell apart in the damp, buggy climate of Liberia. The settlers often asked for writing supplies. Peyton Skipwith's plea was typical: "Please send me on some writing paper, quills & [ink] wafers and you will be confuring [*sic*] quite a favour on me." His daughter Diana asked for paper in another letter, noting that she had tried to find paper for two days and had located only a single sheet.[7]

Mail delivery was slow and uncertain, which may also help account for the long delays between letters. A postman picked up letters from Bassa Cove each Monday. The mail traveled by boat to Monrovia, arriving on Thursday, and it was then loaded on the next ship departing for America. Settlers often noted that they were writing in haste to get a letter on a soon-to-depart vessel. The colonists and their American correspondents often expressed concern that some of their mail had gone astray. Yet, letters remained the only way to stay in touch with those whom they had left behind.[8]

21

The Love of Liberty Brought Us Here

Early on the morning of August 24, 1847, a single cannon shot boomed from Monrovia's Central Fort Hill to announce the dawn. The shot might have awakened the whole town, except most people were already up and preparing to celebrate the birth of their new republic: the country had officially declared its independence the month before. More than a thousand people lived in the capital, and all of them would be participating in or watching the ceremonies.[1]

In the harbor, ships from foreign ports hoisted their national flags to snap in the brisk morning breeze. Atop the promontory, business owners, relieved that their warehouses and stores were closed for the day, prepared for the festivities. Several of Monrovia's leading men and seven specially selected women took extra care in dressing, conscious of their public roles in the day's historic events. The men's frock coats and top hats and the women's full-skirted dresses, multilayered petticoats, and bonnets would be too warm, but everyone wanted to look their best. It was a momentous occasion. Children shouted and laughed, giddy with the excitement that crackled through the air.

At 8:30, the First Regiment's commissioned and noncommissioned officers assembled at the courthouse. Captain McGill's company of light infantry and Captain Barbour's State Fencibles gathered in formation on Broad Street.

The *African Repository* captured the exhilaration: "The unusual activity and bustle in the streets—the rattling of drums, and the huzzas of boys testified how heartily all classes and descriptions of people entered into the business for which the day had been set apart. . . . the people were pouring from all quarters in the direction of Government Square, and the Government House and piazzas were already crowded to overflowing with ladies."

At 11:00, the smartly dressed military companies marched to Government House and formed a sharp line that faced the building's stairway. The seven ladies charged with presenting the new flag—sewn by Monrovian women—stepped from the door of Government House and paused as the troops below presented arms. The women solemnly descended the steps toward the governor, who stood a few paces in front of the troops. The women—Susanna Lewis, Martha Fenton Hunter, Mrs. R. Johnson, Mrs. C. Hazel, Eliza M. Teage, Mrs. C. Ellis, and Willy Ann Yates—formed a row.

Susanna Lewis, wife of John N. Lewis, the associate editor of the *Liberian Herald,* and sister of Jane Waring Roberts, the governor's wife, stepped forward, handed the flag to Governor Roberts, and delivered a stirring patriotic speech.

"At the conclusion of the speech, three cheers went up from the troops and the assembled multitudes . . . the waving of hats in the streets and handkerchiefs from the piazzas and windows, testified how heartily everyone was pleased," the *African Repository* reported. "The governor received the flag with his accustomed gallantry, unfurled it, and handed it to the standard-bearer, who, on the present occasion, was Captain F. Payne, of the Monrovia Militia. He then replied, in the best speech we have ever heard him make. . . . Three lusty cheers announced the conclusion of the ceremony—the ladies retired, and the flag with the guards took the center of the line."

Citizens of the newly minted republic sang their national anthem, stumbling over the not-yet-familiar words.

All hail, Liberia, hail!
All hail, Liberia, hail!
This glorious land of liberty shall long be ours,
Tho' new her name, green be her fame,
And mighty be her powers. And mighty be her powers.
In joy and gladness with our hearts united,
We'll shout the freedom of a race benighted.
Long live Liberia, happy land.
A home of glorious liberty by God's command.
A home of glorious liberty by God's command.

The flag Susanna Lewis handed to the governor bore red and white stripes, a single white star on a blue field, and the republic's new motto.

At noon, Captain Payne hoisted the flag up the flagpole for the first time. A twenty-one-gun salute echoed between Central Fort Hill and Signal Hill. The troops formed around Governor Roberts and the other dignitaries and paraded up Johnson Street to Chavers's corner, down Waring Street to the corner near the Presbyterian church, down Broad Street to Wilson's corner, and up Gurley Street to the Methodist Episcopal Church. Crowds along the route cheered and waved.

Jammed inside the church, the crowd sang, prayed, and listened to the Honorable John B. Gripon read the republic's Declaration of Independence. Then Reverend James S. Payne delivered a lengthy oration that must have seemed interminable to those sitting on hard benches in the stifling church. The service closed with a prayer, the doxology, and a benediction.

The crowd poured from the church into the fresh air and bright afternoon sunlight. The troops formed again and escorted the governor and sweating dignitaries back to Government House. An afternoon and evening of elaborate luncheons, parties, and banquets followed as the citizens celebrated their new status: free men and women living as citizens in a free country.

"It was a day which will be long remembered," the *African Repository* article concluded. "During the ceremony of presenting the flag, many eyes were suffused with tears. And, indeed, who that remembered the past could forbear to weep?"

Outside the capital city of Monrovia, down the coastline and up the rivers of Liberia, every small settlement and town—including Bassa Cove—celebrated the republic's birth with similar pomp.

In fewer than three decades, Liberia had expanded from a tiny, almost-failed settlement into a commonwealth, and finally into a true republic. Americo-Liberians—those freeborn and emancipated black people who emigrated from America and their descendants—had led the effort for independence.

Just a few months earlier, Dr. Lugenbeel, the colony's white physician, had watched part of the legislative proceedings: "I think that the manner in which the subject has been decided is highly creditable to the wisdom and judgment of the representatives of the people. . . . that [sovereignty] was discussed in the Legislature with all that calmness and consideration which its weight and importance demanded; and that the people generally are well convinced, that they are about to assume a solemn and weighty responsibility."[2]

As the colonists advanced toward self-governance, some white observers, long mired in theories of racial inferiority, were surprised by how competently the settlers managed their republic. US Navy commander Samuel Mercer recorded his changing attitude after observing the Liberian legislature: "It was, indeed, to me, a novel, and interesting sight, although [I am] a Southern man, to look upon these emancipated slaves legislating for themselves, and discussing freely, if not ably, the principles of human rights, on the very continent, and perhaps, the very spot, where some of their ancestors were sold into slavery. Who can foresee what may yet spring from this germ of freedom for the regeneration of Africa?"[3]

The path toward independence had started late the previous year, when citizens of the Commonwealth of Liberia voted to call a constitutional convention. Governor Roberts wrote in January 1847: "Liberia is destined by the Almighty to be the free and quiet habitation of thousands, perhaps millions in the future; and a land for the oppressed to flee to and be happy. . . . Here the human mind, untrammeled by unequal laws and unawed by unjust prejudices, will expand with new wings, and gathering strength with its flight, will feel its native force, and reach the summit of human perfection."[4]

By July of that year, a constitutional convention was in session and drafters unanimously passed a resolution agreeing that all territorial matters be resolved by a compact between the Republic of Liberia and the American Colonization Society.

The black men who drafted the Liberian Declaration of Independence recalled with bitterness their lives in America and their decision to come to Africa:

We uttered our complaints, but they were unattended to . . .
all hope of a favorable change in our country was thus wholly
extinguished in our bosoms and we looked with anxiety for
some asylum. . . . In coming to the shores of Africa, we indulged
the pleasing hope that we would be permitted to exercise and
improve those faculties which impart to man his dignity; to
nourish in our hearts the flame of honorable ambition; to cherish and indulge these aspirations which a beneficent Creator
had implanted in every human heart, and to evince to all who
despise, ridicule, and oppress our race that we possess with them

a common nature; are with them susceptible of equal refine-
ment, and capable to equal advancement.[5]

Eleven years earlier, Reverend Amos Herring had spoken at the quarantine grounds on Staten Island before joining the Majors and Harlans
aboard the *Luna*. Now he added his signature to the Liberian Declaration
of Independence.

The drafters of Liberia's constitution modeled it on the US Constitution, but with important differences. They included a provision outlawing
slavery. They reserved the rights of citizenship to male property owners who
were "Negroes or persons of Negro descent." White people—including colonization society employees, teachers, and physicians—were barred from
becoming citizens. The constitution also barred indigenous people from
land ownership and the right to vote. Indigenous men could obtain these
rights if they became adequately "civilized"—residing at least two years
in the colony, exhibiting good moral character, adopting American dress,
and speaking English. The country's motto, "The love of liberty brought us
here," made it clear that the founders considered Liberia a country formed
for the colonists and their descendants and ignored the thousands of indigenous people who had lived on the land for generations.[6]

In short, drafters of the constitution created a two-tiered society much
like the one they had left behind in America. Their decision to do so would
have tragic consequences.

Joseph Jenkins Roberts, a former shopkeeper, public works superintendent, and governor, became the nation's first president on October 5,
1847. Political positions in Liberia were not lucrative. In 1850, Roberts
wrote to the American Colonization Society, citing a lack of funds and asking if Liberia would receive compensation for managing the settlement of
recaptives.[7] Settler families—some struggling for their own survival—took
in the recaptives, and fed, clothed, and housed them. They also benefited
from their labor; adults from the *Pons* were indentured for a period of seven
years. President Roberts had taken five of the people from the *Pons*, captured in 1845, into his home. The US Congress approved $40,000 to reim-
burse Liberia for expenses related to the *Pons* recaptives.[8]

Other leaders in the nation's new government kept their day jobs. The
chief justice and the secretaries of state and treasury earned their livings as
storekeepers; the attorney general was a blacksmith.[9]

Still, despite the new republic's shortcomings, many of Liberia's citizens who had suffered in America wrote about finding a new sense of per-

Joseph Jenkins Roberts, a free-born Virginian man of mixed ancestry, became governor of Liberia in 1841 following the death of Thomas Buchanan. Roberts was the first non-white governor of Liberia and became president of the republic in 1847. (Daguerreotype by Rufus Anson, Library of Congress Prints and Photographs Division, LC-USZC4–4609)

Jane Rose Waring (daughter of Colston and Harriet Waring) married Joseph Jenkins Roberts and became Liberia's first First Lady in 1847. (Daguerreotype by Rufus Anson, Library of Congress, Prints and Photographs Division, LC-USZ6–1922)

Senate Ex doc No 11.d Sess 33° Cong.

PRESIDENT ROBERT'S HOUSE, MONROVIA.

Joseph Jenkins Roberts and Jane Roberts lived in the Executive Mansion in Monrovia, Liberia. (Wagner and McGuigan's Lithography, Philadelphia, Library of Congress, Prints and Photographs Division, LC-USZ62–107635)

sonhood, dignity, and autonomy in Liberia. Many letter writers alluded to the scripture Micah 4:4 that evokes an image of independence, peace, and security: "But they shall sit every man under his vine and under his fig tree; and none shall make them afraid. . . ."

Henrietta Fuller wrote, "Here we Sit under our own vine & Palm Tree. Here we enjoy the same rights & privileges that our white brethren does in America. It is our only home."[10]

Sion Harris wrote, "If they leave It to me I am going to sit here under my fig trees & orange trees About five hundred years longer & then bid Africa good by and try to go to Heaven to live forever."[11]

Hilary Teage, a Monrovia merchant, editor of the *Liberia Herald,* and one of the signers of the Liberian Declaration of Independence, wrote, "The tenants live happy under their own vine and fig tree, or literally true, under banana and plantain, and wondering why our friends in the United States think us foolish for fleeing from contempt in America to respectability in Africa."[12]

22

Men of Advanced Views
on the Subject of Education

On a sunny spring day in 1850, Ben Major and local schoolteacher Asa Starbuck Fisher took a stroll through the dense walnut and maple grove on the outskirts of town. Vivid green leaves unfurled against the dark bark of the trees, and a light breeze stirred the new grass.

At the top of a knoll, Ben stopped and turned to glance back at a piece of land east of the school building. He looked Asa squarely in the eye and said, "On that rise, we intend to build a college and we want you to be president."[1]

Ben and others in Walnut Grove wanted high-quality schools for their community. "They were all men of advanced views on the subject of education," Elmira Dickinson wrote. "[They] recognized the establishment of schools of a high order were essential in the great work of developing the resources of the Prairie State."[2]

Ben's views were influenced by and echoed by his church. The Disciples of Christ strongly supported education, including the education of women and girls. In an issue of the *Millennial Harbinger* published ten years earlier, W. C. Channing wrote: "To educate a man is to unfold his faculties—to give him the free and full use of his powers and especially his best powers. It is first to train the intellect, to give him a love of truth and to instruct him in the processes by which it may be acquired. It is to train him in soundness of judgment, to teach him to weigh evidence, and guard him against the common sources of error. It is to give him a thirst for knowledge, which will keep his faculties in action throughout life."[3]

Ben and Lucy likely educated their children at home initially. Ben bought two copies of *Smiley's Geography and Atlas* in May 1837; he probably used these and other books to teach his children. He also helped provide an education for one of his nieces, paying tuition in May 1846 for fifteen-year-old Mary, Chastine's daughter.[4]

The first institution of learning in Walnut Grove was a small school for girls held in a log structure near the home of Disciples elder John T. Jones. His wife, Emily, and daughter, Susan, taught the students. The school didn't last long. A virulent strain of measles broke out in the winter of 1847–48; many of the students became ill and one died. The school closed its doors and didn't reopen.[5]

Undeterred, in August 1848, Ben and other residents of Walnut Grove hired a recent college graduate, Asa Fisher, to teach a ten-month school term in a small frame building (sixteen by sixteen feet). Fisher boarded in Ben's home. Pleased with the teacher's work, community leaders asked him to stay on as both teacher and principal. Fisher agreed but negotiated several conditions: an addition to the schoolhouse, furnished with seats and desks; an assistant; and arrangements to board out-of-town students. He also wanted to collect the net income from tuition as his salary. Townspeople agreed to his conditions and hired carpenter William Bogardus in April 1849, paying him $45 to build the addition to the school, which more than doubled the space.[6]

Sue Jones, John T. Jones's daughter, was hired as the assistant teacher. Organizers named the school Walnut Grove Seminary and published an announcement in the summer of 1849.[7]

The second session of this Institution will commence on the First Monday of September next. The directors hope to have their new building completed, and ample boarding accommodations will be provided for all students attending the Seminary from other localities.

The course of instruction will include Reading, Penmanship, Arithmetic, Geography, English Grammar, History, Algebra, Geometry, Trigonometry, Surveying, Rhetoric, Logic, English Composition, Chemistry and Natural Philosophy.

The academic year will close on the 4th day of July, 1850. The price of tuition will range from eight to fifteen dollars per session, according to the branches studied. Those attending from other localities can obtain boarding, fuel and lights included, at from one dollar to one dollar and twenty-five cents per week.

THE ACADEMY

Ben Major founded Walnut Grove Academy (originally Walnut Grove Seminary) in 1848. The school became Eureka College in the early 1850s. The college is still in existence and was one of the first in the nation to admit women on an equal basis with men. (From Elmira J. Dickinson, ed., *A History of Eureka College with Biographical Sketches and Reminiscences* [St. Louis, Mo.: Christian Publishing Company, 1894])

> The Walnut Grove Seminary is located in Walnut Grove . . .
> about twenty miles east of Peoria. For health of climate, beauti-
> ful scenery, intelligence and morality among the people, the
> community is not surpassed by any locality of the State.
>
> —A. S. Fisher, Principal

Enrollment was high and a steady stream of applications for admittance convinced Ben and the other trustees to expand. Ben proposed they raise $2,500 for a new two-story brick building and rename the school Walnut Grove Academy.

"Many of those present expressed grave doubts as to the probability of raising a sum of money so large," Elmira Dickinson wrote. "Mr. Major said, 'Brethren, this is a matter very dear to my heart. You all know that I have long entertained the hope of witnessing an institution of high order established in our midst. . . . I believe we can raise the money.'" Ben, along with two other men, immediately committed $150 each toward the effort. William Davenport canvassed the community and acquired enough pledges to meet their goal within a few weeks.[8]

In January 1850, Ben wrote to his brother Joseph about the school. "We have in successful operation a male and female seminary . . . with 60 or 70 students in attendance and only room to swell the list to double their number. We have determined, this coming season, to raise a brick edifice 30 x 42 [feet], 2 stories high, which is to be the foundation of a male and female college. We . . . only want a few more hundred dollars donated to insure the work to be completed by September or October."[9]

Benjamin J. Radford, a former student of rare wit, reminisced about the school in a Founder's Day speech decades later: "The academy measured about thirty by forty feet. What must have been the pressure of intellectuality per square inch in that shell? The library was about ten feet square and most of the space was occupied by vacancy. The apparatus room on the second floor was of the same dimensions and contained all that there was of the physical and chemical laboratory. . . . Desks were homemade and primitive and the blackboards were of the same fashion, portable and inclined against the wall. Crayons were unknown. Chalk was bought in huge chunks and broken into convenient chunklets."[10]

Ben had even bigger plans and, on that spring walk, proposed to Fisher that a college be built. In November, William Davenport traveled to Kentucky to raise funds for the nascent school; by the time he reached Louisville he had secured leads on acquiring sixty books and a $100 money order for the school.[11]

By 1852 the school's library housed about three hundred volumes. That year, thirty-eight boys and thirty girls were enrolled in the upper level classes. In a few years the humble two-story school became Eureka College. (The town of Walnut Grove was renamed Eureka in 1850. Faculty member John Lindsey—son of Ben's friend James Alfred Lindsey and a Greek and Latin teacher at the school—suggested the new name.)[12]

In keeping with the Disciples' support of education for women and the recent Women's Rights Convention held in Seneca Falls, New York, women were admitted to Eureka College on an equal basis with men. Eureka was only the third college in the nation to do so.

The founders sought to instill cultural values beyond what could be learned from a textbook. These included communication and persuasion, manners and orderliness, fraternalism, temperance, tolerance, and leadership.[13]

The first board of trustees of Eureka College included Elijah Dickinson (Elmira's father), William Davenport and his son William Horace Davenport, John Lindsey, John Major (Ben's son), and William T. Major (Ben's brother).[14]

Asa Fisher, the young teacher who had stood atop the knoll with Ben, dedicated thirty-eight years of his life to the institution.

23

I Am a Free Man
in a Free Country

Tolbert placed the sturdy wooden box on the table. It wasn't small, but not a crate either—perhaps two feet long, a foot wide, and a foot tall. It was heavier than it looked. The box was addressed to him in Ben's neat script.

Tolbert slid a hatchet blade between the end of the box and its lid. He pried upward and nails screeched as they pulled from the wood. He set down the hatchet and lifted off the box top. At first he saw only straw, but he dug past it and pulled out several envelopes and small corked jars filled with dried plant material. Each was neatly labeled.

He removed some of the straw and dug deeper into the box. He extracted a large oilcloth bundle, placed it on the table, and unwrapped it. Inside he found small cloth drawstring bags filled with seeds. Tolbert smiled in anticipation of the next season's crops. He pulled out the remaining packing materials and discovered several books. He read the titles, then set them aside.

Liberia
Bassa Cove
Grand Bassa County
June 23d, 1848
My Dear Father,

*   I received your letter dated August 1847 and though it has been written nearly a year, yet it came safe to hand—which gave me great satisfaction, but I heard nothing that was at all dissatisfactory in the least. My wife is at present very well indeed, as is the case with myself. I have at this time two children: Sarah Agnes & Ann*

Eliza—the former was born the 20th Oct. 1843 and being nearly five years old, goes to school and can read a little. The latter, having been born as late as the 9th Sept. 1846, is not quite old enough as yet to go to school and so she stays home with me.

Agreeable to your request, I shall endeavour to write a letter to you at least twice a year, but whenever I see an opportunity of writing, I shall not fail to do so.

I received the medicines and books which you sent me and was very glad of them and that you were so mindful of me and I shall, as far as my poor ability will allow, conform to your advice set forth in the letter.

We are very thankful for the few seeds you sent us, as much so as if you had sent a bushel of each kind, seeing you show a willing mind to do a good part by us, and I intend to try and do the same by you, but as poor Lazarus said to the rich man, there is a great gulf between us.

We have not received the cards which you sent nor even heard of them. . . .

I only received four kinds of medicine, viz Bayberry Bark, Hemlock, No. 4 or Bitters, Lobelia Seed. I do not know whether they are all that you sent or not. . . .

The books that you sent me will answer for my children; they are in my estimation valuable books.[1]

Tolbert included the full names and birth dates of his daughters: Sarah's middle name was likely in honor of her grandmother Agnes Harlan, and Ann Eliza may have been named in honor of Ben's daughter of the same name who died in 1829 in Kentucky. Tolbert didn't mention his two sons who had come to Liberia with him or the new baby boy he had written about in May 1839. His words—"at this time"—hint at the grief of losing all three of his sons.

Ben had also sent botanical medicines to Tolbert. Decades before, Ben had experienced health problems and had tried a system developed by Samuel Thomson. Thomson's followers commonly used bayberry bark, lobelia, rhubarb, cayenne, cinnamon, witch hazel, licorice root, bitterroot, chamomile, slippery elm, and other botanicals for treatments. Thomsonian practitioners rejected what they called "mineral doctors"—practitioners of more traditional medicine—many of whom were still using treatments such as bleeding, blistering, leeches, and "remedies" made of arsenic, lead, and calomel, a toxic compound derived from mercury. Those who had seen

Pearson Cholera Syrup
1 lb Poplar
1 " Bayberry
1 " Cherry
1/4 " Prickly Ash Berries or Bark
1/2 " Valerian
1/8 " Scullcap
1/4 " Golden Seal
1/8 " Hemlock.
Boil in five galls water,
Mock 1 gall of strong No 6
2 gall melasses

Ben Major collected formulas for various Thomsonian treatments, tonics, and liniments. This page preserves his recipe for cholera syrup. (Major Family Private Collection)

loved ones die from traditional treatments were eager to try these more natural approaches.

Ben embraced the Thomsonian system and began practicing it. He often provided compounds and advice to family and friends. His brother Joseph sometimes provided him with ingredients for various remedies. Once, when Joseph's wife was quite ill, he lamented to Ben, "I fear it will be a long time before she recovers. It would be a very pleasing thing to me were we situated nearer together [so] that I could have your advice in this case."[2]

Ben collected formulas for various Thomsonian treatments, tonics, and liniments, recording them in a three-by-five-inch notebook; these included formulas to treat consumption (tuberculosis), whooping cough, rheumatism, hemorrhoids, and cholera, one of the most feared diseases of the time.[3]

Cholera, a bacterial infection, causes extreme vomiting, diarrhea, eventual dehydration, and death in 50 to 60 percent of cases. In one outbreak in Campeche, Mexico, four thousand people died in a month. People in Walnut Grove knew cholera intimately. There had been a bad outbreak in 1834, the year that Ben and his family moved to the area. Ben collected at least three different formulas for treating cholera.[4]

The Liberian colonists used the Thomsonian method, too. Robert M. Page wrote to America in 1849 asking for a Thomsonian medical book, noting that he found it to be more useful than "real doctor medicine."[5]

Tolbert thanked Ben for the seeds and books he had sent. Books were scarce in Liberia. Like writing paper, books rotted in the wet climate or became infested with bugs. Settlers, eager to educate their children and themselves, frequently asked for books in their letters to America, often specifying Bibles, dictionaries, atlases, and grammar, math, geography, and theology texts. Colonists promoted literacy in a variety of ways. The *Colonization Herald* reported in 1838, "In some places, as at Bassa Cove, literary societies are formed for mutual improvement. . . . At Bassa Cove and Monrovia, there are public libraries for the use of the people. The one at the former place numbers 1,200 or 1,500 volumes."[6]

Tolbert's letter continued:

> *We are getting along pretty well indeed. We have lived together without any dispute or disagreeing as yet, and I hope we never will disagree or have disputes and quarrels.*
>
> *I am exceedingly happy. We did on the 29th July last by own representatives solemnly declare ourselves a free sovereign and independent people thereby dissolving all political connection between the Col. Society and ourselves, and we have established a new form of government, viz a "Republican form" and it is my pride and joy that I am a free man in a free country, and can enjoy the free mild and equal government which has just been established, and where I can have an equal share of republicanism—*

Tolbert's statement about getting along with one another is remarkable given the trials, tribulations, and tragedies that had beset the family since their arrival in Liberia. Even the best people crack under stress and grief, yet—perhaps because they had to rely on one another—the Majors and Harlans got along.

Perhaps most importantly in this letter, Tolbert celebrated his life as a free man. He had been born into slavery and spent the first three decades of his life as someone else's property. He was overjoyed to be free and to be able to participate in governing his country.

Back in Illinois, Ben was thinking about liberty and colonization, too. He had been asked to make a speech on the Fourth of July 1848, celebrating the seventy-second anniversary of the nation's independence. He had been reading the May issue of the *African Repository* and found a report on the Kentucky Colonization Society. Ben pulled out a scrap of pale blue paper and scribbled down key points about the American Colonization Society: "1, The History of A.C.S.; 2, The Object of A.C.S.; 3, Effects of A.C.S.: Upon this Nation, [Upon] Coloured population of US, Upon Africa." He noted, "England and France have given to all blacks their freedom, but US alone is placing them in a situation where that freedom may be enjoyed."

Ben then carefully tucked his notes into his issue of the *African Repository*, where they were found 168 years later.

Tolbert's letter continued:

> *The general occupation of the citizens of this country, natives included, is farming. The merchants appreciate their farming more than all their commercial business. Rice—corn—cassavas—potatoes—arrowroot—ginger, etc., grow to perfection. At the same time may be seen [in] every person's garden, salads of every description which Liberia will afford. Eatable herbs and here and there is pictured most beautiful flowers, etc., etc. . . . the staple production [is] also palm oil—which we use in the place of lard.*
>
> *I may say that the women do nothing but would tell a little story that is not true. They sew and wash and sometimes they may be seen weeding out the garden and doing other petty jobs of the same nature. We raise cattle in this country, but the oxen here do not work like those in America; we also have sheep, goats, hogs, ducks, and chickens and we are making a start at turkeys.*

Tolbert revealed his sense of humor when he wrote, "I may say that the women do nothing but would tell a little story that is not true." Ann, Silvay, and Agnes were undoubtedly busy most of the time. Ann was stepmother to sixteen-year-old Mary. Silvay had two little girls. Although Agnes's surviving sons—Asbury and Wesley—were young adults, she probably helped grow and prepare food, wash clothes, and care for the whole family, including her grandchildren.

Rice, sweet potatoes, okra, and boiled greens would have been familiar to the settlers who had come from the southern United States. However, after twelve years in Liberia, the settlers had probably also learned to prepare traditional West African dishes, including palm butter, fried plantains, *palava* sauce, and *fufu* and *dumboy* (starchy cassava dough balls eaten with soups and stews). Native dishes were seasoned with ginger, onions, and fresh or dried melegueta peppers, which gave the region its nickname, the Pepper Coast. (The peppers were also called Grains of Paradise, the source of a second nickname for the area, the Grain Coast.)

The beautiful flowers Tolbert mentioned might have included lilies, ylang-ylang, and orchids brightening the forest's edge.

> *There is also a variety of poisonous reptiles in this country, such as snakes, lizards, scorpions, centipedes, etc. There is a kind of lizard whose bite is said to be fatal; it is called in this country the salimango. I do not know its natural historical name.*

Liberia is home to some of the most poisonous snakes in the world, including vipers, adders, cobras, green mambas, and the more aggressive black mamba—the largest venomous snake in Africa. One Monrovia settler wrote in a letter to America that he had seen a red, pink, and black snake between fifteen and eighteen feet long on the bank of a river. This same man killed a nine-foot snake in his mother's house. Another man, the good-humored Sion Harris, wrote to the colonization society's William McLain that he had caught a nineteen-foot-long boa constrictor. He wrote, "It eats hearty. What is it worth in your country? Don't you want a pet for your children to play with?"[7]

> *We are not fixed in a way to make cloth, so every yd of cloth that is used in this country is bought. Cotton grows and, was it cultivated, would be very plentiful. Neither can we make sewing cotton [thread], and at this very moment, it is in great demand; any price almost would be paid for it. The above are not fables but realities.*
>
> *As to paying you a visit, I hardly know what to say. At this time, I am not in a way for paying visits and I have changed my notion as I won't be able to come for a couple of years yet. But I shall endeavour to send you some coffee. I would have sent it by the [brig] La— Pack-*

et, but not receiving your letter in time, I could not get it in readiness to send . . . I received your letter only a couple of days previous to the starting of the vessel and we have no machines in this country, but have to work with our own hands. When she makes another trip across the ocean, I will be sure and send it.

I really do wish to see you and mother, and sometimes, when I study about past days, it distresses me most wonderful.

What you wrote concerning my brother's wife & children gives me a great deal of satisfaction and comfort. Please remember my love to John Major, your son, and Judith, your daughter, and all the rest of your children. I would have written to them all but for want of time and paper, I could not. Paper is a scarce article.

My love to Chastine Major and his family, to Mr. Davenport and family, to William Major and all of his family, to Joseph Major and his family, to Edward Watkins and his family.

It is not clear to whom Tolbert is referring when he writes about "my brother's wife." Would this have been Austin's former wife, or was George Major, whom Tolbert mentioned in his first letter, his brother, and this refers to George's wife? Or did Tolbert and Austin have another brother?

Dear Mother and father, pray for me, and by the assistance of God, I shall endeavour to do the same for you. I hope the Lord will make a way for me to see you all again this side of the grave. I am yet striving to lay up treasures in heaven where moth corrupteth not nor thieves break in and steal.

This puts me in mind of the time when I came from the iron-works, and you had gone off to Illinois and left me, and when I study about that, it makes the tears rise in my eyes.

Tolbert alluded to a scripture from Matthew 6: "Lay not up for yourselves treasures upon earth, where moth and rust doth corrupt, and where thieves break through and steal: But lay up for yourselves treasures in heaven, where neither moth nor rust doth corrupt, and where thieves do not break through nor steal: For where your treasure is, there will your heart be also."

He understood this scripture in a literal way. People had broken into his home and stolen the supplies he needed to care for his family. In the hot, humid climate of West Africa—where the air felt like a wet towel—any number of treasures could decompose and be gone.

The passage from his letter is filled with nostalgia and sentiment. When Tolbert wrote about the ironworks, he was apparently referring to the time when Ben had hired out his enslaved people as he prepared to move from Kentucky, but before he could free them for colonization. Tolbert likely labored at the ironworks located between the Tennessee River and the Cumberland River in western Kentucky, in a region now known as the Land Between the Lakes. At the time, Kentucky was the third-largest iron-producing state in the nation, with seventeen iron furnaces blazing in the area.[8]

As he often did, Tolbert included greetings to many people in America, then added a closing and postscript.

> *Farewell, father & mother,*
>
> > *Tolbert Major*
>
> *My mother-in-law, Enoch Harlan's wife, was very glad to hear from you and says give her love to all her acquaintances. Wesley Harlan is married.*

Most of Tolbert's letters ended with "yours" or "yours truly" or another standard closing. This is the only time he ended a missive with "farewell."

Neither Ben nor Tolbert had any way of knowing that it would be Tolbert's last letter to his friend in America.

Austin sent a letter to Ben the same day.

> *Bassa Cove, June 23d, 1848*
> *Dear father & mother,*
>
> *We received your letter and was very glad that you thought so much of us as to send an answer & we also was glad to hear of your healths, which seemed to be good—& now I must tell you something about our health & the health of our families. My family is well; my wife & daughter is in good health.*
>
> *I have only one child living, which is Mary & she is nearly grown! She can read tolerably well. But she does not go to school everyday at this time. My wife can also read tolerably well & Mary can write some, but not having had a good chance . . . she cannot*

write better. You will be please to write to me separately so that I may
receive my letters without so much trouble, as it appears that there
has been some miscarriage in them.

I must say something more about Mary. She is a schoolteacher
& she has also embraced the religion of Jesus Christ & is now a full
member in the Methodist church. If you will, please to write to me
whether old mother Rebecca is yet living or not. . . .

I must say also that I am a class leader & a steward in the
Methodist Episcopal Church in Bassa Cove & according to your
request, I am trying to live agreeable & serve the lord to the best of
my knowledge.

Austin's life seems to have been more stable when he wrote this letter than
it had been when he had last written to Ben in 1840. His reference to Mary
as his only living child confirmed that his other children had died. Tolbert
had written in 1843 about Thomas's death, but nowhere in the surviving
letters do Austin or Tolbert reveal what happened to little Caroline. She
was only seven when she came to Liberia. Four of the original five Major
children were dead not quite twelve years after their voyage on the *Luna*.

Ben would have sympathized. He and Lucy had lost their nine-year-
old daughter, Ann Eliza, when they still lived in Kentucky. His brother
Joseph had lost a son. William Davenport had buried four of his children.
In an era without antibiotics and vaccines for common childhood illnesses,
parents often lost half of their children before they grew up. The losses
for the Liberian Majors would have been nearly overwhelming, yet they
believed that heaven was real and they anticipated a reunion with those
who had preceded them in death.

Austin was proud of Mary, who was about seventeen at the time. She
could read and write some and was teaching school. With the shortage
of teachers in the republic, it would not have been surprising for a young
woman with even a basic level of education to become a teacher for younger
pupils. Austin also noted that she belonged to the Methodist Episcopal
Church, and that he himself was a class leader and steward of the church.

He inquired about "old mother Rebecca," but there is no way to determine her identity, or to confirm if she was truly his mother, or if this was a
term of affection or respect for an unrelated woman.

With regard to fruits, we have corn & cassavas, sweet potatoes
& arrowroot—ginger & plantains & soursops & bananas & the

palm trees yields abundantly—& the pawpaw & cotton we can raise in the greatest abundance & fowls—hogs & goats, sheep—there is plenty [of] deers in this country & also a very ferocious animals called the leopard & the bush cat, etc. . . . I have not done much farming as yet, but I am trying to get ready to do so.

Almost twelve years after Austin had arrived in Liberia, he had still not done much farming. He seems to have been a reluctant farmer at best, and his early letters indicated a stronger interest in trading.

Bell Wiley wrote in his book *Slaves No More*, "As a rule, emigrants did not take to agriculture. Native crops were strange, land was hard to clear, and there were few, if any, work animals to lighten the burden of work. Barter with natives was a much easier way to obtain a livelihood."[9]

However, by the late 1840s more settlers were committing to working the soil. The June 30, 1848, *Liberian Herald* reported, "From all parts of the republic . . . they are turning their attention to this most important of all branches of industry."[10]

Austin continued:

With regard to my seeing you again, I never expect to see you again in this life, but I hope to meet you all in the King[dom] of Eternal glory where we will meet to part no more forever—for I am so very well satisfied in this country—the land of my forefathers, where I enjoy all the rights & privileges of a free man & can worship my God & there is none to make me afraid or oppress me in so doing. You will please to excuse me for writing so to you, but I wish not to brag, but only to state the satisfaction of my mind in the land of my fathers or ancestors in which the Lord has been so good as to send me. . . . My wife is just as well satisfied as I am in this country—I oft times think of the many good advices that you have given me in the house, for my aim is to live in peace with all men & when done with this world, get to heaven at last.

In this passage, Austin alluded to the verse from Micah about the vine and fig tree, and expressed his deep satisfaction with the country. His remark about Ben giving him "good advices" provides a hint about his relationship to Ben in America. Perhaps Austin was a house servant, which would help account for his reluctance to farm. Most of the letters in Bell Wiley's book *Slaves No More* were written by or for black people who had been domestic servants, artisans, drivers, or who had held supervisory positions—people closely associated with their owner's family.[11] On the other hand, since Ben did not own a large number of enslaved people, it is likely that each fulfilled multiple jobs. Maybe Austin worked both in and out of the house.

> *My daughter says she wishes you to send her something to remember her & we all want to send you something to remember you all & what is convenient, send to us as a memorial & now our Lord Jesus Christ himself guide you in the paths of righteousness & at last bring you into his heavenly Kingdom is our sincere prayer.*
> *Yours very sincerely & most affectionately,*
>
> *Austin Major & family*

On the other side of the ocean, Ben had been reading about Liberia. The American newspapers continued to publish articles about the burgeoning country and the ongoing colonization movement.

In 1848, Liberia acquired the New Cess region, site of the only remaining slave factory along the coast. The owner of the slave factory wrote to President Roberts, asking if it was true that Liberia now controlled the region and that the slave trade was outlawed.

Roberts promptly replied: "Mr. S. A. Benson, acting on the part of the American Colonization Society and the Government of Liberia, concluded, on the 19th ultimo, a purchase for a valuable consideration, of the entire New Cess territory from the King and Chief of that country; at which time a regular transfer deed, executed in the presence of competent witnesses, was duly sealed and delivered. . . . I need not inform you, sir, that traffic in slaves is contrary to the laws of this government and cannot in any degree be tolerated by the authorities here."[12]

The September 1848 issue of the *African Repository* provided details of the agreement. The society would cede its ownership of public lands to the republic (setting aside some lots for future immigrants), and the society and the republic would work together to develop new settlements. The republic would take ownership of the government house, Fort Johnson, and munitions. The society would retain ownership of its public farm, store, lot, and wharf, and shipments of supplies for settlers would be duty-free.[13]

In early April 1848, President Roberts, his wife, Jane Rose (Waring), and his daughter; settlers Sion and Martha Harris; and several others left Monrovia, bound for the United States. Roberts hoped to conduct business, promote his country, and make a case for American recognition of the new republic. The president and some of the others also spoke to several gatherings in New York, including groups interested in moving to Liberia.[14]

The editor of the *New York Recorder*, covering one of President Roberts's speaking engagements, wrote, "We saw the African race under a new aspect. . . . The tone of conscious inferiority and servility, so universally and so naturally characteristic of the race here, had given place to a manly bearing which at once commanded respect."[15]

President Roberts and several commissioners from Liberia met with the American Colonization Society Executive Committee to develop an agreement that formalized the ongoing relationship between the new republic and its former sponsoring organization.

America—still locked in long-held attitudes of racism and led by men acutely sensitive to divisions over slavery—did not extend official recognition to Liberia until 1862, despite President Roberts's ongoing efforts. American officials were unwilling to formally receive black people, even if they were official representatives of another nation.[16]

24

Send Me Some Carpenter Tools (and Bonnets)

Austin was glad the rainy season was almost over. When the rains came, it was hard to earn a living farming. Back in Kentucky, he used to do some carpentry work now and then. If he only had the right tools, he could do that when he couldn't farm—maybe bring in a little money. Bassa Cove had grown; there were more than two hundred people in town now and there was always a need for someone to build or repair homes and businesses.

Maybe Ben Major could help. Come to think of it, there were several other things he needed from America.

> Oct 19th 1849, Bassa Cove & County of Liberia
> Dear father & mother,
>   I embrace this opportunity of addressing you with these few lines, hoping they may find you & family enjoying good health as the same leaves me & mine at present. Since I have been to Liberia, I enjoy, as a general thing, tolerable good health and also family and all the others.
>   It has been some time since I hear from you & mother. I sent some letters by the Packet when she was out time before last, but whether they got to your hands or not, we cannot tell. I would be very glad to hear from you all indeed and I hope [illegible] you get this letter, you will answer it—in order that we may know how you are doing &c, &c.

Settlers relied on ships to get their letters back to the United States and to a post office at the port of arrival. Austin put his missive directly into the hands of one of the American Colonization Society's representatives to ensure its safe delivery to Ben.

Below the address panel on his letter, Austin had written "the Rev Mr Gurley on Bord the Liberian Packet." The Reverend Ralph Gurley was involved with the American Colonization Society for fifty years (1822–72), first as an agent, then secretary, vice president, and finally honorary life director. He had also set up systems to aid widows, orphans, and the sick in Liberia, and created a colonial advisory council to involve settlers in governing the colony. The colonists knew him and trusted him.[1] The *Liberian Packet* was a ship built by the society in 1846; she made three trips between Liberia and America each year.[2]

Austin opened his letter by asking about Ben's health and that of his family and providing a report on his own family's health. These were not hollow courtesies. Without other means of communication, letters were the only way for the Majors on both sides of the Atlantic to know how friends and family fared.

> *My wife & Mary sends their best respects to you & mother and they hope you would cherish this opportunity to send them a bonnet each. And sir, above all, please send me the age of both myself, wife, & daughter, for we cannot tell them ourselves . . . as my daily occupation is farming, do avail yourself the opportunity to send me some tools.*
>
> *Please send some carpenter's tools, as I can do some at that business: 1 handsaw, some files, & augers & chisels, pliers, and a good hatchet.*

Austin's wife, Ann, and daughter, Mary, needed new bonnets. This was probably a request for practical sunbonnets to shield them from the fierce African sun, rather than a request for fashionable chapeaux. A shipment of bonnets from the American Colonization Society had just arrived in Bassa Cove; perhaps Austin was not yet aware of them or—more likely—Ann and Mary had already checked them out and found them wanting.

Stephen A. Benson, still a shopkeeper, wrote to the society, thanking them for the shipment. "The case of bonnets was safely rec'd—the colours of the most of them are not admirable by our Liberian ladies. . . . Cheaper bonnets of about half the price of those sent this time—straw, (Tuscan) &c.—will sell admirably well in Bassa."[3]

Stephen Benson, a freeborn man from Maryland, was a shopkeeper, secretary to Governor
Thomas Buchanan, and a businessman. He was
vice president of Liberia from 1854 to 1856 under
President Roberts and was the second president of
the republic from 1856 to 1864. (Daguerreotype
by Rufus Anson, Library of Congress, Prints and
Photographs Division, LC-USZ6–2075)

Austin asked Ben to provide his age and that of his wife and daughter. Enslaved people had no calendars, and most were not able to write and
record family events. They often marked their birth dates by season, and
many had only a rough idea of their ages.[4]

Austin also asked for carpentry tools. Settlers who had vocational
skills were fortunate; they could subsidize their incomes when crops were
bad and during the rainy season, when farming was not possible. The average annual rainfall on the Liberian coast is between 170 and 180 inches—
more than fourteen feet of rain each year.[5] One writer reported, "It did not
rain, but poured down like a waterfall."[6] Villagers couldn't walk far without
getting mired in the mud, and fields couldn't be plowed or planted for several months each year.

At the time Austin wrote this letter, Bassa Cove had 260 residents; about 20 percent were from indigenous groups and the rest were from America. A US Navy commander, John Marston, visited the area a few months later. His correspondence gives a glimpse of the settlement. "All these places are regularly laid out into streets running at right angles and the squares are three hundred feet, allowing each building lot to be sixty feet by a depth of one hundred and fifty. The buildings are constructed chiefly of wood."[7]

There would have been plenty of work for carpenters. In 1840, a Liberian carpenter could make 75 cents to $1.25 per day at a time when a cow cost $18. Wages were not equal for women. Thirteen years later, a female correspondent wrote that she could earn only 25 cents a day: "You Know that is too hard for a poor widder to get a long at that Rate and have three Children to find Vitels and Cloths."[8]

> *Dear father, I hope you are acquainted with Liberia, that is—I mean that it is hard to get anything like good cloth to make clothes except for very thin, so please send me some blue jeans to make some good wearing clothes & also some good calico for wife & daughter, and also please send some paper, as it is very scarce here, which cannot be gotten unless I pay fifty cts. per gr.*

Paper was always scarce in the colony. Many who wrote from Liberia pled for paper and ink. John N. Lewis extended his thanks for some paper that arrived in 1847 aboard the *Liberian Packet*. "The supply of Stationary came very opportunely—I wish there had been a little larger supply of Paper and Quills, and I might then have supplied the State, as there is none to be had at present. If circumstances will warrant it, will you not bear this in mind on the return of the *Packet?*"[9]

Austin requested books and cloth—"blue jeans" and calico. Denim, the fabric from which jeans are made, had been widely used in America since the late 1700s. It was durable and would wear well. Calico was a cotton print fabric often used for women's clothing. Ben's household records confirm that he purchased such fabrics, some of which he shipped to Liberia.

The Liberian settlers did not know the Africans' world; they knew only their own world, and they tried to recreate it in their new homeland. Immigrants across history have done exactly the same thing. The men of Monrovia wore frock coats and top hats; the women wore American-style dresses, bonnets, and shawls. The settlers established schools and churches, primarily Protestant denominations. They continued to speak English, gave English names to their children, and built American-style frame houses.

In 1851, the publishers of the *Unabridged Edition of Webster's English Dictionary: The American Dictionary of the English Language* sent a copy to Liberia's president. They enclosed a letter. "The English language will be spoken by the millions who are to constitute the population of this Republic. . . . It is desirable, also, that the language should be preserved, and be written and spoken in accordance with the best standards." The president promptly sent a thank-you note to the publishers.[10]

Lamin Sanneh wrote about the colonists' habit of clinging to English and familiar customs: "It was as if the fact that Liberia was a place in Africa was merely incidental. . . . The colony had America in its eyes while it turned its back on Africa; though it was necessarily in Africa, it was preferably not of it."[11]

New settlers were likely shocked by indigenous people wearing little or nothing other than wigs, body paint, colorful skirts, head wraps, and loincloths, and sporting tattoos and ritual scars. The bush societies, fetishes, music, and dances of the indigenous people would have all been unfamiliar and maybe alarming to settlers from America.

However, had the colonists abandoned western clothing and customs and tried to fully embrace the culture of their new homes, it is unlikely that they would have been readily accepted by the indigenous people, and it is probable that they would have been condemned by their sponsors. The settlers knew that Americans were closely watching the great colonization experiment. At least in the first decades of the colony, the colonization society made the rules and held the purse strings, and settlers were unlikely to deliberately alienate them. They had gone through tremendous culture shock as well, and probably clung to familiar habits of dress and behavior for comfort.

> *Please give my love to Chastine Major; tell him I think very hard of him for not writing & he has never wrote me since I have here been. My love to Wm. Major & family, Jo Major & family, Wm. Davenport & family. My wife say give her love [to] Sarah Tenly . . . please give our love to John Major and tell him to remember his old father that raised him. I hope he has not forgot him because he is in Africa. Give my love to Wm. Major; tell him to send us something, too, for us to remember him, & also Benjamin Major. Tell him send us some things also so as for us to remember him.*

Austin sent greetings to several people in America, including John and Benjamin Major, Ben's sons. He asked Ben to tell John, "Remember his old father that raised him." John, the oldest of Ben and Lucy's five sons, would have been fourteen when Austin left for Liberia. Austin was only twenty-eight at the time, hardly an old man. Yet the request to be remembered seems to indicate a special relationship. (Ben and Lucy had had three more children in the years since they had seen Austin: Joseph in 1834, Anna Elizabeth in about 1836, and Chastine, named for Ben's brother, in about 1842.)

Austin also sent greetings to William and Joseph Major (Ben's brothers) and their families, and to William Davenport and his family. He asked especially to be remembered to Chastine, Ben's youngest brother: "Tell him I think very hard of him for not writing." Austin seems to have been genuinely hurt that Chastine, who was about eight years older than he, had never written to him.

> *Mary is a teacher of the Sabbath School of the M. E. Church and also a member of [the] Christian Church. She is, I am happy to say, stood among the first in society in [Sabbath School]: Church & State, and I expect before this letter gets to you, she will be married & she will be very happy if Mrs. [illegible] Thalis would lend her some things to set her house up. So, if you or she either comes out here, I shall be prepared to receive you.*

Austin was very proud of Mary, his only surviving child, who was eighteen at the time. It is not clear who Mrs. Thalis was or what her relationship to Mary might have been. No families named Thalis, Thails, or Thales appear in the Christian County 1830 or 1840 censuses.

> *I am now a leader of a class of the M. E. church. Please send me some good books and a drawing [knife?] as I have none. Please send some 5"& [illegible] nails five & eight penny nails.*
> *Nothing more, but remains yours*
> *Respectfully,*
>
> *Austin Major*

Other settlers made similar requests. New immigrants Peter Ross and Robert Carter wrote, "We shall be glad to receive also a supply of nails to build our houses, as we have none & no means to get them; they are hard to obtain here & come high."[12]

Austin's letter ends with a postscript: "P.S. my best respects to [illegible] Thails & Lucy Major. Tell them to send ~~me~~ wife & Mary a bonnet for we lost almost [all] our things in the war. AM." It appears that Mary—not her father—wrote the postscript, which is in distinctly different handwriting. The postscript writer first wrote, "send me a bonnet," but then crossed out "me" and replaced it with "wife & Mary." In tiny, flowery script beneath Austin's signature, the name "Mary" appears.

Of all the letters in the Major collection of letters from Liberia, this one includes the longest list of requested items. Austin asked for tools, nails, cloth, paper, books, a drawing knife, bonnets, and wedding gifts for Mary. It is not possible to know if Austin was being greedy or presumptuous or if Ben had previously urged the settlers to let him know if they needed anything. Not all former owners were willing to continue to purchase supplies and ship them at their own expense to Africa.

We Have Not Lived in Vain

In March 1846, Ben Major's niece, fifteen-year-old Margaretta, who lived in Bloomington, Illinois, penned an essay titled "Faith, Hope, and Charity." She sent a copy to her uncle. Her prose was flowery, but her formal tone was offset by a whimsical drawing of a young woman with her hair piled atop her head. Making a pun on her mother's maiden name of Shipp, Margaretta wrote "composed by her Lady Shipp" on the essay. She wrote of worldliness and division between religious denominations, but concluded that by living a Christian life, the faithful could draw others to Christ, and "In the last day . . . we [will] have not lived in vain nor labored in vain."[1]

By 1849, Ben and his family and Christian County friends had not lived or labored in vain. They had led productive, meaningful lives in Illinois for fifteen years. They had built homes and established farms, businesses, churches, and schools in Walnut Grove, Mackinaw, Bloomington, and nearby towns, and had formed tight-knit communities centered on their faith.

They had dealt with malaria, measles, and other diseases, and survived tornadoes, prairie fires, and snowstorms. They had fought wolves, wildcats, and snakes and watched great clouds of passenger pigeons darken the skies. They had hunted duck, geese, quail, deer, and squirrels and fished the streams. People had worked together, helping build one another's homes and barns, and had gathered for weddings, funerals, church services, corn huskings, elections, and quilting bees. The children had played games such as town-ball (a precursor to baseball) and marbles, and the men had played horseshoes. Together, they had built a true community.[2]

Ben had supported local merchants Henkel Danforth and Gaunt Willard, buying household supplies that included tin cups, whiskey barrels, a coffee pot, nails and screws, a saw, shoes, sugar, molasses, tea, whalebone, thread, buttons, needles, pins, and fabric. He had ordered several slat-back and bent-back chairs for the house and bought a New Testament and hymn books, schoolbooks, and pencils and paper, some of which he sent to Liberia.[3]

He had also purchased ingredients for his Thomsonian formulas, including ginger, cayenne, myrrh, lobelia seed, and bayberry. Ben was always doctoring his family, friends, and neighbors free of charge. Sue E. Grant (former schoolteacher Susan Jones), who knew the family, wrote, "Ben Major, everybody's 'Uncle Ben,' was always ready to leave his work to answer calls of distress." Elmira Dickinson recalled, "He was almost a physician without price, as his services were nearly always gratuitous. If any of the neighbors were sick, he would leave his work and stay with them until the danger was past."[4]

In the same tiny notebook that Ben used for his Thomsonian formulas, he had collected recipes for currant wine, grape wine, and cordials. Unlike many of the Disciples of Christ, he apparently didn't support the growing temperance movement.

Ben was a trusted and respected leader in the community. Several people wrote to him from other states, asking his advice about moving to Illinois. Friends and family still in Kentucky counted on him to resolve disputes or collect debts from mutual acquaintances. He became involved in civic matters, penning a petition in early 1852 related to construction of a county road. He had not only helped launch Walnut Grove Academy, but also supported the school with his leadership and personal funds.[5] Ben had raised sheep and farmed his land and Joseph's Illinois tract, planting grapevines, apple trees, wheat, and corn.

Meanwhile, Joseph had continued to waver about selling his Illinois land. Potential buyers included his brother Chastine, his son John, and others. In the end, he kept the acreage until 1851, when he finally sold it and relinquished any idea of living in Illinois.

In Bloomington, young Margaretta's father, William T. Major, had founded the First Christian Church. Like Ben and so many other Disciples of Christ, William was a great believer in education. He had donated heavily to Eureka College and served on the board of trustees. He had also supported other colleges and founded a girls' preparatory school in Bloomington.

Margaretta's essay is intelligent, thoughtful, and filled with grace. Had she lived to adulthood, she might have followed her father and uncle into leadership roles in the church. She could have taught at Eureka College (which had female faculty members almost from the beginning), served on the Christian Women's Board of Missions (founded by a female teacher at Eureka), or even served as an ordained pastor (the Disciples of Christ was one of the first denominations to ordain women). It was not to be.

In July 1849, William T. Major sent an urgent note to William Davenport. "Our dear Margaretta is no more. Her pure spirit left her body at 6 o'clock this morning. Her remains will be buried in the afternoon of tomorrow. Can you come and preach her funeral?" The grieving father did not reveal how nineteen-year-old Margaretta had died.[6]

26

He Was Killed by Those Barbarous People

T olbert yawned and glanced at his brother-in-law, Asbury Harlan. All was quiet in Fishtown. Still, given the settlers' history with the Fishmen, it was probably a good idea to station guards.

Garrison duty was often boring. Usually there were five men on guard and he had someone to talk to besides Asbury. The two men had known each other their whole lives; they knew one another's jokes and stories. This morning, though, the other three guards had volunteered to help build houses for some new arrivals.

From his vantage point, Tolbert glanced toward the settlement and could see the men working on the new buildings. It looked like a normal morning to him. Mrs. Briggs, her baby on her hip, walked through the village. Mrs. Mabry had fetched a bucket of water and was scrubbing her three kids.

Tolbert turned to speak to Asbury. Out of the corner of his eye he spotted movement in the underbrush.

December 26, 1851   *Bassa Cove, Republic of Liberia*
Dear Father,
    Since I heard from you last, many has been my trouble. Tolbert Major, my husband, volunteered to go to Krootown on 22 of March. After being there 4 months, he moved his wife and children down there, and the President come down and employed him two months longer; his time being up for the 4 months, he enlisted again . . . thinking all things was well and the natives seemed friendly and kind . . . the 5 of November, the massacre took place and he was killed by those barbarous people . . . there was 8 other persons got killed in

The group of indigenous people known locally as the Fishmen attacked Fishtown, near Bassa Cove, in November 1851. They killed nine settlers. (Robert K. Griffin, circa 1856, Library of Congress Prints and Photographs Division, LC-USZC4–8195)

the massacre besides my husband, women and children, and I lost all I had and the rest of them that was there lost all they had.

Silvay Major wrote the final letter to Ben from Liberia, conveying horrific news. Her husband, Tolbert, forty-eight, was dead, killed by local warriors. Silvay was a twenty-seven-year-old widow, left alone to care for her three young children.

Tolbert had volunteered in March 1851 to go to what Silvay called Krootown, actually Fishtown, about three miles from Bassa Cove. The cove at Fishtown provided a good landing place, accessible year-round, and ships from around the world stopped there to obtain water and fuel. British and French traders purchased goods from indigenous people, including palm oil and rice.

Tolbert had brought Silvay and the children there in the summer. He had served out his militia term and then reenlisted. The militia, comprising all males over fifteen years old, had been formed for defense of the colony following the 1835 attack on Port Cresson. Recaptives from the *Pons* provided additional reinforcements.[1]

The Fishmen had harassed the settlers in and near Bassa Cove for decades, launching attacks, setting fires, and committing robbery and murder. In December 1843, Governor Roberts reported complaints that some of the other local groups had against the Fishmen. "They were unwelcome intruders upon their territory, and [the other groups] had long been anxious to get rid of them but had not the force to drive them out. Some said they were troublesome neighbors, constantly committing outrages not only upon foreigners but also upon the American settlements and even themselves, and they could bear it no longer."[2] Roberts described the Fishmen in another letter as "a restless and ambitious people, who have given us more trouble than all the tribes along the coast together, and who, backed by one or two designing foreigners, have been the principal agents in causing all these difficulties."[3]

However, things had settled down. People living in and near Bassa Cove believed they were finally on good terms with Grando and his Fishmen, but in 1851, Grando, allied with the leaders of Tabacconee, New Cess, and Tradetown, launched a series of attacks. They started with the raid on Fishtown on November 5.[4]

Upon receiving news of the attack, President Roberts quickly drafted a letter to the American Colonization Society. In response, the society published a lengthy article about the assault in the *African Repository*:

> Under the guise of friendship, [Grando] managed to throw the settlers off their guard; and in this state, while they were altogether unsuspicious of his real intention, he suddenly appeared in the new settlement, at the head of about three hundred men, and unceremoniously commenced butchering the inoffensive inmates of the houses; nine of whom, two men, two women, one boy, and four children (one an infant) were murdered. The savage assailants then plundered the settlement of everything worth carrying away and set fire to the houses. Those of the inhabitants who escaped being murdered, fled for safety to the town of Bassa Cove, about three miles distant.[5]

The *African Repository* reported the names of those killed: "Asbury Harlan, Talbert Majors [*sic*], Mrs. Mabry and her three children, Mrs. Briggs and her infant, and a boy named Charles, about 16 years old." After they had been shot to death, the victims' bodies were mutilated, "horribly cut and mangled."[6] The warriors then burned the garrison, the lumberyard, and ten houses, and carried away everything they could.[7]

Captain Preston at Bassa Cove had heard rumors of trouble and had confronted some of the Fishmen early that morning. He had not received satisfactory answers to his questions and resolved to double the guard at the garrison. However, Grando and his men reached Fishtown before Preston could do so.[8]

President Roberts wrote of Grando that he was "the most consummate villain I ever met" and said of the attack, "It is most unfortunate, and deeply to be regretted, not only in view of the lives that have been sacrificed, but it will inevitably involve us in a war."[9]

Silvay continued:

> *I was at the Krootown myself, me and my children, and only made my escape the 3 days before the massacre took place, and it was through the mercy of God. They also killed my brother and now I have only one left & he has lost one of his eyes in this war, for those native attacked Bassa Cove on the 15 of November and a bloody war ensued and my brother got shot through the nose and that occasioned the last of his eye . . .*

Silvay's brother Asbury, twenty-six, had been killed alongside Tolbert. They were the only men killed. They lost their lives trying to defend the men, women, and children of the settlement. Her only surviving brother, twenty-four-year-old Wesley, had been grievously injured and subsequently lost an eye.

Stephen A. Benson described the attack:

> There seemed to be no end to their numbers, and they were as fearless of cannon as if they were popguns. After they fired the first volley, they made a rush, and when within about forty yards of the cannon, loaded and fired bravely, nor would they give an inch, for thirty minutes, until Tarplan, Grando's principal warrior . . . was shot down dead, within thirty yards of the cannon's mouth. When he fell, and his war-horn ceased, a general panic ensued; a few more rounds set them to flight. . . . I have never seen such quantities of blood as was seen on examining the battleground; from thirty yards from the cannon's mouth on the

fort below the first pawn on the beach, the bushes and paths are dyed with blood—in some places, it stands in puddles. . . . We do not think that the killed and wounded can be less than forty to fifty. We could distinctly hear the cry and wailing of the wounded at the distance of a quarter of a mile.[10]

President Roberts appealed to Captain Pearson, the commander of a US ship, the *Dale,* then in Monrovia harbor, to take him to Bassa Cove. The *Lark,* a Liberian government schooner commanded by Reid Cooper, accompanied the *Dale.* It was equipped with four cannons and a company of seventy-five armed men. The arrival of the president, the armed men, and the two ships halted a planned second attack and discouraged further hostilities.[11]

William Lawrence, who represented British trading interests, was accused of instigating the hostilities; the charge implied that British traders were encouraging Africans to rebel against Liberian authority. That, in turn, might force British intervention.[12]

Matilda Lomax wrote about the attack and its aftermath to her former owner, John Hartwell Cocke of Virginia: "Our people has just returned from a campaign [against Grando] at Trade town. Perhaps they had harder fighting than has occurred since the formation of the Colony. The loss on our part was greater than in any former battle, being 6 killed and 25 to 30 wounded. The strongest & most populous native town on this part of the Coast was taken, burned & the natives completely routed. The natives force is said to have amounted to 1500 men well armed & equipped. The war is supposed to have been excited by British traders on the Coast."[13]

Bassa Cove was one of only two ports of entry into Liberia; the other was Monrovia. Liberian ports faced numerous challenges. Although Liberia claimed to control more than two hundred miles of coastline, their authority was not universally recognized. Many foreign governments didn't respect the black president or the republic's laws. Although Liberia relied on taxes and tariffs on imported goods for income, it had little power to compel foreign nations to comply.

The British had long tested the settlers' authority over the Liberian coast, refusing to pay anchorage fees or comply with port regulations, in an apparent attempt to dominate trade in the area.

The Fishmen likely had their own reasons for the attack, unrelated to British or Liberian interests. Because most of the indigenous groups did not have written languages, it is difficult to find documentation that tells their side of the story.

The *American Baptist* published an article that said, in part:

> The attack upon Fishtown is said to have been unprovoked. But this, it should be remembered, is the version of the colonists themselves. Could the other side be heard, the matter might be placed in a far different light. The instincts of commercial and military colonies impel them to the acquisition of territory and the extension of power; and the history of the measures by which these ends have been sought is, in general, a history of secret fraud and circumvention, or of undisguised oppression. It would be strange if, in this respect, the African colony should prove to be an exception.[14]

Silvay's letter continued: "Now I am left without a home with three small children—2 girls and one boy, about 2 years, one girl about 8 years, and the other six. I am now depending on the mercy of friends for a home ... so you see that I am a poor distressed creature and any assistance you can render me I will be glad of and very thankful." Regardless of whether the British or the Fishmen instigated the November 1851 attacks, the result was the same for Silvay; she was a young widow with three children. She made a plea for general assistance to Ben, but had only a single specific request in her letter:

> *Young Joseph Major, my son, sends word to young Benjamin Major for a pair of hounds ... if you send me the hounds, please to send a [illegible] and a dog male and female, for they are very useful in this place. ... My children often inquires after you and more so since the death of their father ... although my husband is dead, yet that do not hinder me from writing to you whenever I can get an opportunity. My mother sends her love to you and would like to know where all the Harlans have gone to and if you do know, please [write] to her so when I write to them I may know where to direct my letter to. Austin and his family are well. I would like you to write to me as often as you can.*
> *I remain yours truly,*
>
> > *Silvay Major*

Silvay's children had never met Ben; they were all born in Liberia. Tolbert and Silvay may have spoken frequently to their children about the man they sometimes called Father Ben.

Of the Majors and Harlans who had arrived on the *Luna,* ten were dead by the end of 1851—Lewis, Asbury, Coke, Fletcher, and Tyloa Harlan, and Tolbert, Washington, Thomas, Caroline, and Thornton Major. Only Silvay; her mother, Agnes; sister, Ann; brother-in-law, Austin; niece, Mary; and brother, Wesley, were still alive.

Although Silvay's letter was dated the day after Christmas 1851, it was not postmarked in Baltimore until March 9, 1852, and was probably not delivered to Ben in Illinois for a week or two after that.

Ben likely knew of Tolbert's death before he broke the red wax seal on Silvay's letter. An acquaintance named B. J. Campbell, traveling on business in Pennsylvania, had written to Ben on February 17: "At [Pittsburgh], while reading a paper upon file in the reading room, I seen an account of the death of Tolbert Major of Fishtown, Liberia. The thought struck me immediately that it was your Tolbert; he with eight others were murdered by one Grando, a native at the head of others."[15]

Ben and his formerly enslaved people had been the most faithful of correspondents, maintaining contact across the Atlantic Ocean for more than fifteen years. Ben had hoped for a better life for his former bondspeople when he sent them to Liberia. Now more than half of them were dead.

27

I Thirst to Meet You in Bright Glory

Ben slumped wearily in a hard, wooden chair next to his sister's bed. He glanced at her ashen complexion and fear knotted his gut. The morning— an ordinary spring morning—had started in such an everyday way. He and Lucy had been eating breakfast when a messenger pulled up his horse in front of the Major home, leapt down, and pounded on the door. That wasn't unusual; people in town frequently turned to Ben when there was illness or an emergency. But this time the news hit home—Eliza Ann was gravely ill.

Eliza was Ben's only sister, the baby of the family, seven years younger and dear to his heart. Ben abandoned his breakfast, grabbed his bag and his notebook of Thomsonian remedies, saddled and mounted his horse, and galloped to the Davenport home. There, he tried all the various treatments for cholera he had collected over the years, but to no avail.

Several days earlier, Eliza's husband, William, had returned home ill from a trip to St. Louis, but with Eliza's careful nursing he had recovered. Everyone thought that perhaps he had been exposed to the grippe, but what Eliza had was clearly cholera, and perhaps William had brought the disease home.

Now it was evening. Ben had been there all day. He and William had changed the bed linens and her gown multiple times. His older nephews carried the soiled linens out to be burned. The windows were open, but a strong stench still hung in the room. Ben feared she was beyond his help. Through his tears, he prayed that God might still save her life and spare William yet another loss.

The couple had already faced so many tragedies—the deaths of two

Ben Major in his later years. Ben died in 1852 at the age of fifty-five. (Major Family Private Collection)

baby girls and two little boys. Eliza's death would crush William and his other children.

Ben finished his prayer and reached for his sister's hand.

Eliza Ann Davenport died of cholera in May 1852. Ben, grief-stricken, returned to his home accompanied by his nephew Joseph. By morning it was clear that both Ben and Joseph were sick, too. Ben seemed to know his own case was hopeless. Still, he tried to direct others to prepare the Thomsonian formulas to treat Joseph.

After many hours of suffering, Ben died. Joseph died later the same day. John Davenport, William and Eliza's oldest son, also died. Ben was fifty-six; Eliza, forty-nine; John, thirty-two; and Joseph, twenty-four. The Major and Davenport families had had four deaths in a matter of a few days.[1]

A newspaper article recalled the 1852 cholera epidemic that hit central Illinois. "In the spring of that year, the awful scourge of Asiatic cholera spread rapidly all over the United States. It was worst in the river towns and cities, where it claimed victims by the thousands. Whole families were

Lucy Ann (Davenport) Major, Ben Major's wife,
in her later years. Lucy was the youngest of five
children of Jonas and Alice (Redd) Davenport. Her
father died shortly before she was born, her three
sisters died in childhood, and her mother died
when Lucy was twelve. Lucy and her only surviving
sibling, William, were raised by an aunt. She married Ben when she was nineteen. (Major Family
Private Collection)

wiped out in a few days. Men would go to their places of business in the
morning, well and hearty, to be brought home before night dead or dying."[2]

Ben's widow, Lucy, and his family grieved deeply for this man who
seems to have been a decent, caring, and honorable person. He was a man
of faith who put his faith into action. He believed in God, family, friends,
and education. Decades later, one local historian wrote of Ben, "His name
became known far and wide because of his great heart and his devotion to
the interest of others."[3]

With the deaths of Tolbert Major and Ben Major—just six months apart—the remarkable correspondence between Bassa Cove and Walnut Grove ended. Silvay's letter is the last one in the collection, but it was not the last interaction between the Liberian colonists and the Major family in America.

Four years later, in June 1856, twenty-nine-year-old Wesley Harlan—now Reverend John Wesley Harland—boarded the westbound *Mendi* in Monrovia.[4]

Crossing the Atlantic took several weeks. Wesley had plenty of time for contemplation and prayer as he stood at the rail, watching the sea. He recalled his first voyage two decades earlier, when he had come to Liberia as a boy. This trip was much the same—sky, sea, wind. Passengers still battled seasickness, and boredom mingled with anticipation. He thought of the others who had sailed to Monrovia on the *Luna*. So many of them were now gone—all of his brothers and most of the Majors. Wesley looked forward to his reunion with them in God's heavenly realm.

But this trip was different in so many ways from his voyage on the *Luna*. Wesley was a grown man, married, and a minister with the Methodist Episcopal Church. He was now on official business for the colonization society.[5]

As a teenager, he had yearned to visit America. His dream was fulfilled when the *Mendi* docked in New York City on June 27.

His visit to America was not without risk. Slavery was still vigorously defended in the southern states, and the US Congress had passed the Fugitive Slave Act six years previously. The act required that law enforcement officers throughout the United States, in the South and North, arrest anyone suspected of being a runaway slave. Many freeborn black people and formerly enslaved people were pulled into this net and, having no legal recourse, were sent South to live in slavery for the remainder of their days. Wesley's distinctive appearance—his scarred face and perhaps an eye patch over an empty socket—might have drawn undue attention. He would have had to exercise great caution while in the land of his birth.

On the other hand, Wesley may have been perceived as an exotic foreigner—an African—rather than a former slave, a transformation brought about by years of living in a country where he was free, educated, respected, and able to determine his own fate. Being black in Africa was very different from being black in America. Wesley carried that experience with him. Furthermore, the American Colonization Society provided settlers

Ben Major died of cholera in May 1852. His grave is in the Olio Township Cemetery in Eureka, Illinois. (Photograph by Susan E. Lindsey)

with documentation to prove they were Liberians when they traveled in the United States.[6]

Few details have been discovered about Wesley's time in America, but his visit was apparently a long one. A colonization society conference was held in September 1858 in Peoria, just twenty miles from Walnut Grove, now called Eureka. Wesley may have attended the Peoria conference and then visited friends nearby. He made his way to Eureka, where people who had known him as a boy back in Kentucky greeted him with joy and hospitality. They noticed that his Kentucky accent was gone, replaced by the lilting cadence of West Africa.[7]

An attentive and curious crowd filled the Eureka Christian Church when Wesley spoke about the formerly enslaved and freeborn black people from America who had colonized Liberia. He described the new republic, its laws, its schools and churches, its towns, and the exotic animals. He told them about some of the tribulations the settlers had faced—the bouts of fever, the difficulty establishing farms, the war in which he had lost his eye, and other battles with indigenous people. But he remained optimistic about Liberia. He told the crowd that prospects for the country's future were good.[8]

After his speech, Wesley descended the steps of the church and, with Lucy Major, members of her family, and several other old friends, walked to the town cemetery. There he stood solemnly before the grave of Ben Major, bowed his head, and prayed.

Elmira Dickinson chronicled the 1858 visit to Eureka from a Liberian man. "One of the Negroes, whose father and mother had been slaves of Mr. Harlan and Mr. Major, was sent to this country on official business for the colony, and while in the United States, visited Eureka and spoke in the old church, and gave an account of their manner of living. . . . He thought the prospect for the future of Liberia was good." She also wrote of his visit to Ben's grave. Dickinson does not name the visitor, but without a doubt it was Wesley Harlan.[9]

After visiting the United States, Wesley returned to Liberia. Fifteen years later, he became a member of the Liberian House of Representatives, representing Grand Bassa County.[10]

Wesley had once said that he overcame all downfalls with ambition and that he delighted in his country. He had watched the legislature in action while he was still a teenager. His success perhaps represented all that Tolbert, Austin, and Agnes had hoped for when they landed in Bassa Cove. It seems that Wesley indeed had found a way to live under the vine and fig tree.

Conclusion
Under the Vine and Fig Tree

Freeborn black people and formerly enslaved people migrated from America to Liberia to find freedom, peace, safety, and control over their lives—to sit under their own vines and fig trees where no one could make them afraid.

The former slave owners likewise sought to free themselves of the moral, spiritual, and physical burdens of owning other people, to build new lives without unpaid labor, and to find peace and security in a new state.

Tolbert had been born into slavery; Ben into a slaveholding family. Tolbert could not legally own anything; Ben was a wealthy man, and much of his family's wealth had been accrued through the labor of enslaved people. Yet they had much in common. Both were committed to their families. Both were Kentucky natives and farmers. Each of them had a strong faith and solid values. Both were risk takers and open to change. Both of them died caring for others: Tolbert while guarding a village and Ben after nursing his sister.

Did they succeed in finding peace and security? How would the lives of the white Majors and Harlans have been different if they had stayed in Kentucky? Ben Major, George Harlan, and other Kentucky slave owners certainly would have lost their enslaved people when the Thirteenth Amendment passed. Eureka College would not exist. On the other hand, they would have avoided dividing their families over the issue of slavery, they would have fit better into their society's culture, and they would have acquired more wealth and retained it longer.

How would the lives of the black Majors and Harlans have been different if they had stayed enslaved in Kentucky? Without the risk of war with indigenous people, perhaps Tolbert, Asbury, and Washington would have lived longer. Wesley would not have lost an eye. Lewis Harlan would have avoided malaria and lived longer. However, they likely would have remained enslaved for another thirty years. Despite the abolitionists and those who advocated gradual emancipation, slavery in America became more—not less—entrenched in the decades preceding the Civil War. Had the Harlans and Majors stayed in Kentucky, some of the male slaves might have crept away from the plantations on a moonlit night and made their way north to join Union troops near Bowling Green. Agnes and her children might have joined the groups of "contrabands"—enslaved people who escaped to Union lines during the Civil War.

On the other hand, any or all of them might have been sold South before or during the war—joining the thousands who labored on cotton, rice, indigo, and tea plantations. Or they might have been caught up in the panic over a rumored slave revolt in Christian and Trigg Counties in Kentucky, and in nearby Stewart County, Tennessee, around Christmas 1856. The insurrection was imagined, but the results were real—six suspected slave conspirators were executed before white panic subsided.[1]

All of the enslaved Majors and Harlans would have been freed after the Civil War, but life in the South during Reconstruction and the early years of the Ku Klux Klan would not have been easy or without risk. Black people in the postwar South were no longer enslaved, but they also did not have full rights of citizenship in a white-dominated society.

Elmira Dickinson wrote that the Majors and Harlans had to be persuaded to go to Liberia. It is impossible to know if she was correct, yet the emigrants don't appear to have regretted boarding the *Luna*. Their letters expressed homesickness and sorrow at being parted from loved ones. They faced multiple hardships and tragedies. Many of them died prematurely. Yet they never expressed disappointment about Liberia. On the contrary, Tolbert, Austin, and Wesley all wrote about their satisfaction with their new country. Perhaps they preferred the possibility of death as free people to longer lives under enslavement. At some undefined point, "home" had ceased to mean America.

Bell Wiley summarized his thoughts about the Liberian settlers: "Most of them appear to have been respectable people possessed of an earnest desire to make good in the land of their forefathers. . . . [they] were ambitious for their children, were intimately acquainted with hardship, bore their misery with a minimum of complaint and demonstrated an enormous capacity for suffering . . . the majority were resourceful, well-intentioned, generous, compassionate, and reliable."[2]

For the thousands of black people who migrated to Liberia, their freedom and new lives came at a price. At least some of them understood the risks before they left America but emigrated anyway, cherishing the notion that—although their own experiences might be harsh—their children and grandchildren would at least be able to live out their lives in freedom.

All evidence indicates that Ben Major never regretted freeing his enslaved people and leaving Kentucky. He established a prosperous farm in Illinois and built a successful life for his family there. His continued correspondence with his formerly enslaved people and his willingness to send them supplies indicate that he cared about them, wished them well, and wanted them to succeed. He not only responded to their letters, but actively sought to hear from them on a regular basis and encouraged Tolbert to return to America for a visit.[3]

George Harlan also seems to have been content in Illinois. He lived to be an old man, with plenty of land and his daughters and two of his brothers living nearby.

It appears that Majors and Harlans—black and white—all found some measure of security and peace in their lives, albeit at a high cost.

Afterword

The Majors and Harlans in Liberia

Attempts to find out what happened to the Majors and Harlans in Liberia after Tolbert's death have not been successful, except for the discovery of limited information about Wesley Harlan. It is unlikely that the settlers—striving to survive—kept extensive records of births, deaths, marriages, land purchases, and so forth. Joseph Jenkins Roberts complained to the American Colonization Society as early as 1842 about poor recordkeeping. "The records of the Colony, I regret to say, have been kept very loosely; several important documents . . . cannot be found."[1]

Those records that were kept were vulnerable to damp, insects, and mold. Some archives were ruined by torrential rains, and many of the government buildings that housed such records were destroyed during the country's civil wars from 1989 to 1996 and from 1999 to mid-2003. Many of the oral historians—the guardians of the stories—were killed during these wars.

There is a Liberian family group with the surname Major; however, leads on possible descendants of Tolbert Major have yielded no new information.

There is a tantalizing hint about the fate of the Harlans in Africa—a town called Harlandsville in Grand Bassa County, Liberia. It is just east of Bassa Cove (present-day Buchanan), where the *Luna* dropped off its passengers on that hot August day in 1836. Did some of Agnes Harlan's descendants survive and thrive in this small Liberian village?[2]

Harlandsville is in Grand Bassa County, Liberia, east of Buchanan. It may have been founded by one of the Harlans who migrated from Kentucky or some of their descendants. (Photograph by Jeanine Milly Cooper and used with permission)

Ben Major's Family

Ben Major left behind his widow, seven children, and three grandchildren. His estate included extensive landholdings and altogether was valued at $10,000.[3]

Ben died without a will. A few months after his death, estate administrators announced an auction to sell his horses and mules, seventy steers, 180 sheep, eighty hogs, hay, a thousand bushels of harvested wheat and oats, a crop of corn still in the field, tools, lumber, and an early McCormick reaper.[4] One of his family members boxed up his books and bundles of periodicals.

Lucy Major was fifty when she became a widow. Her youngest child was only seven. She and her family continued to live in Woodford County, which had been created from the northern parts of Tazewell and McLean Counties in 1841. By 1860, she shared a household with her sons Chastine and Jo, who had been named for Ben's brothers. She kept house and her sons farmed. At that point Lucy had $7,000 in real estate and $200 in personal property.[5]

Two years later, her son Jo enlisted in Company A, 86th Illinois Volunteer Infantry, and fought in the war that finally resolved the slavery issue in America. He attained the rank of captain and fought in pivotal battles, including those at Stone River, Lookout Mountain, and Chickamauga, and participated in Sherman's March to the Sea. Two of his cousins who had remained in Kentucky—daughters of his uncle and namesake Joseph Major—married men who fought against him in the Confederate Army. Jo survived the war and came home to his bride, Mary. In 1870, Lucy shared a household with the couple and her two granddaughters.[6]

Lucy outlived her husband by nearly two decades. She died on January 16, 1876. Her family buried her beside Ben in the Olio Township Cemetery in Eureka, established on land Ben had donated to the community.

The small school Ben founded grew into Eureka College and received a charter from the Illinois legislature in 1855. Majors, Davenports, Dickinsons, Radfords, Lindseys, and others from Christian County, Kentucky, served on the school's board of trustees. Many of their children and grandchildren attended the college. Eureka College continues its mission of providing a high-quality education to this day and boasts among its alumni the fortieth president of the United States, Ronald Reagan.

Traces of the Major and Davenport families remain in Eureka, a town of about five thousand people—Davenport Elementary School, Major Street, and Ben Major Hall at Eureka College. Descendants of Ben Major still live in the area.

William T. Major, Ben's older brother, died on January 11, 1867, and is buried in Evergreen Cemetery in Bloomington, under the epitaph "Here lies a Christian." A contemporary who knew William said of him, "His countenance wore the expression of a saint. He was always ready with a kind word and a smile, and always willing to succor the distressed."[7]

Ben's youngest brother, Chastine, had moved to Illinois with his wife, the former Joanna Hopkins, and their large family. They originally settled in Danvers Township but were living in Bloomington by 1860. Chastine died in late 1884; he is buried at Evergreen Cemetery in Bloomington, near William.

Ben's brother Joseph remained in Kentucky. He married Henrietta Catlett, and the couple had eleven children. Though Joseph owned land in Illinois and considered moving there, he never did. In an 1839 letter he wrote to Ben, "It is highly gratifying that your labors have been thus blessed, your prospects are favorable, country healthy, and above all, contentment and peace. Your situation [is] enviable; I am still struggling in the land of slavery."[8]

Joseph continued to live in Kentucky and continued to own slaves. He died in the fall of 1864, about six months before the Civil War ended. After his death, his personal estate—"except the negroes"—was sold at auction for $4,147.[9]

Ben's brother-in-law and friend, William Davenport, lost his wife and two sons in the cholera outbreak. He had inadvertently brought the disease to his community, and it is not difficult to imagine that guilt was interwoven with his grief. He had fathered eleven children; his wife and nine of his sons and daughters died before him.[10]

Davenport was a preacher and lawyer, and known as "a man of exceptional oratorical power." However, he struggled with debt his entire life. In a moving message penned in the back of his family Bible, he wrote of his net worth diminishing from $7,000 to $1,200 in Kentucky before he moved to Illinois and "commenced the world anew." For two or three years he stuck to a vow to avoid buying on credit, but eventually succumbed to persuasive merchants and started to again accrue debt. He wrote, "I have been involved in debt ever since, and in all probability, it will result in the ruin of my property a second time." He urged his children "to always pay for what they buy—and if they have not the means to pay with, never to go into debt." While traveling in 1844, he scrawled a desperate letter to Ben after learning a suit had been filed against him for debt. "Sell anything I have to pay my debts . . . I feel very near like going crazy."[11]

Davenport died on June 24, 1869, in Nebraska City, Nebraska, at the home of his son, Benjamin Major Davenport, whom he had named in honor of his friend and brother-in-law. His obituary indicates that he, like Ben, had emancipated some of his enslaved people and sent them to Liberia.[12]

In 1930, on the seventy-fifth anniversary of its founding, Eureka College presented a historical pageant to the community. Descendants of the Majors and Dickinsons portrayed their own ancestors. Student actor Ronald Reagan portrayed William Davenport.[13]

More than 160 years after the *Luna* landed in Bassa Cove, the General Board of the Christian Church (Disciples of Christ)—the church that had had such a powerful influence on Ben, William, and Chastine Major and William Davenport—issued a formal apology for not doing enough in the nineteenth century to oppose slavery.[14]

George Harlan

George Harlan, who had owned Agnes and her family, left Christian County in 1833 and settled in Macoupin County, Illinois, about 140 miles southwest of where Ben settled. It is likely that George hired out his enslaved people to Christian County neighbors until arrangements could be made for their eventual emancipation and transportation to Liberia in 1836.

George's family consisted of his third wife, Margaret (King) Harlan, and their two children. The couple probably also took George's fourteen-year-old son from his second marriage with them to Illinois. George's children from his first marriage were young adults by 1833. He left behind in Kentucky the graves of two of his children and the graves of his first two wives. After the family settled in Illinois, he and Margaret had three daughters.[15]

George had been a slave owner much of his adult life; it would have been an adjustment for the family to do their own labor and maintain a household. He was no longer a young man—fifty-seven when he moved to Illinois. He bought numerous tracts of land in Macoupin County, eventually accumulating several hundred acres.[16]

Macoupin County was formed in 1829, only four years before the Harlans arrived. In 1830, the population of the entire county was under two thousand. In this frontier setting, the Harlan family established a farm and joined the local Presbyterian Church. When elections rolled around, George voted for the Whig candidate.[17]

Margaret Harlan died in 1842, at the age of forty-four. Her much older husband was left to raise his remaining children alone. The 1850 census lists seventy-four-year-old George in a household with his three youngest daughters, ages eight to sixteen. He died in 1851—the same year that Tolbert Major died—at the age of seventy-five. He is buried in Macoupin County.[18]

Despite the letters that Agnes and the other settlers repeatedly sent to George Harlan from Liberia, no evidence has been found that he ever contacted his formerly enslaved people after freeing them.

The American Colonization Society

The images in a kaleidoscope constantly shift as the bits of colorful glass tumble in the tube. No two images are ever alike even though the same bits of glass form all of them. Similarly, the motives of colonizationists and viewpoints about colonization change as they are viewed through various perspectives—black and white, proslavery and antislavery, American and Liberian—and at various times—from four decades before the Civil War, through the war, during Reconstruction, and in modern times.

Did formerly enslaved people voluntarily go to Liberia or were they deported or exiled? Were the settlers immigrants or invaders? Was the American Colonization Society racist, patronizing, paternalistic, proslavery, and manipulative? Or was it abolitionist, antislavery, well intentioned, and humanitarian? A case could be made for any of these positions, for all of these positions. It depends on who is peering into the kaleidoscope, when they are looking, their personal attitudes and experiences, and how the facts tumble into place.

"Colonization, then, was an amalgam of humanitarianism, racism, commercialism, missionary purpose, and even diluted abolitionism," historian Randall Miller wrote. "However impractical it appears in retrospect, it was not a wild visionary scheme. Short of war, there was no other means of ending slavery in the South."[19]

Ben and the others in this story lived in nineteenth-century America. They applied what they knew, what they believed, what they valued, to their decision-making process and filtered it through their own experiences and the culture in which they lived. Although they knew that slavery was a divisive issue and many felt that it was wrong, they had no way of knowing that a great war over slavery would split the country asunder in only a few decades.

An open letter to American clergy, published in the May 1845 issue of the *African Repository*, summarized the reasoning of many colonizationists:

> The colored people in our own country, whether bond or free, are in circumstances which challenge for them our sympathy. They are degraded in the scale of human existence. They are in a very inferior condition. The very framework of society around them tends to depress them still lower. . . . In this country, they never can rise above the very lowest grade of society. You may say that this state of society is all wrong; may call it *prejudice* that keeps them down; and all this may be admitted without improving their condition in the slightest degree. The facts remain the same. And if we are to wait till the whole constitution of society is remodeled—till every root of evil is eradicated,

and everything is managed exactly right, before we do anything for the elevation of the colored race, how many generations will die unblessed?[20]

The letter acknowledged that the colonization society "never expected to remove the whole colored population by voluntary contributions! The plan was to remove those who were willing to go and could be taken by the means the Society could command, and to locate them in Liberia with reference to further results and ulterior ends. An experiment was to be made."

In the decades before the Civil War, the American Colonization Society sent 143 expeditions to Liberia. Willingness to emigrate and donations to the society fluctuated with politics, news of slave revolts, increasingly stringent slave codes, and laws restricting the rights of free black people. The 1831 Nat Turner revolt and subsequent acts of vengeance against enslaved people and free black people triggered renewed interest in colonization, as did the Fugitive Slave Act of 1850 and the *Dred Scott* decision in 1857.[21]

Migration to Liberia increased in the 1840s and 1850s, in part because the practice of freeing slaves in wills increased. More free black people from the South chose colonization, and even many from the North decided that Liberia was a better alternative to life in the United States under the Fugitive Slave Act and restrictive state statutes.[22]

Uncle Tom's Cabin; or Life among the Lowly, Harriet Beecher Stowe's pivotal novel about slavery, was published in 1852. It became the best-selling novel of the nineteenth century. The Fugitive Slave Act inspired Stowe to write the book, and the main character was based on Josiah Henson, a Kentucky slave who had escaped to Canada in 1830. Another character in the book, George Harris, decided to migrate to Liberia. (An early edition of *Uncle Tom's Cabin* was found in the attic of the Major family home, built by Ben's son after the Civil War and occupied by the family since.)

Many prominent black abolitionists—who had once viewed black supporters of colonization as dupes, puppets, or race traitors—shifted their views after passage of the Fugitive Slave Act. Martin Delaney argued for migration to the West Indies or South America. Delany led the National Emigration Convention in Cleveland in 1854, and five years later he visited West Africa with the notion of establishing a settlement there, an idea he later abandoned. H. Ford Douglas argued for emigration to Canada; he moved there in 1856 and became the proprietor of an abolitionist newspaper. Mary Ann Shadd Cary, the first black woman publisher in the United States, moved to Canada after the Fugitive Slave Act passed.

In the late 1850s, the American Colonization Society grew stronger, funded by legacies and some federal money. Abraham Lincoln—not yet president but becoming increasingly prominent on the national political scene—expressed an interest in colonization and regularly read the American Colonization Society's publications.

The list of subscribers to the *African Repository,* now archived at the Library of Congress, included Ben and William T. Major and William Davenport, as well as the Honorable A. Lincoln of Springfield, Illinois. The multi-year entry for Lincoln includes a notation on the row with his address: "Changed to Wash. D.C., President," confirming that he continued to receive colonization publications after his election. Lincoln also served on the board of managers for the Illinois Colonization Society in 1858.[23]

Lincoln knew at least some of the Majors. Starting in 1837, three years after the Major brothers settled in Illinois, and continuing until 1860, Lincoln was one of the circuit lawyers for the Eighth Judicial Circuit: fourteen counties in central Illinois covering 10,000 square miles. An *African Repository* article noted that Lincoln "associated with and was well known to the leading citizens of each county." When Lincoln made his famous Lost Speech on May 29, 1856, which established the Republican Party in Illinois, he spoke at a Bloomington public hall built and owned by William T. Major. (The speech was known as the Lost Speech because it is said that those reporters who heard it were so caught up in Lincoln's eloquence that they stopped taking notes. No complete, accurate copy of the speech exists.)[24]

Lincoln also spoke on the campus of Eureka College. Young Benjamin Radford, a friend of the Majors, was in the audience:

> In the fall of 1856, Lincoln delivered in the Eureka College chapel a speech in advocacy of the candidacy of Fremont. . . . The chapel was on the ground floor. It was a pleasant moonlit evening and the windows were open. . . . Pretty soon, one of Lincoln's anecdotes put the house into a roar of laughter. At about the second explosion of merriment, some of the outsiders came up to the windows to see what it was about. Little by little, others came up and crowded around the windows, and in the first quarter hour, the speaker had those wild colts tamely feeding out of his hand.[25]

William T. Major was a client of Lincoln's, and the rail-splitter frequently visited the Major home in Bloomington. William Davenport was a political supporter of Lincoln and a "warm personal friend."[26]

It is likely, but unproven, that Ben also knew Lincoln. If so, one wonders what Lincoln thought of Ben's choice to colonize his formerly enslaved people, if the two men ever discussed their shared interest in colonization, or if Ben showed Lincoln his letters from Africa.

In November 1860, Lincoln was elected president of the United States, and he took the oath of office in March 1861. Shortly after his election, southern states started to secede from the Union. The long-simmering issue of slavery—discussed, debated, delayed, and compromised for decades—finally came to a boil. Within a month of Lincoln's inauguration, the nation was at war. Eventually 178,895 black soldiers would fight in the Union armies—23,703 of them from Kentucky.[27]

The Emancipation Proclamation of 1863 did not abolish slavery or free all the nation's enslaved people. It freed only those who were enslaved in Confederate states. The proclamation did not apply to those slave states that had remained in the Union: Kentucky, Missouri, Maryland, or Delaware. It was not until the Thirteenth Amendment was added to the US Constitution in December 1865 that slavery was finally abolished across the country.

Kentucky—the native state of Ben Major and presumably that of his formerly enslaved people—did not ratify the Thirteenth Amendment until 1976, more than a century later.[28]

The Fourteenth Amendment, passed in 1868, granted black Americans full citizenship, and the Fifteenth Amendment, passed in 1870, ensured their right to vote, a right that was quashed for decades. The war essentially halted migration to Liberia, but it increased again after the war.[29]

The American Colonization Society continued to struggle financially. It had been alternately attacked and supported by abolitionists and slave owners and attacked and supported by white and black people. Some of the wildly disparate narratives about the colonization society are likely due to the fact that the organization relied on donations and membership dues for its existence. The society's publications tended to paint a rosy picture of the colony and glossed over problems in the hope of inspiring donations and adding new members. The society's detractors reported only the negatives and ignored any positive news coming out of the colony. The truth about colonization is likely somewhere between the two extreme narratives.

However, the financial instability of the organization meant that support for Liberian settlers fluctuated. The settlements in Liberia struggled—many settlers died and those who survived faced daily challenges, discouraging others from emigrating.

In early 1867, the society celebrated its fiftieth anniversary. By then, nearly twelve thousand people had left the United States for Liberia; half were emancipated with colonization in mind, including about 650 from Kentucky. The independent Maryland Colonization Society sent another 1,227, and 5,722 recaptives also settled in Liberia.[30]

Even after the Civil War, support for colonization remained controversial, particularly in the South, where racism ran deep. A Baton Rouge newspaper reported on the 1870 meeting of the colonization society. "Once a year, a number of antiquated gentlemen . . . meet in New York to discuss the condition of the Liberian Republic and aid Sambo in running his government machine in the country of his curly-headed ancestors. . . . It seems that the treasury of the society is now nearly exhausted; which is hardly to be wondered at, considering what it costs to rid the country of even one pickaninny."[31]

By the time the society finally ceased operations in 1913, about sixteen thousand black Americans, most of them formerly enslaved people, had migrated to Liberia.[32] In the end, the American Colonization Society, "this stupendous scheme of philanthropy," as Governor Buchanan called it, did not—could not—eliminate the institution of slavery, but that was never one of the organization's goals. Many critics of the colonization movement claimed that the organization's primary motive was to remove all free black people from the United States, a claim the society denied. "It is not true that the friends of colonization are actuated by no higher motive than 'to try to get clear of the colored people.' They do not propose to *send* them to Liberia contrary to their own wishes. . . . If we wish to *get clear* of them, and this only, we certainly are laboring with but very little prospect of obtaining our wish."[33]

In 1860, nearly 4 million people were in bondage in America. The colonizationists recognized that it was impossible to free 4 million people, transport them all to Africa, and settle them in a land already occupied. They also clearly understood that many—maybe most—black people who had been born and raised in the United States wished to remain.[34]

An article in the February 1851 *Colonization Herald*, published by the Pennsylvania Colonization Society, defended the group's efforts. "Who refuses food to a hungry man because he cannot feed all the starving? We can send *some*, and those we send cease to be chattels or inferior."[35]

The colonization movement did have some successes. The society secured emancipation for several thousand enslaved people who may never have been freed had that option not existed.

Colonization started to shift white viewpoints about the capabilities of black people. Many white people, including some of the proponents of colonization, believed that black people were naturally subservient, ignorant, and incapable of independent thought. The roles of enslaved people and owners had been scripted long before, and white males—particularly those who owned slaves—were at the top of hierarchy. In slave states, everyone knew his or her place; most dutifully recited the lines assigned to them. Enslaved men (and most women of any race) learned to skillfully play roles to survive. Over time, white people came to believe the "ignorant darky" fiction, or at least pretended to believe it. The success of the Liberian settlers at governing themselves, building businesses, churches, and schools—building a nation—stunned many white people in northern and southern states.

A circular published in 1830 (seventeen years before Liberian independence) addressed these conflicting notions. "It is the opinion of some, that the negro race can never be capable of conducting the affairs of empire. But in forming our estimate of their mental qualifications, great allowance should be made for prejudice and the circumstances in which we have seen them, without education or any means of intellectual improvement. When raised from their present degraded condition and properly educated, there is no reason to suppose that they will be incapable of self-government."[36]

Finally, efforts of the Liberian settlers did help end the slave trade along the Liberian coast, and in this way formerly enslaved people were able to help save thousands of others from lives of bondage.

The Republic of Liberia

What if Liberia had not been colonized? Would it be better off today? Or would it have been snatched up by a European country during the days of empire building? Without colonization, might Liberia have been ruled by a distant king or queen, by white people instead of people of color?

Liberia is one of only two African nations that were not colonized by European powers. There is a distinct difference between colonization and colonialism. Colonialism is exploitive and focuses on commodification of land and resources; *Merriam-Webster* defines it as "control by one power over a dependent area or people." From the beginning, founders of the American Colonization Society intended that the colony they established would eventually be governed by its residents. Article II of the colony's 1820 constitution notes that the society would make rules for governing the settlement "until they shall withdraw their Agents and leave the settlers to the government of themselves."[37]

When the white governor Thomas Buchanan died, Joseph Jenkins Roberts, a man of mixed ancestry, was appointed governor. The society's 1843 annual report noted, "Among the reasons for this appointment was the desire, ever cherished by the Society, of placing the political destinies of the Colony in its own hands, as soon as might be consistent with its welfare."[38]

When Wesley visited Eureka in 1858, he spoke about good prospects for Liberia. He was not alone in predicting a bright future for the republic. Dr. Lugenbeel wrote in 1845, "The advantages enjoyed by the children and youth of Liberia in acquiring knowledge induce me to believe that the little ship of state will never become a wreck for want of competent officers to direct her in the proper course."[39]

Their predictions were optimistic. The country has been divided socially, politically, economically, and culturally throughout its history.

Present-day Liberia is about 59,900 square miles in area and has a population of about 4.3 million. It is bordered by Sierra Leone, Guinea, the Ivory Coast (Cote d'Ivoire), and the Atlantic Ocean. Fishtown, where Tolbert Major and Asbury Harlan were killed, was renamed Buchanan in honor of the former governor; it expanded to envelop the original Bassa Cove settlement.[40]

The descendants of those who had immigrated to Liberia from America became known as Americo-Liberians. Indigenous people often referred to them as "Congoes" (sometimes spelled "Congaus"), adopting the term that had first been applied to the recaptured slaves; it was often used in a derogatory manner. In turn, the Americo-Liberians referred to the indigenous people as "country people."[41]

Although Americo-Liberians were a minority of the population (never more than 5 percent), they became leaders in the social and political structure of the country. They dominated the republic's politics from 1877 to 1980.[42]

The Roman poet Horace wrote of immigrants, "They change their sky, not their soul, who rush across the sea." The Americo-Liberians carried across the sea the culture, traditions, and values of the American South, which they attempted to recreate in Africa. For many of them, success meant replicating the plantation class they remembered from home, and as time passed, the Americo-Liberians remained stuck in the mythos of the American South.

The ruling class adopted the best and worst of American culture, politics, and beliefs, including attitudes about race. Many of the settlers were of mixed ancestry, and light-skinned people often held an advantage in Liberian society and business, as did settlers who had been freeborn rather than those who had been enslaved. Among former slaves, those who had been house slaves often considered themselves superior to those who had been field hands. Those who migrated from northern states looked down on those who came from southern states.

Some Americo-Liberians were accused of abusing the pawn system or holding indigenous people in slavery or forced labor. Some ethnic groups were dismayed at the settlers' misunderstanding of their local customs. The Gola had long placed children in homes of important people from other ethnic groups as a means to build alliances, and they likewise placed some of their children in the homes of colonists in Monrovia. However, as Warren d'Azevedo noted, they were dismayed to learn that these children were then treated as slaves. Indigenous people were generally excluded from civic life and positions of power.[43]

On the other hand, many colonists did mingle peaceably with indigenous people and some intermarriages occurred. The settlers traded with local people and often relied on their superior knowledge of plants, animals, and treatments for various ailments.[44]

The two groups were never completely segregated, but they were not truly integrated either. Settler towns were often established near indigenous villages, and the newcomers frequently relied on indigenous labor, especially at first because they lacked the knowledge or skills to do the necessary work. Many Kru lived in the colonists' coastal towns, close to the ocean and maritime work they'd always done. Most of the indigenous groups were polygamous, and some of the married Americo-Liberian men took "country wives" and had "outside children."[45]

One settler, Edward Wilmot Blyden, an educator, journalist, writer, diplomat, and politician, was a pivotal figure in the early days of the Republic of Liberia. He was deeply involved in the struggle to determine what historian Robert July characterizes as "a philosophy of life which might resolve the conflict between African and European standards by accepting from Europe what appeared beneficial to Africa while preserving the best of the traditional African way of life."[46]

Blyden was born in the West Indies in 1832. He showed early scholastic aptitude and rare linguistic ability. (In his lifetime, he mastered Spanish, Greek, Latin, Hebrew, and Arabic.) In 1850, a Presbyterian minister who recognized Blyden's potential sent him to the United States to study. Unable to gain admission to segregated seminaries, he was sent by the New York Colonization Society to Liberia to study. He became principal of the Presbyterian High School in Monrovia, taught classical languages at Liberia College, and went on to serve as the Liberian secretary of state and secretary of the interior. He was also an ordained Presbyterian minister.

An African nationalist, Blyden urged former slaves in America to come to Liberia to build a great African nation, including centers for higher education and a culture that preserved African values, instincts, and racial purity, and that, while religious, was independent of European Christian churches.[47]

Liberia never became what Blyden or the colonizationists had hoped for.

In 1936, Englishman Graham Greene spent four weeks trekking through Liberia, a trip he chronicled in *Journey without Maps*. He started in Sierra Leone, hiked south through the interior of Liberia (known as the hinterland), then west to the coast at Grand Bassa County, and finally traveled north again by steamer to Monrovia. A full century after the Majors and Harlans arrived in Liberia, Greene painted a dismal picture of the capital city. "Monrovia is like a beginning . . . a beginning which has come to little beyond the two wide grassy main streets intersecting each other and lined with broken-paned houses all of wood and one storey."[48]

He wrote, "There is a pathos about these stunted settlements along the coast, the grassy streets, the follies on the rocky hillside, the pathos of a black people planted down, without money or a home, on a coast of yellow fever and malaria to make what they can of an Africa from which their families had been torn centuries before. No one can pretend they have made much of their country."[49]

The country's economy and infrastructure gradually improved over the decades, and Liberia remained relatively stable under Americo-Liberian presidents.

Liberian Leymah Gbowee described the Monrovia of her childhood in the 1970s and early 1980s. She wrote first of her neighborhood's concrete houses, topped by corrugated metal roofs, then continued:

The settlement on Old Road wasn't luxurious; there were no

paved sidewalks or air conditioners to break the constant,
muggy heat. But our homes had televisions, bathrooms, modern kitchens . . . the rest of Monrovia was beautiful, too, a long
narrow city of a few hundred thousand, framed by the Atlantic
on one side, the Mesurado River and its mangrove swamps and
creeks on the other. It was clean and modern; almost nothing
but the Masonic temple with its ornate white columns was
more than a few decades old. . . . In the center of town, where
we went to buy clothes and shoes, white and pastel two-story
apartments lined the narrow streets, their balconies decorated
with wrought-iron railings. Roads ended at brilliantly white
sand beaches with tall palm trees.[50]

Despite the progress that was made, discontent, bitterness, and resent-
ment grew among the typically poorer and marginalized indigenous people.
William R. Tolbert became president in 1971. In April 1979, his admin-
istration proposed a 50 percent increase in the price of rice—a staple of
the Liberian diet. The new price was about $30 for a bag, difficult to afford
when the average monthly income for Liberians was $70 to $80. It was
the last straw for many Liberians who were fed up with Americo-Liberian
dominance.[51]

Protesters flooded the streets of Monrovia. Dozens, perhaps more
than a hundred, were killed and buried in a mass grave. The president
quickly rounded up his political opponents and rescinded the order raising
the price of rice. Agitation and opposition to the government continued
and finally boiled over a year after the rice riots.[52]

In April 1980, seventeen soldiers, led by Master Sergeant Samuel Doe,
invaded the executive mansion and assassinated President Tolbert after first
disemboweling him. They quickly rounded up, tried, and publicly executed
thirteen of his government ministers. The men were tied to posts on a pris-
tine white sand beach and shot by a firing squad. Doe suspended the constitution. The value of the Liberian dollar plummeted and corruption ran
rampant. The economy deteriorated. Historical and government records
were destroyed.[53]

One author, writing in the early 1990s, described the state of the
national archives building. "The Ahmed Sékou Touré National Archives
Building overlooked the road: it was closed, of course, its plate-glass door
punctured with neat bullet holes. The building, as far as I could tell, was
now empty of papers; they had either been looted, burned, or moved away

for safety. It was possible that the nation's entire historical record had been destroyed or irredeemably dispersed."[54]

In September 1990, Doe was captured and tortured to death, his grisly end videotaped and shown throughout the country. An interim president, Amos Sawyer, served for four years, followed by the chairman of the Council of State.

Charles Taylor, who had worked for Doe's government, became president in 1997. Taylor's father was Americo-Liberian; his mother was Gola. Taylor plunged the country into disorder and despair for many more years.

The progress Liberia had made vanished during the war years. Hundreds of thousands of Liberians were mutilated, raped, tortured, or killed. Gangs led by opposing warlords roamed the countryside, looting villages and murdering their occupants. Warlords kidnapped children, fed them drugs to make them pliable and dependent, traumatized and corrupted them, armed them with AK-47s, and set them loose on the countryside. Schools were demolished, and teachers fled or were killed. Homes, roads, and commercial buildings in Monrovia were destroyed; shell casings littered the streets.

Those living in rural areas fled to Monrovia; those living in Monrovia who could afford to do so fled to other countries. Foreign investors and businesses deserted the republic. Liberia's entire infrastructure was demolished, including telecommunication, power, water, and sanitation systems.

Charles Taylor resigned in 2003 under growing international pressure and internal pressure from a group of determined, peace-seeking Christian and Muslim women, led by Leymah Gbowee and Tawakkul Karman. These women rallied thousands of their sisters to force the government to move toward peace.

Taylor's resignation paved the way for a transitional government, followed by the 2006 election of Ellen Johnson Sirleaf, the first female elected head of state in Africa.

Leymah Gbowee wrote:

We had to confront the magnitude of what had happened to Liberia. Two hundred and fifty thousand people were dead, a quarter of them children. One in three were displaced, with 350,000 living in internally displaced persons camps and the rest anywhere they could find shelter. One million people, mostly women and children, were at risk of malnutrition, diarrhea, measles, and cholera because of contamination in the wells.

More than 75 percent of the country's physical infrastructure, our roads, hospitals and schools, had been destroyed. . . . To a person, we had been traumatized. We had survived the war, but now we had to remember how to live. Peace isn't a moment—it's a very long process.[55]

In 2011, Leymah Gbowee, Tawakkul Karman, and Ellen Johnson Sirleaf received the Nobel Peace Prize for their efforts to bring peace to Liberia.

Charles Taylor was convicted in 2012 of eleven counts of war crimes and crimes against humanity in Sierra Leone, including murder, systemic mutilation and rape, slavery, and use of child soldiers. (The two civil wars involved both Sierra Leone and Liberia, but only crimes committed in Sierra Leone were within the court's mandate.) Taylor was sentenced to fifty years in prison. His sentence was upheld in September 2013, and he will remain in prison the rest of his life.[56]

During the wars, many Liberians fled their homeland. The Liberian diaspora in the United States comprises between 250,000 and 500,000 people, according to Liberian American organizations, many times the number of black Americans who fled to Liberia in the 1800s. In this reverse migration the Liberians have left behind their beloved country, familiar culture, and family and friends, much as the original colonists had when they left America more than a century before.

After the election of Ellen Johnson Sirleaf, Liberia stabilized. As of the writing of this book, the country has been at peace for many years. The Firestone Rubber Company and other businesses have returned to Liberia. But Liberia remains one of the poorest countries in the world. No basic services (electricity, water, sewage systems, and garbage disposal) exist in much of the country. Roads are poorly maintained or nonexistent, fuel is hard to get, public transportation and postal service are nonexistent, and the police force has limited resources. Health care and educational systems remain inadequate. Unemployment is high; the economy has not fully recovered. The horrific 2014 outbreak of the deadly Ebola virus brought more misery to the country.

In 2017, professional soccer player George Weah replaced Ellen Johnson Sirleaf as Liberia's president.

The vine and fig tree scripture comes from the book of Micah. Preceding that verse is this one: "They shall beat their swords into plowshares, and their spears into pruninghooks: nation shall not lift up a sword against nation, neither shall they learn war any more."

Perhaps the day will come when all of the good people of Liberia will be able to work together to build a stable nation where they can live in peace under their own vines and fig trees.

Appendix

The Major Collection of Letters from Liberia

Tolbert Major, Austin Major, Wesley Harlan, and Silvay Major sent letters from Liberia to America. Most of their letters were addressed to Ben Major or his brother Joseph Major. A few were sent to James Moore. The Major family donated their surviving letters from Africa to the McLean County Museum of History in Bloomington, Illinois. Two of the letters sent to James Moore were published in the *African Repository*, a publication of the American Colonization Society.

The letters in Bloomington are very old. The paper is fragile and yellowed. A few letters have small holes in them. One letter has a significant hole, about two by three inches. The letters are on paper about sixteen inches long and ten inches wide. The writers folded the paper to create four panels. They used three panels for the text of their letters and the fourth as an address panel. The letters were sealed with wax—red stains and bits of wax still cling to the yellowing paper.

In some places, the faded ink is difficult or impossible to read. The old-fashioned handwriting, poor spelling, and missing or misused punctuation often make it difficult to understand what the authors of the letters were trying to convey.

I started with the museum's transcriptions of the letters based on the work of Kristine Gebhardt and James Amemasor. My research assistant and I carefully scrutinized each original and compared it to the transcription. I have read each missive multiple times, word by word, sometimes letter by letter, often with a magnifying glass. I sometimes interpreted handwriting differently than did the original transcribers. Despite my careful and intense efforts at transcribing the letters, some sections still don't make sense.

I've reproduced the letters in this appendix in as close a form to the originals as possible, including spelling and grammar errors, random capitalization, incorrect punctuation, and strikethroughs. Square brackets indicate my additions. When I quote from the letters elsewhere in the book, I have inserted missing words and corrected spelling and punctuation to facilitate reading.

Tolbert Major to Joseph Major, September 1836

Bassa Cove Western Africa
Sept. 1836
Dear Sir,
    We have all landed on the Shores of Africa & got into our houses. We have been here 3 weeks. So far I am well pleased ~~so far~~ to my master in Illinois. remember me affectionately Tele him that none of us have been taken with the fever yet. We have a prospect of war with the natives. I hope it will be settled without bloodshed. To Joseph Major & his family I want my love & compliments. It rains here almost every day more or less. when the rain is over we com out to over 8 gallen as the Soil is Sandy. we have not got our farms laid out yet. each of us will get 40 acres. Which will be ours when we clear 2 for every 10—that is 8 acres. we have a Sunday School here 3 missionary white men 2 baptists & a Methodist. as it respects living here it is altogether deffarint to that in America here we have Palm oil & rice. sweet potatoes plantain & Banana. & Copada a root something like artichoke tastes very well when boiled. we have pine apples—limes etc. though the principal article of food is rice & palm oil. To W. Woolridge & his family & Ed. my love & Compliments—tell George Major & Henry that it is my desire for them to come to this Country. they need not fear the heat. it is not so hot as in America & we never expect to see frost again. this is now the winter here & the trees are as green as Spring. Tell Master Jo. Majors to please to let them come. my love to Mr. Moore in Hopskinsville. to Gid Overshiner my respects. to F. Wheatly & his family.
Your &

Tobot Major

Tolbert Major to Ben Major, May 20, 1839

Bass cove May 20th 1839
My Dear Master,

it is a long time since I hav seen you I have seen very many thing since I have seen you Some are new & interesting in the highest degree & some a gain are to horrible to mension but the Lord has carried us through them blessed be his nam he does all things well I have hav the honor of being marriad to a very worthy woman & we have been blessed with a boy we are all well thank God for hiss goodness he is good & his kind care is over all his work I hav found somthing in Afraca that I could I could not find in America that I could not fin in the Lord Jesus Christ whome to know is live eternal

we were geting along very well & I though I would be able to take it to America in a For we were all getting along very well, that is Tho Austin Wa & Thorton and Myself old aunt Hanah is dead, she died & her both of her sons. Why sir, your endowed family was all doing well we had learn how to be our own Masters [illegible] but we have had war & that has de-stressed all very much indeed we hav had the most of things destroyed Washington was shot in the war he was shot in the back near his left Shoulder the ball is not out yet & he is not able to do any thing. We are all needy & should be glad if you would send us out some things if you pleas we are trying to get along a gain.

tel all of your family howde Dear Sir I am in hast & must bid you good bye

Bengemen
Magers

Your humble
Servant Tolber magers
Bassa cove Liberia

Tolbert Major to James Moore, May 20, 1839

A short note addressed to a "Mr. More" accompanied Tolbert's letter of May 1839. The letter has a two-by-three-inch hole in it.

Bassa cove May 20th 1839
Dear Mr ~~Hopkins~~ More
I take this opportunity
to write you a few lines to inform [you]
that I & my wife's health is well. Please tell

Mr. George	that Agnes Harlin
& her daug	ell but her two
sons are	died first he
Died soon [illegible]	here & Henry
has been de	six months he
died in the cou	ect that he had a
good deal of	his mother was none

off better for it. For he was alone amonge
the coutry people. & agness says that she
wishish that her good Mastir Harlin
pleas to send her some necessarys
for she is needy for we hav had
war with the natives & and they destroyed

The Major collection of letters includes a folder with two fragments of a letter. Folds in the two fragments align. On the bottom of the second fragment, James Moore's name (spelled More) and Hopkinsville appear. Just to the right of Moore's name are Tolbert's name and Bassa Cove. The handwriting matches Tolbert's and these fragments seem to be part of the May 20 letter. If so, the final sentence of the letter, which starts, "... for we have had war with the natives and they destroyed ..." concludes: "everything I had & I find it very hard to get along, for my two small boys [illegible] able to help me for I have to help them Tel my uncle [illegible] Harlin that I want him to pleas to send me out some things for I am very needy at this time the war has destroyed us so that we do not know what to do I like the place very much indeed &"

The left side of the second fragment is missing the first three lines, and the whole right side of the fragment is missing. The words that remain are:

the war has not [illegible] we should have been very Give my
lov to all of my fa
tel them that I want to see th very much indeed
To More James   Tolbert M

Hopkinsvill   Bassa cove Libe
Christan Count   West Af
US

Tolbert Major to Ben Major, October 17, 1840

Bassa Cove October the 17th 1840

Dear father

I was very happy to here from you and the more to So to see the much regard you have for me I recived your letter aug the 8th 1840 I am well & family I have marriad sence I arived hear and happy to say that I have a vary good in dustris wife and one that may be apended on and if she had a chance she could do much more with Such as whells cards. Lums and thir utenshuls not with standing Sence I left you I have met with a grat misforthon when I arrived here I was put in a thatch house where I was taken down with the fever and the natives brook in upon me and takin every thing I had in this world. I like this country vear well all to that one can not rase as much here as they can in the Stats on account of the roug & Sence I was robed I have been oblig to take up all of my time in working for people to suport my Self & famly.

We have rice for brad & cassavar & yams & potatos we use Palm oil for lard meet is very Scarce here the Palm tree which I have jest menchened is I beleve the gratis in this country & I thenk Eneay other first is the oil Second it gives wine thirdly it gives cabages that is as good if not beter then those with you in fact I be leve its match is not to be found on the globe at least not in this country the fig & bananas is veary good three of the plantin speches which is Also veary good and plenty in these parts this plant never bears but ounce but yeat always hath another ciont [scion, a shoot or bud] ready to thake [take] its place

I was veary much oblagated to you for the thing which you sent me or rather us but whether we recved all that you Sent us or not I can not tell I Recived five peces of cloth namly one of mixed catin [cotton] one of caloco thirty four yard three peces of on bleched catin three Roals [rolls] of raw catin containing about a lb each I Also recived 125 scans [skeins] of whit thread I would be veary glad Sir, if you would to us how much you

Sent us and the defant amt with thir thir nams & thir numbers
the box we received was brook opin when we recived it pleas to
try help us all you can tobacco cloath larg wash Basons is grat
[for] Sail in this country we stand in grat need of Seed Such
as cabag seed ounan [onion] mustard & bucwheat Seed if you
Shuld Send us eny thing do Send us your Son John to bring it
or put it in veary Strict hands

I am Sir yours Talbeart Magor

P.S. Friend is veary scace sence [we] had hour [our] misforthon no one hath ever been so good as to give us the worth of a
pin it apears that the people here strives to Eat each other in the
stad [instead] of thriving to help each other I [am] happy to tell
you that for christ cake [sake] cummited my soul

Austin Major to Ben Major, October 17, 1840

Oactober the 17th 1840 B. cove
Dear farther
    I in barche [embrace] this oppotunity to writ you these
fue lines which will in form you of my heth which is good at
the presan in complinace with your requast I now give you a
statment of my condishon soon after I arrived hear I was put
in a thratch house were I was taking daw sick with the fever
and when helpless the natives came in an taking everything
that I pur-sessed in this world fater which thay come again in
about two years and burnd my house with all that I had make
to geather my sickness held me at least two years I have sufard
much Sence I come here but the dark clouds begin to disaper
again if you can Send Send us Sum fue artickels of trad such
as to bacco [tobacco] clouth pipes beed such as china beed it
will be a proffit to both of us I can by [buy] palm oil cam wood
ivory & I and return to you that is if you can make it cunvenent
[convenient] to send these things as goods is so dear hear I can
not by them and make eneay profit at all do try to Send these
artickels for which you shall not loose
    I am happy to in form you of the goodness of god to my soul
senc i come here the lord have Spook [spoke] peace to bouth of

195

our Souls or all of our Souls if I never see you in this life I thrist [thirst] to meet you in bright glory these misfourtins [misfortunes] which I have told you of have caused us to laber hard to suport our famlys but after chrismas we expet to clear farm land and commence try to do Some thing for our Selves if you do Send these things do try to Send them by Some veary partiler pourson [particular person] we wont seep much hear I thank god that I do in tend [intend] to strive to live as much above boure [above board] as posabe [possible] yours Auston Magor

PS you will pleas to writ george harlin to write to my motherinlaw Enoch harlins wife and She have meet with a grat misfoarthin She have loast three of hir Sans [sons] this is four letters I have sent I reci one Excuse the very [bad] hand writing for we have got about one of the worst pensman that we hav

Tolbert and Austin Major to Ben Major, August 7, 1843

Bassa Cove

August the 7 1843

My Dear mush beloved father it is with Plesher that I take this opperunity of wrighting you this letter to informe you that we are all well and I sinserley hope father these few lines may find you & your mush Beloved famley in the same as well as the Blessing of God But I am Sorry to informe you that Washington Tommous is Both Dead Washinton Dide with a Bledding it was thought that some of his Blode vessels Brock frome the wonde [wound] he reseved in the wore [war] 2 or 3 years a go. Tommous Dide with a long lingerring diszese But nevr the less the Lord workes all thinges for the Best a nother thing I am Sorrow to informe you of and that is thise I hade the mis forchen to get my House Burned in ashes a Bout 2 monthes a go my Loss wus grate and hade it not have Bine for my Plantation I do not know what I would have don But I do not fele no wase discorriged at all for as Long as Life Lastes and my helth is good I do not fele discorriged I wud send you Some of the Produce of this country But I have no one to Send it By and a nother thing I do not know where to send theme so you can get

theme But if you will Send me word where to Send I will Send
you Some coffy and ather thinges if it will be ecseptabl [ac-
ceptable] With you and Some groundnuttes and meney other
thinges

We ar well Satisfide in this country and I will Say this is the
Place for the mane of Coller [man of color] if we can not get
as mush of the Benfites of this Country as you do in yours or as
we did the country that giv us Borth [birth] But you may know
in all new country how it is and as this is the Commensment
of things we will do all that we can do and leve the Ballance for
the rizeing ginaration and God or [our] father

I did wright you one letter Befor this But if you reseved it I
do not know or [our] wives sendes thare Love to you all wer-
emane [women] yours truly

it is Tobers House   Tolbr Mages

Burnte   Austin Magers

Wesley Harlan to Ben Major

Mr. Magers

Deare Sir it [is] with plusher that yore Humbel Survant at-
tompes to inform you that he is well and it is my hontes Diszer
[honest desire] to have this to find you Sir and famly in the
Same all of my Pepel is well and ar doing as well as can Be es-
pectted in a new country. I my Self have had meny don fals lick
[many downfalls like] others But with ambishshon [ambition]
it is that I overcome theme all and if there is any one delites in
this country it shorley is me But I want you to have the goodness to Condecend So much as to Wright me if you please
where Mr. Gorge Harlan is or his famley as I have sunte and
[sent a] short letter But no anser do Dear Sir do me this faver I
remane yours with Due Respect
Wesley Harland

PS I wanto come over to See you all Wright me if you think
Best to com and remane a few monthes with you or not

WH

Wesley Harlan to Ben Major, April 4, 1844

Bassa Cove West Africa Liberia
April the 4–1844
Deare frand

I am hoppay that I have this opperetunity of wrighting you a few lines this leves me well and I do hope you a in good helth and all your fambley Deare sir thare is nothing very strang that I have to Relate to you at this time it would be a Plesher to me to have a Regular communication with you so that we would be abel to have information frome on [one] coutenent [continent] to the other not that I am so mush consurnd a Bout the a fares in the U States but it would be Some Satesfaction to me in deed to know the State of thinges I hope the United States ar all mot [almost] giv up the habbet of slave holding and I think if thay would God would Bless them more it is sumthing varry strang to me that white men that hase the Gospel Rather the Bible to giv them all the information that is nesserry for the Salvation of thare soles not with standing it semes to theme as Creme [crime?] it is time that Crisendom would let heare [her] Light Shine ~~on the~~ & La a sid [lay aside] sish darkness and a Bomanations[abominations] and crimes that know if truly ar clare of eany thing ealce that a Lone [are clear of anything else that alone] will sink theme be Low the Sodamites I am a shamed of the U States or that Part that indalges in this a caursed thing slaveray and I do not know why they do in dulg in it with out it is low enug to make a [illegible] of the collerd pepel and whites it seems as it is all most imposubel for so menay collerd pepel to Live thare in slaveray however it is all wease the Best to Stand Still and see the Salvation of God as the israelites Did whane thay whene thay hade the tiranickel [tyrannical] yok of Bondige on I hope God will offer the Pepel Eys that thay may see as they are Blined like ~~he did~~ the Poor Blind man that cald on him thouth Son of David have murcay [mercy] on me) (So ends the subject at Present)

The next thing that comes under aur notice is to giv you a Brefe a count [a brief account] of this common welth in all the Settelmantes thare ~~may Be Beed~~ ar Beteen 4 & 5 thousand 4000 or 5000 in habletans [inhabitants] or panlatations [plantations] ~~the place is~~ the seltelmentes mentes the most Pauler [popular] ones are on the Sea Biord [seaboard] we have some seltemont up the River the common welth is aBaut 20 or 23 yare old it is governed by or it is a Republican government We send 10 caunselers Anuley [counselors annually] to Legislat for us and make Lawes The next thing the corrancay [currency] of this commanwelth is not Acknalliged by forran countrays the corrancay is paper monay formed on came wood thare ar no gold nor silver in cercolation [circulation] Came wood may Be hade in Lage quntilays if men hase goodes suttabl [suitable] for the marcut [market] of wood But thare ar no wood none the sea Bord it is all in the interior of this countray and merchants Bys it frome the natives But the setters never gos thare owing to so menay Difficultays that thay would have to contend with Pame [palm] oil this is a thing that ar made on a varry Large skil the natives makes a grat dele of it and a man for 25 leves of tobacco my By 2 gallons or 2 gls of is as good as 621/2 cts and this are of the Best thinges that we have heare for the market of this countray as thare is not tobacco made heare The next thinge that we will notice is farming this may be come [common?] here But it is one thing to have a farme and a nother thing to make that farme make monay [two crossed-out words] farming in this countray is not Like farming thare it is 2 yores all after a man comes to this countray be for he cane larne the arte of farming and thane it is five yores before he cane make any thinge on that farm that will be woth a Brass cent coffey can be made in that time and thore is nothing Else that will be of any [illegible] to hime without he wantes it for his own fambley and and he may make a Living at the Bisness But not a verry good one Rice yames potatoes Casaders [cassavas] or the Bread frutes is Sowersope [soursops] guavers plantans Bananners papawes ornages Limes Lemmons thare is no nesetay [necessity] or it is not worth while for me to tell you what the Porduce of this countray is as you Know all a Bout all the zones and that more thane I cantell you the Land is tarabel [terrible] good back frome the Sea Shores a Bout 20 or 36 miles good a nufe to make anything by me saying that it is not Poor Livving in this canntray understand me under the Present sucomstance [circumstance] with the Poor class of pepel a manege [I imagine] the men that have Been in this canntray 15 or 16 yores Lives as well as any man in the U States that is if he is a indutres [industrious] man and Better than menay But if a man comes to this Countray if he hase not any monay nor goodes he nevr will get up under [crossed-out word] 16 or 17 yores as I say the men that have been here that Long Lives will if this shet [sheet] of paper wud hold all I woutell you a bout it he hase to work hard all day if he hopes for [illegible] ℔ of tobacco and thane sometimes it is so badly that he can not sell it at other times for 2 Komod [common?] Hankechifes Work a hole day and glad to get work at this Rates it is a harde thinge for a poor man to make a nofe [enough] for his fambley to live of[f] or by in this countray whane he fars come the first 6 monthes he is sick and he givs oblig to you in debt for thinges for the soport [support] of his fambley Some 2 or 3 hundred dollers and it five or 6 yores befor he is abel to Pay this and thane it is five or six more befor he can do any thinge for hisself wod say more But not Rome [room] am your Respefuley

Wesley Harlan

Wesley wrote in the margins of the letter:

Will you be so good as to see where Georg Harlanes fambley is and wright to them for me also any of the Harlanes as I do not know where thay is also Jhon J. Grifons of Kantuckay of Ciriston countray also the Bradsawes fambleys see if Shebay Bradshaw hase anythinge of John J grifon and his fambley as the Place that [illegible] or belonged to Shelvay Bradshaw so wright me and tell me all a Bout every thing that I wud like to know do [not] forgit G Harlan fambley

Wesley also wrote an additional note in very tiny script on the address panel of the letter. In order to read the note, the letter has to be folded in the manner in which it was mailed. The note is incomplete since two spots (marked here by ellipses) are illegible:

by me wrighting in this way I hope you will not let it get in the slave stalls for it may be the means of making some slaves disabeont to thare masters I hope that I will be able to see you befor long as I am coming to America befor Long or next Spring or sumer if I hade silver monay a nofe [enough] after I got to New York . . . if you will as[k] Mr. Harlanes . . . wrighte to them if they could in close as draft one way or thron [the other?] of a Bout 50 dollrs in cash and will settel for it; if they do and send me the draft in a letter and when I a Rives [arrives] in New York I will draw the mony and come on not that I am dipons [dependent?] on this money forever or dependes on them, but I manley wanto borry [mainly want to borrow] after I getes to New York as well. Send no silver WH

Wesley Harlan to James Moore, January 18, 1846

Bassa Cove,
Jan. 18, 1846.

This leves me well, and I hope you ar the same. I was verry glad to hear from you indeed, and more asspechel [especial], becaus that wase the first letter that I reseved from you sace my arival in this countray. It semes to me that the pepel have forgot me altogether. I hope we will be abel to cepe [keep] up a regular correspondence with each other hereafter.

The firs thing that I will consider, is the condition of the collonay. From the information that I have reseved since my arival, I am hapay to say this is a very good countray; and any man may make a living in this countray if he will.

Let us notice the land. The land is good. The land in one mille of the ocion [ocean] is good enufe to rase any thing most on it; and the father you go back the better the land is. The land is not very large timber, but verry good. I have some timber in this countray four feet in diameter. But I do not think that is as large as timber in the U. States, tharefor I say it is not verry large. The land is verry well timbered—that is, thar is plenty of it.

Hillay Land. —The land is not very hillay—it is as level as any countray, or as any part of the U. States I have scene. Thar is a chane of mountains that runs from the norther extremety of Africa to the Cape of Good Hope. Thes ar verry large mountains. This I have from modderon travelers.

Produce of Africa. —There is palm oil, rice, casander, yams, potaters, coffay, cabbish, water mellons, and many other things that I might name, sugar can &c., &c. Cattle, sheep hogs, goats, and fouls of various kinds, &c.

Crimes. —Thar is indeed some crimes in this country of a very bad natcher, but not a grate menay of them.

Religion. —This pepel is a religis pepel, thare is no queston about that. Thay ar a Church going pepel. They go to meeting evry Sabbath. I had the pleshur of being at the last Anul Conferance at Monrovia, on the 9th instand, and I remaned thare for some days, and was verry mutch grattefide, hevving some verry abel ministers.

The number of settlements. — Thar ar ten or fifteen settlements, but Monrovia is the largest—that also is the seat of government. We have legislatter every yere, commensing on the 5th of this month. The business is maniged very well, indeed, this I am a witness to, I have been in the legislater and seen them myself. Myself and my mother's family—my mother is well, and my sister and two brothers; Asberry and mother, the pepel that came to this countray with us, the Majers thare is three men and two wimmen alive; Hopkins, two alive; Alexander Horland, mother and two of his sisters—he is dead, the most of his pepel did not die with the fever, some of theme was shot in the last ware with the natives. As for the pepel, they ar all employed in doing something. Thar is not any of the very lazzy, by this do not understand me to say there is no lazzy ones among us, for thar is. I expect to come to the U. States before long, if you think it advisabel. I am doing a littel of most everry thing. I am yours,

Wesley Horland.

This letter is not all I will send, I will send another letter soon. H.

Wesley Harlan to James Moore, January 19, 1846

Bassa Cove,
Jan. 19, 1846.

I told you that I would say something more in my next [letter] that would afford you more satisfaction, as it regards this countray. The next thing that I will notice, is the situation of the settlements. Monrovia is the Cappetel of the Colony of Liberia. The pepolation of Monrovia is about one thousand men, wimmen and childring. This settlement is on a Cape extending in the Atlantick ocion [ocean], and it is a verry elevated place. It is bound on the north by the ocion, on the este by the Sent Pal's river, and on the west by the ocion. The buildings is made of wood, stone and bricks; the pepel that live here is those that follers merchandizing. The revenue is somewhere between eight and ten thousand dollars a yare. Thare is mechanickes also in the place of almost everry kind, so thare is not much need of me moveing the different employments. There is also three or four settlements up the Sent Pal's river. There pepel are farmers, so they live without having anythinge to do with trading; these settlements is about 18 miles the fathis [farthest] settlement; thar is some misshingnerry [missionary] stations the other side of the settelments. Marshall or Junk.— This settlement is somewhare about 50 miles south of Monrovia, situated on the Junk river, bound on the south by the mane branch of the river, on the west by the Atlantick ocion, and on the este by the north branch of the said river. Ediner.— This is a fine little settelment, 40 miles south of Marshall, situated on the north side of the Sent John's river; the pepel of this settelment is improving verry fast both wase; they ar the most of them farmers; this settelment is one that have been blest; they have never had an inserecshen [insurrection] sense the settelment of that place. It is situated on the north side Sent John's river, bound on the este by the Meehlen river, on the west by the ocion. Bexley.— This settlement is six miles from Ediner, on the north side of the St. John's river. Bassa Cove.—This little place is had more to contend with than the most of the settelments. It hase bin consumed by fier by natives; but we have nothing to dred at this time. This settelment is the cappetal of the country of Grand Bassaw. This is a verry fine settelment and the best that I have seen since I have been in this countray. This settelment is one mile south of Ediner, situated on the south side of the St. John's river, bound on the este by the Benson river, on the weste by the ocion. Senoe.— This settelment is somewhare about 100 miles south of Bassa Cove. Cape Palmas.—This settelment is somewhare between 200 or 150 miles south of Senoe.

Monrovia settled twenty yares ago; the popelation 1,000, without the upper settelments: the upper settelments have between 5 and 600; Marshall 80—Ediner have been settled ten or fifteen yares; popelation between 75 and 120—Bexeley have been settled six yares; it has somewhare about 150—Bassa Cove somewhare about the same—Cape Palmas have somewhare about 150 or 100.

This I think will answer for the settelments. As for myself, I am, by endevering [endeavoring], by the assistance of God, to do the best I cane. I am indevering [endeavoring] to Preach the Gospel of Crist, and this I think nothing less than my duty. I am a member of the Methodist Church. I have not been sick two weeks since I have been in this countray, and if the Lord is willing, I intend to see yore face once more. I do hope you will advise me what to do in this respect. I would like to come thare verry well; but I do not know the law that you have among you as yet. I would be glad if you would wright me all the newse. Wright to my pepel for me. This leves me well.

I remane yours truly with respect,   W. J. Horland [Harlan]

Tolbert Major to Ben Major, June 26, 1847

Africa grand bassa county June 26th 1847
Dear fother
    I write you these few lines to in form you of my helth which is good at this time present & I hope these few lines may find you and your family in good helth the Sheep in this country affordes no wole they have Strait hair Like a dog when I lived with you I was used to eating meat 3 times a day but if I get it once a weak here I think that I am a doing very well in dead for I have to pay 37½ cents a pound of meat flour is $300 dolars a barrel I did think once that I would come home but I have decline coming untill I make one or 2 good crops So that I can have some thing to bring with me the woman would do more

than what they do but but they have no looms to weave cloath
and all the cloath that we get we pay from 75 to 50 & 25 cents
a yard for it I want to See you and your wife and children very
bad I for got one thing and that is this my children talks abut
you and mother very much please to have the profile of you and
your wife drawn and Send it to me for my children to loock at
when I am dead My oldest dautor Sarah is a bout 5 years old
and She can read a little She is considered to be a ver Sence a
ble [sensible] child by the people to her age and my motherinlaw enock Harlans wife in Quiers [inquires] very much about
you and Should Like to hear from you at all times her and her
children She told me to write a few lines for for her She Still
remains a widdow She is a bout 50 years old and She loocks to
be a bout 26 years old and her hair is as black as ever it was and
She Still is a Striveing to Serve the Lord yet and She is got 4
children Living wesley is married and She Says that She wants
you to in Quier for George Harlands famly and write her a bout
them She says that She has wrote so often to them and nevr got
any anser She wants you to write to her a bout them

Please to remember me and brother aston magors we want to
write to you 2 times a year but we have no paper

Please to Send me Some paper

your truly tolbert Magors

Tolbert Major to Ben Major, June 23, 1848

Liberia
Bassa Cove
Grand Bassa County
June 23d 1848
My Dear Father
I received your letter dated August 1847 and though it has
been written nearly a year yet it came safe to hand—which gave
me great satisfaction but I heard nothing that was at all dissatis-
factory in the least

My Wife is at present very well indeed as is the case with
myself I have at this time two children Sarah Agnus—& Ann
Eliza—the former was born the 20th Oct 1843 and being

nearly five years old goes to school and can read a little the latter having been born as late as the 9th Sept 1846 is not quite old enough as yet to go to school and So She Stays home with me—agreeable to your request I shall endeavour to write a letter to you at least twice a year But whenever I see an opportunity of writing I shall not fail to do so I received the medicines and Books which you sent me and was very glad of them and that you were so mindful of me and I shall as far as my poor ability will allow conform to your advice Set forth in the letter We are very thankful for the few seeds you sent us as much So as if you had Sent a Bushel of each kind Seeing You show a willing mind to do a good part by us and I intend to try and do the Same by you but as *Poor Lazarus* said to the Rich man there is a Great gulf Between us—We have not received the cards which You sent nor even heard of them We are getting along pretty well indeed We have lived together without any dispute or disagreeing as yet and I hope we never will disagree or have disputes and quarrels I am exceedingly happy. We did on the 29th July last by own representatives Solemnly declare ourselves a free Sovereign and independant people thereby dissolving all political Connection Between the Col. Society and ourselves and we have established a new form of Government viz a "Republican form" and it is my pride and Joy that I am a free man in a free country and can enjoy the free mild and equal Government which has just been established and where I can have an equal Share of Republicanism—

The General occupation of the citizens of this country natives included is farming the merchants appreciate their farming more than all their commercial Business Rice—Corn—capadas—Potatoes—arrow Root—Ginger etc Grow to perfection at the same time may be seen every persons garden sallads of every description which Liberia will afford eatable herbs and here and there is pictured most Beautiful flowers etc etc Rice capadas potatoes ginger arrow root etc is the staple production also palmoil—which we use in the place of Lard I may Say that the women do nothing but would tell a little story that is not true they sew and wash and some times they may be seen weeding out the garden and doing other petty jobs of the same nature

We Raise cattle in this country but the oxen here do not

work like those in america we also have Sheep Goats Hogs Ducks and chickens and we are making a Start at turkeys

There is also a variety of poisonous reptiles in this country Such as Snakes lizards Scorpions Sentipedes etc there is a kind of Lizard whose Bite is Said to be fatal it is called in this country the Salimango I do not know its natural Historical name.

We are not fixed in a way to make cloth So every yd of cloth that is used in this country is Bought Cotton Grows and was it cultivated would be very plentiful neither can we make Sewing Cotton and at this very moment it is in Great demand any price almost would be paid for it The above are not fables but realities—I only received four kinds of medicine viz Bayberry Bark Hemlock No. 4 or Bitters Lobelia Seed I do not know whether they are all that you Sent or not as to paying you a visit I hardly know what to say at this time I am not in a way for paying visits and I have changed my notion as I wont be able to come for a couple of years yet But I Shall endeavour to Send you Some coffee I would have Sent it by the [brig] La— Packet but not receiving your letter in time I could not Get it in Readiness to send as I received your letter only a couple of days previous to the starting of the vessel and we have no machines in this country but have to work with our own hands when she Makes another trip across the Ocean I will be Sure and Send it I Really do wish to See You and mother and Sometimes when I study about past days it distresses me most wonderful

What you wrote concerning my Brothers wife & children gives me a great deal of satisfaction and comfort Please Remember my love to John Major your son and Judah [Judith] your daughter and all the rest of your children I would have written to them all but for want of time and paper I could not paper is a scarce article My Love to Shastene Major and his family to Mr Davenport and family to to William Majors and all of his family To Joseph Majors and his family to Edward Watkins and his family. Dear Mother and father pray for me and By the assistance of God I Shall endeavour to do the Same for you I hope the Lord will make a way for me to See you all again this Side of the Grave I am yet striving to lay up treasures in heaven where moth corrupt eth not nor thieves Break in and steal This puts me in mind of the time when I came from the

Iron works and You had Gone off to illinois and left me and when I study about that it makes the tears rise in my eyes The Books that you sent me will answer for my children they are in my estimation valuable Books
Farewell farther & mother

Tolbert Majors

My mother in Law Enuck Harlans wife was very glad to hear from you and says Give her love to all her acquaintances Wesley Harlan is Married

Austin Major to Ben Major, June 23, 1848

Bassa Cove June 23d, 1848
Dear father & mother
We Received your letter And was very glad that you thought So much of us as to send an answer & we also was glad to hear of your healths which Seamed to be good—& now I must tell you Some thing a bout our health & the health of our family's my family is well my wife & daughter is in good heath I have only one child living which is mary & She is nearly grown! She can read tolerably well. But She dos not go to school evry day at this time my wife can also Read tolerably well & mary Can wright Some But not having had A good chance better to she can not wright Better. You will be please to wright to me Seperately so that I may Receive my letters without so much trouble as it appears tha their has Ben Some mis carage [miscarriage] in them I must say Something more A Bout Mary She is a School teacher & She has also embraced the Religion of Jesus Christ & is now A full member in the methodist church If you will please to wright to me whether old mother Rebecca is yet living or not & with Regard to fruits we have corn & casidoes sweet Potatoes & arroroote—ginger & plantings & Sower Saps & Banannaes & the Palm trees yields abundantly—& the popawe & Cotton we can rase in the greatest abundance & fouls—hogs & goats Sheep—there is plenty Deers in this country & also A very ferocious animals called the lepard & the Bush cat etc
& with Regard to my seeing you Again I never expect to

see you Again in this life But I hop to meete you all in the King[dom] of Eternal glory whare we will meet to part no more for ever—for I am so very wll satisfied in this country—the land of my fore fathers where I enjoy all the wrights & priviledges of A free man & can worship my God & there is none to make me affrade or oppress me in so doing. you will please to excuse me for wrighting so to you But I wish not to Brag But only to State the Satisfaction of my mind in the land of my fathers or ansesters [ancestors] in which the lord has Ben So good as to cend me & I must say also that I am A class leader & A stewart in the methodist Episcopal Church in Bassa cove & according to your Request I am trying to live agreeable & serve the lord to the Best of my knowlege. I have not done much farming as yet But I am trying to get Ready to do so—My wife is just as well satisfied as I am in this country—I oft times think of the many good advices that you have given me in the house for my aim is to live in peace with all men & when done with this world get to heaven at lass } My Daughter Says She wishes you to send her some thing to Remember her & we all want to cend you Something to Remember you all & what is Convenient cend to us as A memorial & now our lord Jesus christ himself guide you in the paths of wrighteousness & at lass Bring you in to his hevenly King dom is our sincere Prayer
Yours very sincerely & most affectionately

Austian major & family

Austin Major to Ben Major, October 19, 1849

Oct 19th 1849 Bassa Cove & County of Libria
Dear farther & mother
    I embrace this opportunity of addressing you with these few lines hoping they may find you & family enjoying good Health as the same leavs me & mine at present. Sence I have been to Liberia I enjoy as a general thing tolorable good health and also family and all the others. it has been Some Time Sence I here from you & mother I Sent Some Letters by the Packet when she was out time before last but whether they got to your hands or not we can not tell I would be very glad to here from you all

indeed and I hope [illegible word] you get this letter you will answer it—in order that we may knonow how you are doing &c, &c., My wife & Mary sends their Best Respects to you & mother and they hope you would cherish this opportunity to send them a Bonnet each. and Sir above all please send me the age of Both myself wife & Daughter [f]or we can not tell them our selves and as my Daily ocpation [occupation] is farming do avail your self the opportunity to send me some Tuules [tools]

Please send some carpenters tuuls as I can do some at that Buisness 1 hand Saw som philes [files] & orgors [augers] & chisels plairs [pliers] ad a good hatchet and Der farther I hope you are acquionted with Liberia that is—I mean that it is hard to get anything like good cloth to make clothes except—for Very thin so please send me some Blue genes to make some good wareing clothes & also some good calico for wife & Daughter and also please Send Some paper as it is very Scarce here which cannot begotton unless I pay fifty cts. per gr. Please Give my love to Chasteen Mago[r] tell him I think Very hard of him for not writing & he has never wrote me sence I hev I hear Been. My love to Wm. Magor & family Jo. Magor & family Wm. Debenport & family My wife say give her love Sarah Tenly tel her to send her som t. Mary is also a Teacher of the Sabbeth School of the M.E. Church please and also a member of Christn Church She is I am happy to say stood a mong the first in society in Sab shcl: Church & State and I expect before this letter get to you She will be married & she will be very happy if Mrs [illegible] Thalis would lend her some things to set her house of. So if you or she either comes out here I shall be prepard to Receive you home and Little Lucy tel her to send Mary som thing too. and please give our love to John major and tell him to Remember his old father that Raised him I hope he has not fore got him because he is in africa—. Give my love to Wm. Magor tell him. to send us some thing too. for us to Remember him. & also Benjamin Magor. Tell him send us some things also so as for us to Remember him & I am now a Leader of a class of the M. "E" church Please send me some Good Books & a Drawing [knife?] as I Have none. —please send some 5"& [illegible] nails five & Eight Penny nails. — Nothing More but Remains Yors

Respectfully

Austin Magor

P.S. my Best Respects to [illegible] Thails & Lucy Mager tell
them to send ~~me~~ wife & mary a Bonnet for we lost all most our
things in the War
AM

Silvay Major to Ben Major, December 26, 1851

December 26 1851
Bassa Cov Republic of Liberia
Dear Frather
　　Since I heard from you last many has been my trouble
Tolbert Magers My husband volunteered to go to Kroo town
on 22 of March after being there 4 months he move his wife
and children down there and the President com[e] [d]own an
emploud [employed] him two months longer his time being up
for the 4 months he [en]listed again two months longer thinking all things was well and the natives seemed friendly and
kind and the 5 of november the massacree took place an he was
killed by those bardaraus [barbarous] people and now I am left
with out a home with three small children 2 girls and one boy
about 2 years one girl about 8 years and the other Six I am now
depending on the mercy of friends for a home I was at the Kroo
town my self me and my children and only mad my escape the
3 day before the massacree took place and it was through the
mercy of god they also killed my Brother and now I have only
one left & he has lost one of his eyes in this war for those native
attacked Bassa cove on the 15 of november and a bloody War
insued and my brother got shot through the nose and that oc-
caissained the last of his eye so you see that I am a poor drestre-
sece [distressed] creature and any assistance you can render me I
will be glad of and verry thankful young Joseph Magers my son
sends word to young Benguman magas [Benjamin Major] for a
pair of houns and my childre often inquires after you and more
so since the death of their father there was 8 other persons got
killed in the massacree besides my husband women an children

211

and I lost all I had and the rest of them that was ther lost all
they had and suppose the government lost upwards of 5 thousand dollars if you send me the houns pleas to send a [illegible]
and a dog male and female for they are verry useful in this place
all tho my hus is Dead yet that do not hinder me from [wri]ting
to you whenever I can git an opportunity my mother send her
lov to you an would like to know where all the Harrlands have
gon to and if you do know please [write] to her so when I write
to them I may know where to direct my letter to
Austin and his family are well
I would like you to write to me as often as you can
I remains yours truly

Silvay Magers

Acknowledgments

Letters written by four formerly enslaved people—Austin, Tolbert, and Silvay Major, and Wesley Harlan—inspired this book. After their emancipation and migration to Liberia, these four people maintained a very personal connection with two white men, Ben Major and James Moore, across thousands of miles of ocean and land, and across deep-seated cultural barriers. This book would not have been possible had they not set pen to paper more than 180 years ago. I am deeply grateful for their words.

I appreciate the careful stewardship of Ben Major and his descendants, who understood the value of the letters and preserved them for generations, and the editor of the *African Repository* for preserving the content of the letters sent to James Moore. Special thanks go to Deanne (Annie) Major-Dillard and Gretchen (Gigi) Macklin, Ben Major's great-great granddaughters, who generously shared his documents and letters, and their knowledge of the family's history.

My sincere thanks to the McLean County Museum of History in Bloomington, Illinois, for their kind permission to use the letters from Africa. Special thanks are also due to the Kentucky Foundation for Women for their generous artist enrichment grant, and to the management and staff of Wildacres Retreat in North Carolina for the gift of two weeks to focus and write in an extraordinary place.

Very special thanks are due to Pam Robertson, my research assistant extraordinaire—we spent countless hours in courthouses, archives, museums, attics, and cemeteries. Together we logged thousands of miles in my aging Volvo station wagon and her trusty van. This book might not have been possible without her support and help.

I thank my daughter, Carrie L. Grant, and her family, who opened their home to me when I launched my editing business and started this book; my son, Chris Swanson, for his encouragement and support along the way; and my niece, Bryanna Garrett Lindsey, who helped conduct research at the Library of Congress and the National Archives. My sister, Sara McReynolds, loaned her expertise to prepare image files.

I appreciate the skills and patience of Shellee Layman Jones of Rock Paper Jones, who created the family charts and maps for this book.

My sincere thanks go to the staffs of various museums, archives, and collections for their assistance with research. These people include Verlon Stone, Megan MacDonald, and others affiliated with Indiana University's Liberian Collections; William T. Turner of the Christian County Historical Society in Hopkinsville; the staffs of the Disciples of Christ Historical Society, the Filson Historical Society in Louisville, and the Kentucky Historical Society in Frankfort. The staff members of the Library of Congress and the National Archives were extremely helpful, and Katrina Brown at the National Museum of American History helped me locate a critical piece of information.

Dr. Claude Clegg, author of *The Price of Liberty: African Americans and the Making of Liberia*, was kind enough to meet with me early in the process; he provided much-needed encouragement. Others who have been helpful include many members of the Liberian Studies Association, Dr. Junius Rodriguez and Anthony Glass of Eureka College, and missionary kids Annie Hammon and Heath Vogel for their firsthand knowledge of Liberia. Jeanine Milly Cooper, descended from one of the early settler families in Liberia, was kind enough to be an early reader of my manuscript and provided the photo of the Harlandsville sign.

Finally, although writing is usually a solitary practice, I had tremendous support from the members of the Women Who Write and Talking Story writing groups in Louisville, and members of the nonfiction writing group at the Carnegie Center for Learning and Literacy in Lexington, Kentucky. A group of dedicated beta readers, including people in America and Liberia, and skilled editor and friend Susan Salsburg helped me pull the manuscript across the finish line. Anne Dean Dotson and others at University Press of Kentucky have been extraordinarily patient and helpful.

I hope this book honors the memory of the Majors and Harlans, black and white, and serves to further the understanding of the complexities of the colonization of Liberia.

Notes

1. May I But Safely Reach My Home

1. "Departure of the Emigrants by the *Luna*," *African Repository* 12, no. 7 (July 1836): 226–229.

2. The names of other emigrants are from a letter to the editor of the *Commercial Advertiser*, signed "B.," July 8, 1836, and "Brig *Luna*'s Company, Arrived at Bassa Cove, August 1836," *Senate of the United States, Second Session of the Twenty-Eighth Congress*, vol. 9, no. 150 (Washington, D.C.: Gales and Seaton, 1845), 269–271, https://books.google.com/books?id=N4lHAQAAIAAJ.

3. Joseph Major to Ben Major, March 29, 1837, Major Family Private Collection; G. W. McElroy to the editor, *Kentucky Gazette*, August 8, 1836.

4. Isaac Watts, "When I Can Read My Title Clear," 1707 (lyrics from http://library.timelesstruths.org).

5. "Annual Report," *African Repository* 11, no. 7 (July 1835): 221. Proudfit had accepted the office of permanent agent and corresponding secretary for the New York Colonization Society in May 1834, according to the society's annual report.

6. Extracts are from a speech Dr. Alexander Proudfit delivered to a group of settlers departing for Bassa Cove in spring 1835. He likely delivered a similar speech to those departing in July 1836. "Dr. Proudfit's Address to Emigrants," *African Repository* 11, no. 10 (October 1835), 306–308.

7. Details on the departure ceremony are from "Departure of the Emigrants," *Christian Watchman* (Boston), July 15, 1836, American Periodicals, 115.

8. The captain is named in an account of the departure of the *Luna*, published in American Colonization Society, *Twentieth Annual Report of the American Colonization Society for Colonizing the Free People of Colour of the United States, with the Proceedings of the Annual Meeting*, December 13, 1836 (Washington, D.C.: American Colonization Society, 1837), 7–8, https://books.google.com/

books?id=1scCAAAAYAAJ&pg=RA3-PA21&lpg=RA3-PA21&dq=Donelson+and+L
iberia&source=bl&ots=A890EM3lQB&sig=-NS5Qt0P_R—SgICU5cEOIIYqao&hl
=en&sa=X&ved=0ahUKEwjHvan1zOrJAhVK5yYKHUeZBOkQ6AEILzAE#v=two
page&q=Donelson&f=false; the description of emigrants providing personal information is from G. W. McElroy to editor, *Commercial Advertiser,* June 27, 1835.

9. Marie Tyler-McGraw, *An African Republic: Black and White Virginians in the Making of Liberia* (Chapel Hill: Univ. of North Carolina Press, 2007), 138; "Brig *Luna's* Company," 269–271; "Departure of the Emigrants by the *Luna,*" 226–229.

10. G. W. McElroy, letter forwarded by "a subscriber" to the *Kentucky Gazette* (Lexington) and published August 8, 1836, Kentucky Digital Library, http://nyx.uky. edu/dips/xt7x3f4kmt95/data/3364.pdf.

11. G. W. McElroy, letter to the editor of the *Commercial Advertiser,* dated August 27, 1835 (published December 8, 1835); the background information is from letters to the *Commercial Advertiser,* June 27, 1835; October 5, 1835 (republished in the *New York Spectator,* December 31, 1835); and July 21, 1836.

12. G. W. McElroy letter to the editor, *Louisville Courier-Journal,* May 24, 1836.

13. Donelson died May 23, 1834, and Fisher died between 1827 and 1834; the *Tennessean,* June 5, 1834, and April 5, 1834. Also see "Emancipation," *African Reposi-tory* 11, no. 12 (December 1835): 335–336; Eli Seifman, "The United Colonization Societies of New York and Pennsylvania and the Establishment of the African Colony of Bassa Cove," *Pennsylvania History: A Journal of Mid-Atlantic Studies* 35, no. 1 (Janu-ary 1968): 24.

14. Persons of Color, called Fisher's Negroes, by their next friend, vs. J. Dabbs, Administrator of P. Fisher, Appeal from Chancery Court at Carthage; opinion pub-lished in the *Tennessean,* April 5, 1834.

15. Account of the *Luna's* departure: letter from G. W. McElroy published in the *Kentucky Gazette,* August 8, 1836. Details on McElroy's involvement and their journey from Kentucky to New York: letter to the editor from G. W. McElroy, *Pittsburgh Gazette,* June 10, 1836; and the *Annual Report of the Board of Managers of the Young Men's Colonization Society of Pennsylvania* (Philadelphia: Pennsylvania Colonization Society, 1837), 19–20.

16. James Hall, "Voyage to Liberia," *African Repository* 33, no. 8 (August 1857): 272–273, HathiTrust.org, https://hdl.handle.net/2027/hvd.hwrchv.

17. "Departure of the Emigrants by the *Luna,*" 226–229. Her age, reported as 110 in the news article, merits skepticism. It is unlikely that anyone of that time, but espe-cially an enslaved person, could have lived to be that old.

18. "Liberia," *Christian Watchman* (Boston), November 11, 1836.

2. Slavery and the Troublesome Question

1. Frederick Douglass, *On Slavery and the Civil War: Selections from His Writings* (New York: Dover Thrift Editions, 2003), 30.

2. Wilson Armistead, *Calumny Refuted by Facts from Liberia* (London: Charles Gilpen, 1848), 43. Armistead cites an 1846 speech by Liberian senator Hilary Teage, in which Teage quotes Henry H. Garnett.

3. The number of free black people is from Robert July, *The Origins of Modern African Thought: Its Development in West Africa during the Nineteenth and Twentieth Centuries* (New York: Praeger, 1967), 86.

4. Thomas Jefferson, July 27, 1821, autobiography draft fragment, January 6 through July 27, 1821, from the Thomas Jefferson and William Short Correspondence, transcribed and edited by Gerard W. Gawalt, Manuscript Division, Library of Congress, Washington, D.C., https://www.loc.gov/collections/thomas-jefferson-papers/?q=Thomas+Jefferson%2C+July+27%2C+1821.

5. See Alan Huffman's excellent book *Mississippi in Africa: The Saga of the Slaves of Prospect Hill Plantation and Their Legacy in Liberia Today* (New York: Gotham, 2004) for a detailed account of the prolonged legal battle over Isaac Ross's attempt to free and colonize more than two hundred slaves in his will; Eric Burin, *Slavery and the Peculiar Solution: A History of the American Colonization Society* (Gainesville: Univ. Press of Florida, 2005), 126–131.

6. Occupations of free black people are from Claude A. Clegg III, *The Price of Liberty: African Americans and the Making of Liberia* (Chapel Hill: Univ. of North Carolina Press, 2004), 164.

7. Early Lee Fox, "The American Colonization Society: 1817–1840," Ph.D. diss., Johns Hopkins University, 1919, 33, https://archive.org/stream/americancoloniza00foxe/americancoloniza00foxe_djvu.txt.

8. J. Winston Coleman Jr., "The Kentucky Colonization Society," *Register of the Kentucky State Historical Society* 39 no. 26 (January 1941): 1.

9. Henry Clay, John Randolph, Francis Scott Key, and Alexander Campbell appear on the society's list of life members, and Daniel Webster and Henry Clay appear on the original subscriber list. American Colonization Society Records, microfilm volumes 56 and 57, reel 299, Library of Congress Manuscript Collection, Washington, D.C.

10. "Meeting of the American Colonization Society," *Pittsburgh Gazette,* December 23, 1836.

11. American Colonization Society, "The Constitution of the American Society for Colonizing the Free People of Colour of the United States," Library of Congress digital archives, http://www.loc.gov/item/91898198.

12. Henry Noble Sherwood, "The Formation of the American Colonization Society," *Journal of Negro History* 2, no. 3 (July 1917), https://www.gutenberg.org/files/20752/20752-8.txt.

13. "Gradual Emancipation in Kentucky," *African Repository* 11, no. 8 (August 1835): 256.

14. Harold D. Tallant, *Evil Necessity: Slavery and Politics in Antebellum Kentucky* (Lexington: Univ. Press of Kentucky, 2003), 49.

15. Robert P. Murray, "Whiteness in Africa: Americo-Liberians and the Transformative Geographies of Race," Ph.D. diss., University of Kentucky, 2013, 286n357, Theses and Dissertations—History, 23, https://uknowledge.uky.edu/history_etds/23/.

16. Douglass, *On Slavery*, 36.

17. The number of people transported is from Clegg, *Price of Liberty*, 6.

3. People of Culture and Refinement

1. "Curses of slavery" from Ben Major to Joseph Major, May 3, 1840, Major Family Private Collection.

2. Inventory of John Major's estate; 1810 and 1820 United States census records; Elmira J. Dickinson, ed., *A History of Eureka College with Biographical Sketches and Reminiscences* (St. Louis, Mo.: Christian Publishing Company, 1894), 113–114. See also Daniel Trabue, *Westward into Kentucky: The Narrative of Daniel Trabue*, ed. Chester Raymond Young (Lexington: Univ. Press of Kentucky, 1981, paperback ed. 2004), 81.

3. Dickinson, *A History of Eureka College*, 113.

4. John E. Kleber, ed., *The Kentucky Encyclopedia* (Lexington: Univ. Press of Kentucky, 1992), 324; Trabue, *Westward into Kentucky*, 10, 146–151.

5. 1810 US Census, www.census.gov.

6. *Louisiana State Gazette*, eighteen issues dating from February 4 to December 22, 1818.

7. See Walter Johnson's excellent book *Soul by Soul: Life inside the Antebellum Slave Market* (Cambridge, Mass.: Harvard Univ. Press, 1999) for an in-depth look at the New Orleans slave markets; Henry Louis Gates Jr., host and executive producer, "The Stories We Tell," *Finding Your Roots*, season 3, episode 1, Public Broadcasting Service, 2016.

8. Johnson, *Soul by Soul*, 152.

9. Dickinson, *A History of Eureka College*, 113. The name Christian County has nothing to do with religion; the county was named for William Christian, a Revolutionary War veteran.

10. William Henry Perrin, ed., *Counties of Christian and Trigg, Kentucky: Historical and Biographical* (Chicago: F. A. Battey Publishing Co., 1884), 8, https://archive.org/details/countiesofchrist00perr/.

11. John Major to Ben Major, April 24, 1819, Major Family Private Collection.

12. Marriage records, 1797–1850, Christian County, Kentucky. Most of the information on the Davenport family is from a handwritten transcription of notes in William Davenport's Bible (the transcription is on file in the Kentucky Historical Society in Frankfort); from Nathaniel S. Haynes, *History of Disciples of Disciples of Christ in Illinois: 1819–1914* (Cincinnati: Standard Publishing, 1915); and census records.

13. Dickinson, *A History of Eureka College*, 114.

4. Serious Doubts on the Slavery Question

1. US Census, 1820 and 1830, and Lowell H. Harrison, *The Antislavery Movement in Kentucky* (Lexington: Univ. Press of Kentucky, 1978), 3.

2. Kleber, ed., *Kentucky Encyclopedia*, s.v. "Economy," 280; Harrison, *Antislavery Movement*, 2; Tallant, *Evil Necessity*, 9.

3. Dickinson, *A History of Eureka College*, 111–122.

4. Ibid., 115.

5. Leo Rosten, ed., *Religions of America: Ferment and Faith in an Age of Crisis* (New York: Simon and Schuster, 1975), 83–95; Disciples of Christ website, accessed March 1, 2014, https://disciples.org/our-identity/history-of-the-disciples/. The parentheses are part of the official name.

6. Kleber, ed., *Kentucky Encyclopedia*, s.v. "Christian Church (Disciples of Christ)," 187; Barton W. Stone, *Biography of Eld. B. W. Stone, Written by Himself, with Additions and Reflections from Elder John Rogers* (Cincinnati: J. A. and U. P. Jones, 1847), HathiTrust.org. https://babel.hathitrust.org/cgi/pt?id=chi.26752889;view=1up;seq=7.

7. Dickinson, *A History of Eureka College*, 115.

8. Burin, *Slavery and the Peculiar Solution*, 105, 110.

9. [First name illegible] Fishers of Nashville, Illinois, to the American Colonization Society, March 10, 1835, American Colonization Society Records, microfilm vol. A59, reel 22B, Library of Congress Manuscript Collection, Washington, D.C.

10. Randall M. Miller, *"Dear Master": Letters of a Slave Family* (Ithaca: Cornell Univ. Press, 1978), 32; Burin, *Slavery and the Peculiar Solution*, 102; Huffman, *Mississippi in Africa*, 75.

11. "Colonization Meeting," *African Repository* 11, no. 1 (January 1835): 16.

12. Ben Major's teaching his slaves to read and write is from Dickinson, *A History of Eureka College*, 11; Harrison, *Antislavery Movement*, 10. (Kentucky was one of only a few slave states that did not outlaw teaching slaves to read and write.)

13. Ben eventually accumulated hundreds of acres in Illinois. The portion of Tazewell County where he settled was later annexed and joined to the northern part of McLean County. The new county was called Woodford County. The settlement of Walnut Grove (between Bloomington and Peoria) was later renamed Eureka.

14. Dickinson, *A History of Eureka College*, 116.

15. Coleman, "Kentucky Colonization Society," 6–7.

16. Zebina Eastman, "Black Code of Illinois," *Illinois Historical Survey*, Learning Lincoln Online, http://learningabe.info/Black_Code_Text_Portion.html (accessed May 22, 2019).

17. Kleber, ed., *Kentucky Encyclopedia*, s.v. "Afro-Americans," 14–18; Harrison, *Antislavery Movement*, 2.

18. Joseph Major to Ben Major, March 29, 1837, Major Family Private Collection.

19. Copy of original receipt for wagon maker dated September 20, 1834, supplied to author by Annie Major-Dillard; Dickinson, *A History of Eureka College,* 113. Lucy gave birth to her first child when she was about nineteen years old; she had the last of her nine children when she was forty-one.

20. Charles F. Hinds, "Migration Routes from Kentucky," at the Martin F. Schmidt Research Library, Kentucky Historical Society, Frankfort, Kentucky.

21. Haynes, *Disciples of Christ in Illinois,* chapter 3; Dickinson, *A History of Eureka College,* 119.

22. Haynes, *Disciples of Christ in Illinois,* chapter 3.

23. Dickinson, *A History of Eureka College,* 119. In 1837, Ben built a bigger frame house for his family. He paid a total of $51.50 for the lumber, trading several bushels of wheat for part of the cost, according to a receipt still in possession of his descendants; Benjamin Johnson Radford, *Autobiography of Benjamin Johnson Radford* (Eureka, Ill.: N.p., 1928), 2.

24. B. J. Radford, *History of Woodford County* (Peoria, Ill.: W. T. Dowdall, Printer, 1877), 30.

25. Ralph Gurley to Philip Fendall of the American Colonization Society, April 29, 1836, American Colonization Society Records, microfilm vol. 63, reel 25, Library of Congress Manuscript Collection, Washington, D.C.; American Colonization Society, *Twentieth Annual Report of the American Colonization Society,* 7–8.

26. William Innes, *Liberia; or the Early History and Signal Preservation of the American Colony of Free Negroes on the Coast of Africa* (Edinburgh, UK: Waugh and Innes, 1831), 112–113.

27. Joseph Major to Ben Major, March 29, 1837, Major Family Private Collection.

28. Receipt from the Christian County Colonization Society in possession of Annie Major-Dillard.

5. The Scene of Suffering and Misery Is Beyond Description

1. R. McDowell, "Miscellaneous Information: Attack on Bassa Cove," *Religious Monitor and Evangelical Repository,* January 1836, American Periodicals, 251.

2. *African Repository* 11, no. 3 (March 1835): 85.

3. John Hersey to Elliot Cresson, n.d., published in the *Long Island Star,* November 6, 1834.

4. Samuel Wilkeson, *A Concise History of the Commencement, Progress and Present Condition of the American Colonies in Liberia* (Washington, D.C.: Madisonian Office, 1839), 58–59, https://books.google.com/books?id=J8sNAAAAQAAJ; Tyler-McGraw, *An African Republic,* 137; Clegg, *Price of Liberty,* 145.

5. McDowell, "Miscellaneous Information: Attack on Bassa Cove," 251; Murray, "Whiteness in Africa," 63.

6. McDowell, "Miscellaneous Information: Attack on Bassa Cove," 251.

7. Ibid.; Seifman, "The United Colonization Societies," 23–44.

8. Wilkeson, *Concise History of Liberia*, 61. Wilkeson was a judge and former real estate promoter from New York. He served without a salary as a general agent for the American Colonization Society and then served as president of the society's board; Seifman, "The United Colonization Societies," 23–44. Also see McDowell, "Miscellaneous Information: Attack on Bassa Cove," 251.

9. McDowell, "Miscellaneous Information: Attack on Bassa Cove," 251; "The Colony and Colonization," *African Repository* 11, no. 11 (November 1835): 321.

10. "From Liberia," *Niles Weekly Register,* December 26, 1835, American Periodicals, 288. Also see "Latest from Liberia," *African Repository* 11, no. 11 (November 1835): 337–339.

11. Seifman, "United Colonization Societies," 23–44.

12. Wilkeson, *Concise History of Liberia,* 61, 63, 70; "From Liberia," *New York Commercial Advertiser,* n.d., published in the *Pittsburgh Gazette,* March 8, 1836.

13. "Expeditions to Liberia," *African Repository* 11, no. 12 (December 1835): 373; John Breckinridge and Thomas Buchanan, "The Massacre at Bassa Cove," *Religious Intelligencer* (October 31, 1835), American Periodicals, 347; Seifman, "United Colonization Societies," 23–44; "Conversion of Africa," *Boston Liberator,* December 19, 1835.

14. Thomas Buchanan, "Late and Interesting News from Bassa Cove," *Pittsburgh Gazette,* June 28, 1836.

15. Wilkeson, *Concise History of Liberia,* 63.

16. "Young Men's Colonization Society of Pennsylvania," *African Repository* 12, no. 4 (April 1836): 125.

6. We Have All Landed on the Shores of Africa

1. American Colonization Society, *Twentieth Annual Report of the American Colonization Society,* 7–8.

2. Kru tattoos, Clegg, *Price of Liberty,* 52, 77–78; Charles H. Bell to Reverend Alfred Chester, April 3, 1840, *African Repository* 16 (1840): 294.

3. "Brig *Luna's* Company," 269–271; American Colonization Society, "Census of the Colony of Liberia" in *Tables Showing the Number of Emigrants and Recaptured Africans sent to the Colony of Liberia . . . Together with a Census of the Colony* (Washington, D.C.: American Colonization Society, 1845), 403 (referred to hereinafter as the 1843 Liberian census); letter from Tolbert Major to James Moore, May 20, 1839, Major Collection of Letters from Liberia, McLean County Museum of History, Bloomington, Illinois. Tolbert Major's letter implies, but does not state outright, that Thornton and Washington were his sons.

4. The description of unloading passengers at Monrovia is from Dr. James Hall, "Voyage to Liberia," *African Repository* 34, no. 4 (April 1858): 110–111.

5. "Marine List," *African Repository* 11, no. 11 (November 1835): 341; the

description of Monrovia is compiled from numerous sources, including a summary of a letter from Beverly Wilson, November 1833, published in *African Repository* 11, no. 8 (August 1835): 244; Miller, *"Dear Master,"* 40; Clegg, *Price of Liberty,* 81–82; Mathew Carey, *Letters on the Colonization Society and on Its Probable Results,* 7th ed. (Philadelphia, Pa.: I. Johnson, 1833), 24, 26.

6. All quoted text from the Major and Harlan letters comes from the Major Collection of Letters from Liberia, McLean County Museum of History, Bloomington, Illinois, and is used with permission (with the exception of two letters to James Moore that were published in the *African Repository* and are cited separately).

7. Bell I. Wiley, *Slaves No More: Letters from Liberia 1833–1869* (Lexington: Univ. Press of Kentucky, 1980), 57; Innes, *Liberia,* 2; Clegg, *Price of Liberty,* 86.

8. Clegg, *Price of Liberty,* 68, 69, 160, 230.

9. J. W. Lugenbeel, "Sketches of Liberia. No. 3," *African Repository* 26, no. 8 (August 1850): 230.

10. J. W. Lugenbeel to Rev. R. R. Gurley, January 17, 1844, *African Repository* 20 (1844): 146, Liberian Collections, Indiana University Libraries, Bloomington, Indiana.

11. J. W. Lugenbeel, "Sketches of Liberia. No. 7," *African Repository* 26, no. 12 (December 1850): 377–378; "Forty-First Annual Report of the American Colonization Society," *African Repository* 34, no. 3 (March 1858): 68.

12. "Brig *Luna*'s Company," 269–271. This passenger list/roll of emigrants indicates that nine-year-old Washington Major died of fever in 1836, but subsequent letters from Tolbert indicate that Washington died between May 1839 and August 1843.

13. Innes, *Liberia,* 29, 49–53; Tom W. Shick, *Behold the Promised Land: A History of Afro-American Settler Society in Nineteenth-Century Liberia* (Baltimore, Md.: Johns Hopkins Univ. Press, 1977, 1980), 30.

14. Wiley, *Slaves No More,* 57; Innes, *Liberia,* 51; Murray, "Whiteness in Africa," 3 (citing *Journal of an African Cruiser* by Horatio Bridge, edited by Nathaniel Hawthorne); Lamin Sanneh, *Abolitionists Abroad: American Blacks and the Making of Modern West Africa* (Cambridge, Mass.: Harvard Univ. Press, 1999), 205.

15. "Sentiments in London on African Colonization," *African Repository* 24, no. 2 (February 1848): note on page 49.

16. C. Patrick Burrowes, *Between the Kola Forest and the Salty Sea: A History of the Liberian People before 1830* (Bomi County, Liberia: Know Your Self Press, 2016), 261.

17. Warren d'Azevedo, "Tribal Reaction to Nationalism, Part 1," *Liberian Studies Journal* 1, no. 2 (spring 1969): 6–7, 13–14.

18. Innes, *Liberia,* 98–99.

19. Carey, *Letters on the Colonization Society,* 26.

20. Wiley, *Slaves No More,* 6.

21. Catherine Reef, *This Our Dark Country: The American Settlers of Liberia* (New York: Clarion, 2002), 49.

22. Clegg, *The Price of Liberty,* 86.

23. Miller, *"Dear Master,"* 53.

24. James Amemasor, who examined and wrote about the Major letters for his master's thesis, speculated that George Major and Henry were Joseph Major's sons. Joseph Major did have sons named George and Henry; however, George was born in 1826. He would have been only ten when this letter was written. Henry was not born until 1838, two years after this letter was penned. It seems unlikely that Tolbert would be urging a ten-year-old white child to come to Africa. It seems far more probable that he was referring to two of Joseph Major's slaves who used his surname. James Amemasor, "A Taste of Freedom: The Benjamin Major Collection of Letters from Emancipated American Slaves in Liberia, 1836–1851," Master's thesis, Illinois State University, 2004.

25. Clegg, *Price of Liberty,* 177–179, 187–188.

26. US Census, 1820–1840.

7. Bowing the Knee to Slavery

1. "Elijah Parish Lovejoy: 'A Martyr on the Altar of American Liberty,'" *Alton Observer,* November 7, 1837, reproduced on http://www.altonweb.com/history/lovejoy/ao1.html; "Elijah Parish Lovejoy," National Abolition Hall of Fame and Museum, https://www.nationalabolitionhalloffameandmuseum.org/elijah-parish-lovejoy.html (accessed October 27, 2016); "Elijah Parish Lovejoy Was Killed by a Proslavery Mob," http://www.americaslibrary.gov/jb/reform/jb_reform_lovejoy_1.html (accessed October 27, 2016).

2. See Tallant, *Evil Necessity,* for an excellent exploration of the shift in thinking about slavery.

3. "Bowing the Knee to Slavery," *Pittsburgh Gazette,* December 19, 1836.

4. "The Nullifiers and Abolitionists," *Raleigh Weekly Standard,* June 16, 1836.

5. "Bowing the Knee to Slavery," *Pittsburgh Gazette,* December 19, 1836.

6. "Struggles over Slavery: The Gag Rule," National Archives, http:/www.archives.gov/exhibits/treasures_of_congress/text/page10_text.html; "Slavery and the Making of America," Public Broadcasting Service, http://www.pbs.org/wnet/slavery/; US Congressional Documents and Debates, 1774–1874, 882–883, Library of Congress, American Memory, http://memory.loc.gov/ammem/hlawquery.html; "The House Gag Rule," US House of Representatives, History, Art and Archives, http://history.house.gov/Historical-Highlights/1800-1850/The-House-of-Representatives-instituted-the-%E2%80%9Cgag-rule%E2%80%9D/.

8. We Are All Needy

1. The May 1839 letter has a hole in it, and large sections of text on both the first and second pages are missing. However, an unidentified person long ago handwrote a transcription of Tolbert's original letter to Ben Major. The transcription in this book includes wording from the handwritten transcription in the file.

2. Wilkeson, *Concise History of Liberia,* 70; American Colonization Society, *Memorial of the Semi-centennial Anniversary of the American Colonization Society* (Washington, D.C.: American Colonization Society, 1867), 181, https://books.google.com/books?id=QC4OAAAAIAAJ.

3. G. W. McElroy to Reverend R. R. Gurley, n.d., published in the *Pittsburgh Gazette,* January 13, 1836.

4. Maurice Zwass, "Unpublished Letter from Bassa Cove in 1847 from a Black American Missionary: Political and Medical Significance," a paper presented at the Liberian Studies Association annual meeting, April 1976, Bloomington, Indiana, 3–6.

5. *Colonization and Abolition Contrasted* (Philadelphia: Herman Hooker, n. d.), 14.

6. "Brig *Luna's* Company," 269–271; "Liberia as It Is," *Boston Recorder,* June 15, 1838 (republishing an article that appeared in the *Colonization Herald*), American Periodicals, 96 (found at the National Museum of American History; the initials "T. B." appear at the bottom of the article; possibly Thomas Buchanan wrote it); Clegg, *Price of Liberty,* 153.

7. Clegg, *Price of Liberty,* 154.

8. Ibid., 155–57.

9. Governor Finley was the son of Robert Finley, one of the founders of the American Colonization Society; there is no tribe called the Fishmen and it is unclear to which ethnic group these warriors belonged; Wilkeson, *Concise History of Liberia,* 77; American Colonization Society, *Memorial of the Semi-centennial Anniversary,* 181; see also Clegg, *Price of Liberty,* 146–147; extract of letter from Governor Thomas Buchanan, May 17, 1839, in Svend Holsoe Collection, Liberian Collections, Indiana University Libraries, Bloomington, Indiana.

10. "Departure of the Emigrants," *Christian Watchman* (Boston), July 15, 1836, American Periodicals, 115.

11. "Governor Roberts' Annual Message," *African Repository* 21, no. 5 (May 1845): 132.

12. Peyton Skipwith to John H. Cocke, May 20, 1839, in Wiley, *Slaves No More,* 48–49.

13. "Governor Thomas Buchanan's Dispatch, May 17, 1839," *African Repository* 16 (1840): 50–52.

14. Charles H. Bell to Reverend Alfred Chester, April 3, 1840, *African Repository* 16 (1840): 295, Liberian Collections, Indiana University Libraries, Bloomington, Indiana.

15. Clegg, *Price of Liberty,* 80.

16. Peyton Skipwith to John H. Cocke, April 22, 1840, in Wiley, *Slaves No More,* 53; Simon Harrison to William McLain, September 10, 1853, in Wiley, *Slaves No More,* 242.

17. Description of huts, John N. Lewis, December 8, 1848, originally published in the *Philadelphia Ledger* and republished in the *Maryland Colonization Journal* 4, no. 20 (February 1849), 314–315, Liberian Collections, Indiana University Libraries, Bloomington, Indiana; Wiley, *Slaves No More,* 338.

18. Wiley, *Slaves No More*, 7.

19. Marie Tyler-McGraw, "Patrick Bullock: Abandoned in Liberia." Virginia Emigrants to Liberia, Virginia Center for Digital History, University of Virginia, www.vcdh.virginia.edu/liberia/index.php?page=Stories&section=Patrick%20Bullock.

20. Henry B. Stewart to William McLain, October 20, 1849, in Wiley, *Slaves No More*, 282.

21. "Things Which Every Emigrant to Liberia Ought to Know," *African Repository* 24, no. 4 (April 1848): 111–114; "Outfit for Emigrants," *African Repository* 24, no. 4 (April 1848): 119.

22. "Governor Roberts' Annual Message," 134.

23. Carey, *Letters on the Colonization Society*, 16; Wilkeson, *Concise History of Liberia*, 54; also see "African Colonization," *Louisville Courier-Journal*, August 31, 1836.

9. We Have Had War with the Natives

1. Enoch Harlan was born into slavery in about 1795, probably in Berkley County, Virginia (now West Virginia), to parents whose names are lost in time. His owners, the seven Harlan brothers, moved with their widowed mother to Christian County, Kentucky, sometime after 1812.

2. US census records list four men named James Moore living in Christian County in 1830.

3. 1843 Liberian census.

4. Burin, *Slavery and the Peculiar Solution*, 17.

5. By 1843, colonization officials had realized that the danger from malaria was higher near the shore and at nighttime ("Annual Report of the American Colonization Society," *African Repository* 19, no. 3 [March 1843]: 88). They learned to establish colonies farther inland and to schedule ships to arrive in the dry season. The settlers learned from indigenous people how to treat the disease. These strategies helped reduce the mortality rate.

6. Clayne L. Pope, "Adult Mortality in America before 1900: A View from Family Histories," in *Strategic Factors in Nineteenth Century American Economic History*, ed. Claudia Goldin and Hugh Rockoff (Chicago: Univ. of Chicago Press, 1992), 286. http://www.nber.org/chapters/c6965.

7. Murray, "Whiteness in Africa," 19–20, 166, 176, 197.

8. Alpheus H. Harlan, *History and Genealogy of the Harlan Family and Particularly the Descendants of George and Michael Harlan* (Baltimore, Md.: Gateway, 1914), 104.

9. Ibid., 268. George Harlan was from a well-known family. Harlan County, Kentucky, was named for one of his relatives, and Supreme Court Associate Justice John Marshall Harlan, who wrote the dissent to *Plessy v. Ferguson*, was also related to him. Kentucky Pension Roll of 1835, Ancestry.com, https://www.ancestry.com/search/collections/flhg-kypensionroll/?name=George_Harlan&name_x=s_s.

10. Slaves were not permitted to legally marry, so Agnes and Enoch's marriage would have been an informal one; Christian County, Kentucky, Order Book F, 374–375.

11. US Census, 1830.

12. Harlan, *History and Genealogy of the Harlan Family,* 268–269.

13. Charles A. Walker, ed. *History of Macoupin County, Illinois: Biographical and Pictorial,* vol. 1 (Chicago: S. J. Clarke Pub. Co., 1911); US General Land Office Records, 1796–1907, on Ancestry.com, accessed December 4, 2012. Like Ben, George may have hired out his slaves after he moved to Illinois and before they migrated to Liberia; Samuel H. Williamson and Louis P. Cain, "Measuring Slavery in 2009 Dollars," http://www.measuringworth.com/slavery.php, figure 5, "Real Price of Owning a Slave in 2009 Dollars," recalculated to 2017 dollars using MeasuringWorth.com.

14. Burrowes, *Kola Forest,* 324–325.

10. My Heart Yet Bleeds

1. Information on Emily Thomas Tubman's life comes from multiple sources: "After Many Days" (obituary), *Augusta Chronicle,* June 9, 1885; "Mrs. Tubman's Death," *Augusta Chronicle,* June 10, 1885; Donald Nunnelly, "Emily Tubman: A Disciple Wonder Woman," Disciples of Christ Historical Society; Georgia Women of Achievement, "Emily Harvie Thomas Tubman," http://www.georgiawomen.org/copy-of-thomas-ella-gertrude-clanto; Bettye Lee Mastin, "Liberia's Tubman Had Local Ties," *Lexington Herald-Leader,* May 20, 1980; John D. Simmons, "A Memorial to Emily Thomas Tubman, 1794–1885," *Augusta Chronicle,* July 1985; George Darsie, "Mrs. Emily H. Tubman," in *Churches of Christ: A Historical, Biographical, and Pictorial History of Churches of Christ,* ed. John T. Brown (Louisville, Ky.: Morton, 1904); Russell R. Rechenbach II, "Emily Tubman of Kentucky," an address given in commemoration of Emily Tubman's 200th birthday, March 19, 1994, at Augusta First Christian Church, Augusta, Georgia; "Mrs. Emily H. Tubman," *Christian Standard,* June 1885.

2. His body was later moved to St. Paul's Episcopal Church in Augusta.

3. Burin, *Slavery and the Peculiar Solution,* 123; will of Richard Tubman, Georgia Wills and Probate Records, 1742–1992, from Wills, vol. A–B, 1798–1853, Ancestry.com, https://search.ancestry.com/cgi-bin/sse.dll?indiv=1&dbid=8635&h=499393&tid=&pid=&usePUB=true&_phsrc=oNP1&_phstart=successSource.

4. Emily Tubman to Rev. Ralph R. Gurley, March 20, 1837, American Colonization Society Records, vol. 66, reel 27, Library of Congress Manuscript Collection, Washington, D.C.

5. Wilkeson, *Concise History of Liberia,* 70.

6. Catherine Clinton, *The Plantation Mistress: Woman's World in the Old South* (New York: Pantheon, 1982).

7. Mary Boykin Chesnut, *Mary Chesnut's Civil War,* ed. C. Vann Woodward (New Haven, Conn.: Yale Univ. Press, 1981), 29, https://books.google.com/books?isbn=0300024592.

8. Burin, *Slavery and the Peculiar Solution,* 49–50, 52.

9. "The Late Expedition for Liberia," *African Repository* 26, no. 4 (April 1850): 103–106.

10. See lists of contributors in issues of the *African Repository*; these examples are from vol. 18, no. 13 (November 1842): 34–35; vol. 19, no. 2 (February 1843): 67–68; and vol. 19, no. 3 (March 1843): 85; *Pittsburgh Gazette*, October 7, 1836.

11. "Munificent Donations," *African Repository* 11, no. 7 (July 1835): 211.

12. "Another Expedition Sailed for Liberia," *African Repository* 20, no. 7 (July 1844): 220; Tyler-McGraw, *An African Republic*, 89.

13. Burin, *Slavery and the Peculiar Solution*, 103–104; Wilkeson, *Concise History of Liberia*, 46. Mercer's dedication to the cause was costly to her in terms of reputation in her community and finances. After freeing her slaves, she started a small school to support herself and her family, but she struggled for the rest of her life; Burin, *Slavery and the Peculiar Solution*, 34.

14. John Hartwell Cocke to George Fitzhugh, 1853, cited in Tyler-McGraw, *An African Republic*, 97.

15. Elizabeth Fox-Genovese, *Within the Plantation Household: Black and White Women of the Old South* (Chapel Hill: Univ. of North Carolina Press, 1988), 138.

16. Burin, *Slavery and the Peculiar Solution*, 67; Clegg, *Price of Liberty*, 222.

17. Murray, "Whiteness in Africa," 255–258; Wiley, *Slaves No More*, 333n1; and Tyler-McGraw, *An African Republic*, 169, 177. In recent years, the in-person delivery of the quilt has been disputed.

18. Tyler-McGraw, *An African Republic*, 71, 136.

19. Clegg, *Price of Liberty*, 204–205.

20. Tyler-McGraw, *An African Republic*, 154, 155, 165; Colston's death date, August 12, 1834, is also recorded in the *African Repository* 11, no. 1 (January 1835): 29.

21. Harriet G. Waring to Rev. R. R. Gurley, March 5, 1835, American Colonization Society Records, vol. 64, reel 25, Library of Congress Manuscript Collection, Washington, D.C.

22. Tyler-McGraw, *An African Republic*, 154, 155.

11. We Stand in Great Need of Seed

1. Alice A. Dunnigan, ed., *The Fascinating Story of Black Kentuckians: Their Heritage and Tradition* (Washington, D.C.: Associated Publishers, 1982), 14.

2. One definition for *scion* is a living shoot, bud, or twig of a plant used for grafting.

3. Importation of cassava, Burrowes, *Kola Forest*, 320–321; J. W. Lugenbeel, "Sketches of Liberia. No. 4," *African Repository* 26, no. 9 (September 1850): 279.

4. Buchanan to Wilkeson, December 13, 1840.

5. Bill of Lading for the *May Wilkes*, January 7, 1847, American Colonization Society Records, microfilm vol. 104, reel 51, Library of Congress Manuscript Collection, Washington, D.C.

6. Burin, *Slavery and the Peculiar Solution,* 150, 153.

7. Governor Thomas Buchanan to the board of the American Colonization Society, November 6, 1839, *African Repository* 16 (1840): 71–72, Liberian Collections, Indiana University Libraries, Bloomington, Indiana.

8. Ibid.

9. Ibid.

10. Governor Thomas Buchanan to Samuel Wilkeson, December 13, 1840, *African Repository* 17 (1841): 83, Liberian Collections, Indiana University Libraries, Bloomington, Indiana.

11. "Dr. Hall's Answers to Mr. Key's Questions," *African Repository,* 28, no. 13 (November 1842): 342, Major Family Private Collection.

12. Historical documents spell the location in various ways; the river for which the region is named is spelled both New Sess and New Cess.

13. Governor Thomas Buchanan to Samuel Wilkeson, July 1, 1840, *African Repository* 16 (1840): 277, Liberian Collections, Indiana University Libraries, Bloomington, Indiana.

14. Thomas Buchanan to Sam Wilkeson, August 10, 1839, *African Repository* 14 (1839): 283.

15. Buchanan to Wilkeson, December 13, 1840; Governor Thomas Buchanan to Samuel Wilkeson, June 10, 1841, *African Repository* 17 (1841): 258, Liberian Collections, Indiana University Libraries, Bloomington, Indiana.

16. "Dr. Hall's Answers," 346.

17. Joseph Jenkins Roberts to the executive committee of the American Colonization Society, June 9, 1842, *African Repository* 19, no. 1 (January 1843): 10–11.

12. Affectionately, Your Friend and Brother

1. John D. Trefzger, "Our People, Our Pastors, 1837–1987" (Bloomington, Ill.: First Christian Church (Disciples of Christ), 1987, unnumbered pages; Haynes, *History of the Disciples of Christ in Illinois,* 564; Eugenia J. Hunt, "Pioneer Recalled," *Bloomington (Ill.) Daily Pentagraph,* March 10, 1937.

2. US Census, 1830; his name is spelled as Chasteen Major. His first name is variously spelled on other documents as Chastain and Chastene; John D. Trefzger, "Pioneer Disciple: William T. Major," *Discipliana* (October 1967), 45.

3. Alexander Campbell and W. K. Pendleton, "Our Tour to the West," *Millennial Harbinger* 3 (1846): 204; William Davenport, letter to the editor (Barton W. Stone), *Christian Messenger* 6 (1832), 245; obituary, "Elder William Davenport," *Daily Nebraska Press,* June 28, 1869. A record of immigrants to Liberia through 1843 does not list any settlers with the surname Davenport. That does not disprove the assertion that some of his formerly enslaved people migrated there; many formerly enslaved people chose to change their names when they obtained their freedom.

4. Joseph Major to Ben Major, February 10, 1850, and other letters, Major Family Private Collection.

5. Joseph Major to Ben Major, December 31, 1841, Major Family Private Collection.

6. Joseph Major to Ben Major, September 38, 1837, and February 10, 1850, Major Family Private Collection.

7. US Census, 1820–1860.

8. Ben Major to Joseph Major, May 3, 1840, Major Family Private Collection.

9. Ibid.

10. Ibid.

13. The Dark Clouds Begin to Disappear

1. Miller, *"Dear Master,"* 51.

2. Clegg, *Price of Liberty,* 82.

3. Governor Thomas Buchanan, Dispatch to the board of the American Colonization Society, September 1, 1840, *African Repository* 16 (1840): 334, Liberian Collections, Indiana University Libraries, Bloomington, Indiana; William E. Allen, "Liberia and the Atlantic World in the Nineteenth Century," *History in Africa* 37 (2010): 41.

4. 1843 Liberian census.

14. I Cannot Banish the Horrid Picture

1. Governor Thomas Buchanan to board of American Colonization Society, November 6, 1839, *African Repository* 16 (1840): 74.

2. Ibid., 75.

3. W. B. Hoyt to the editors, December 15, 1845, *African Repository* 21 (1845): 143–144, Liberian Collections, Indiana University Libraries, Bloomington, Indiana.

15. I Will Send You Some Coffee

1. Sue Grant recalled this meeting and Ben Major's words in Elmira Dickinson's *A History of Eureka College,* 218–219. Washington, Illinois, had an auxiliary colonization society; it is likely that Ben belonged to that chapter; American Colonization Society Records, microfilm volume 57, reel 299, Library of Congress Manuscript Collection, Washington, D.C.

2. The roll of emigrants ("Brig *Luna's* Company," 269–271) indicates that Thomas Major died in 1839 of an unknown cause. If that were the case, then it seems likely that either Tolbert or Austin would have informed Ben of the death earlier, perhaps in the letters of October 1840.

3. The 1843 Liberian census lists the Harlans under the name Hubbard.

4. Clegg, *Price of Liberty*, 159.

5. Sanneh, *Abolitionists Abroad*, 214.

6. "Pale faces" in James C. Minor to John Minor, February 11, 1833, *African Repository* 9 no. 6 (June 1833): 127, HathiTrust.org, https://hdl.handle.net/2027/hvd.32044010585735; Abraham Blackford to Mary B. Blackford, February 14, 1846, *African Repository* 22, no. 8 (August 1846): 261, HathiTrust.org, https://hdl.handle.net/2027/hvd.hwrch7; James P. Skipwith to Berthier Edwards, May 31, 1860, in Wiley, *Slaves No More*, 24, 95.

7. William C. Burke to Ralph R. Gurley, March 6, 1857, in Wiley, *Slaves No More*, 197.

8. Graham Greene, *Journey without Maps* (New York: Penguin, 2006; first published in Great Britain by William Heinemann, 1936), 94.

9. Burin, *Slavery and the Peculiar Solution*, 67–69.

10. Clegg, *Price of Liberty*, 187.

11. "Carry Me Back to Old Virginia!" *Detroit Free Press*, January 16, 1859; "Returning to Slavery," *American Advocate* (Kingston, N.C.), February 24, 1859.

16. This Accursed Thing Slavery

1. Wesley Harlan to Ben Major, April 4, 1844, Major Collection of Letters from Africa, McLean County Museum of History, Bloomington, Illinois.

2. Allen, "Liberia and the Atlantic World," 27.

3. Carey, *Letters on the Colonization Society*, 29.

4. *The Liberator*, November 19, 1836, American Periodicals, 188 (found at the National Museum of American History).

5. Governor Thomas Buchanan to the Honorable Council of Liberia, September 5, 1839, *African Repository* 16 (1840): 36–37.

6. "The Slave Trade," *African Repository* 26, no. 12 (December 1850): 361.

7. Wiley, *Slaves No More*, 2.

8. Liberian Constitution of 1839, http://liberianforum.com/articles/constitution1839.htm.

9. Several women from Bassa Cove, including a Mrs. E. Harland (Wesley Harlan's wife), appealed to the colonization society for funds to erect a monument to Buchanan in Bassa Cove; "Monument to Governor Buchanan," *African Repository* 26, no. 11 (November 1850): 338. The date of Buchanan's death is from "Death of Gov. Buchanan," *Raleigh Register*, December 10, 1841.

10. George R. Ellis McDonogh to John McDonogh, May 14, 1844, in Wiley, *Slaves No More*, 133.

11. James McGeorge to John McDonogh, May 20, 1844, in Wiley, *Slaves No More*, 135.

17. Decidedly Antislavery

1. Records of the First Christian Church of Bloomington, Illinois, at the Disciples of Christ Historical Society. (This organization, now in Bethany, West Virginia, was previously in Nashville, Tennessee.)

2. *History of Tazewell County* (Chicago: Chas. C. Chapman and Co., 1879), 552; *Portrait and Biographical Record of Tazewell and Mason County, Illinois* (Chicago: Biographical Publishing, 1894), 432; Lindsey family records and gravestones. (James Alfred Lindsey is the author's great-great-great grandfather.)

3. Will of Thomas Bullock, dated January 1, 1834, copy at Kentucky Historical Society, Frankfort, Kentucky (typed notation indicates it is from Will Book L, 523); US Census, 1820 and 1830. The 1843 Liberian census lists several people with the last name Bullock.

4. Haynes, *Disciples of Christ in Illinois,* 657; N. S. Haynes, "The Disciples of Christ in Illinois and Their Attitudes toward Slavery," *Transactions of the Illinois State Historical Society for the Year 1913* (Springfield, Ill.: Board of Trustees, Illinois State Historical Society, 1913), 52–59, https://books.google.com/books?id=nUgvIFmyZoMC&printsec=frontcover&source=gbs_ge_summary_r&cad=0#v=onepage&q&f=false.

5. Clegg, *Price of Liberty,* 165; Williamson and Cain, figure 5. The authors note that the "real price" attempts to account for the impact of inflation and gives an idea of the purchasing cost of a slave in 2009 dollars. The original figure from 2009 has been updated using the DollarTimes.com calculator.

6. "Proceedings of the American Colonization Society," *African Repository* 11, no. 2 (February 1835): 50; *African Repository* 11, no. 10 (October 1835): 319.

7. James Wrial to the American Colonization Society, May 29, 1848, and James Rial Starkey to the American Colonization Society, July 12, 1848, *African Repository* 24, no. 10 (October 1848): 304–305.

8. James R. Starkey, correspondence with Reverend W. N. Hawks, and the American Colonization Society, May to October 1850, *African Repository* 26, no. 12 (December 1850): 366–368.

18. I Have Been in the Legislature

1. Wesley Horland [Harlan], "Letters from Bassa Cove," *African Repository* 23, no. 9 (September 1847): 279–281. Four men named James Moore are listed in the 1830 census for Christian County, Kentucky—two are listed with no middle initial, one is James W., and one is James S.; Christian County Genealogical Society, *Family Histories: Christian County, Kentucky, 1797–1986* (Nashville, Tenn.: Turner, 1986), 303.

2. Horland [Harlan], "Letters from Bassa Cove." Both letters are lengthy and are extracted in this chapter. In the appendix, they appear as they were published in the *African Repository* 23, no. 9 (September 1847): 279–281.

3. "Brig *Luna*'s Company," 269–271.

4. "Liberia as It Is," *Boston Recorder,* June 15, 1838; "Massachusetts Colonization Society," *African Repository* 20, no. 7 (July 1844): 212.

5. "Cheerful Intelligence from Bassa Cove," *Boston Recorder,* August 10, 1838, American Periodicals, 127 (found at the National Museum of American History).

6. 1843 Liberian census.

7. Austin mentioned his wife in letters written after this, and Silvay herself wrote a letter to Ben in 1851.

8. Joseph J. Roberts to Reverend A. M. Cowan, circa March 1846, published in *Western Citizen* (Paris, Kentucky), May 23, 1846, republished in J. Winston Coleman, *Slavery Times in Kentucky,* 281.

9. Stephen A. Benson to Reverend William McLain, April 7, 1846, *African Repository* 22 (1846): 306, Liberian Collections, Indiana University Libraries, Bloomington, Indiana.

10. See the full text of his letter in the appendix.

11. Murray, "Whiteness in Africa," 107.

12. William Coppinger, "Methodist Episcopal Missions in Liberia," first published in *Christian Repository* and reprinted in *African Repository* 24, no. 10 (October 1848): 293. Payne's occupation is listed in the 1843 Liberian census.

13. Murray, "Whiteness in Africa," 221.

14. July, *Origins of Modern African Thought,* 215–217.

19. I Am Nothing but a Plain Christian

1. Ben Major to Rev. W. McLain, March 29, 1846, American Colonization Society Records, vol. 101, reel 48, Library of Congress Manuscript Collection, Washington, D.C. (Ben misspelled McLain as McLean.)

2. Ben Major to Alexander Campbell, 1829; Alexander Campbell to Ben Major, September 12, 1838; circular and prospectus for *Millennial Harbinger,* 1845; *Christian Disciple* flyer, 1845; and list of *Millennial Harbinger* subscribers, June 14, 1847; Major Family Private Collection.

3. *Portrait and Biographical Record of Tazewell and Mason County, Illinois,* 432–433; Lindsey family genealogical records.

4. Campbell and Pendleton, "Our Tour to the West," 204.

5. William Yates, ed., *Woodford County History* (Woodford County, Ill.: Woodford County Board of Supervisors, 1968), 126.

6. American Colonization Society, *Twentieth Annual Report of the American Colonization Society,* 7–8.

20. I Want to See You and Your Wife and Children Very Bad

1. Lindsey Apple, *The Family Legacy of Henry Clay: In the Shadow of a Kentucky Patriarch* (Lexington: Univ. Press of Kentucky, 2011), 6–7.

2. Miller, *"Dear Master,"* 23.

3. Innes, *Liberia,* 140–141.

4. 1843 Liberian census.

5. William C. Burke to Ralph R. Gurley, December 10, 1856, in Wiley, *Slaves No More,* 195.

6. Matilda Skipwith Lomax to John H. Cocke, September 30, 1850, in Miller, *"Dear Master,"* 105; Miller, *"Dear Master,"* 109.

7. Peyton Skipwith to John H. Cocke, June 25, 1846, and Diana Skipwith to Sally Cocke, August 24, 1837, in Miller, *"Dear Master,"* 83, 88.

8. "From Western Africa," *Pittsburgh Gazette,* September 9, 1836.

21. The Love of Liberty Brought Us Here

1. All quotations in this section and details of the day's events are from "Celebration of the Twenty-fourth of August" and "The Twenty-fourth," *African Repository* 24, no. 1 (January 1848): 14–17.

2. J. W. Lugenbeel to Reverend William McLain, February 8, 1847, *African Repository* 23 (May 1847): 139–140, Liberian Collections, Indiana University Libraries, Bloomington, Indiana.

3. Letter from Samuel Mercer, Commander, US Navy, to Elliot Cresson, Philadelphia, May 12, 1848, *African Repository* 24, no. 10 (October 1848): 290.

4. J. J. Roberts, letter dated January 4, 1847, *African Repository* 23, no. 5 (May 1847): 152–153, Liberian Collections, Indiana University Libraries, Bloomington, Indiana.

5. *Liberian Declaration of Independence,* https://emansion.gov.lr/doc/Presidentialdeclaration.pdf.

6. The requirements for indigenous citizenship are in "Massachusetts Colonization Society," 214.

7. Joseph J. Roberts to Reverend William McLain, July 15, 1850, Liberian Collections, Indiana University Libraries, Bloomington, Indiana; a notation on a copy of the letter indicates the original is in the American Colonization Society microfilm, reel 155, no. 99688.

8. Murray, "Whiteness in Africa," 181; J. W. Lugenbeel, "Religion among the Congoes by the *Pons*," *African Repository* 24, no. 2 (February 1848): 37; J. J. Roberts to William McLain, May 19, 1851, in Liberian Collections, Liberian Letters, 1836–1858, Indiana University Libraries, Bloomington, Indiana.

9. Mercer to Elliott, May 12, 1848.

10. Henrietta Fuller McDonogh to John McDonogh, October 24, 1849, in Wiley, *Slaves No More,* 153.

11. Sion Harris to William McLain, March 3, 1853, in Wiley, *Slaves No More,* 241.

12. Hilary Teage, "Extract from a letter from the Hon. H. Teage to Rev. J. B. Pinney," *African Repository* 29, no. 1 (January 1853): 17, HathiTrust.org, https://hdl.handle.net/2027/hvd.hwrchr.

22. Men of Advanced Views on the Subject of Education

1. Dickinson, *A History of Eureka College*, 25.

2. Ibid., 18.

3. W. C. Channing, "What is Education," *Millennial Harbinger* 4, no. 9 (September 1840): 430.

4. Receipt for Ben Major from Lands and Hawks, May 1837, and receipt from E. D. Perrin, dated May 20, 1846, both in Major Family Private Collection. Ben Major had three nieces named Mary: Joseph's daughter, Chastine's daughter, and his sister Eliza's child, Mary Ann. The Mary referred to in the memo is undoubtedly Chastine's daughter, as Joseph's Mary hadn't been born in 1846 and Eliza's daughter's last name was Davenport.

5. Dickinson, *A History of Eureka College*, 18–19, and Harold Adams, *The History of Eureka College* (Eureka, Ill.: Board of Trustees of Eureka College, 1982), 19–20.

6. Dickinson, *A History of Eureka College*, 21; copy of handwritten agreement between William Bogardus and Elijah Dickinson, dated April 21, 1849, Major Family Private Collection; Radford, *Autobiography*, 1.

7. Dickinson, *A History of Eureka College*, 22.

8. Ibid., 23–24.

9. Ben Major to Joseph Major, January 11, 1850, Major Family Private Collection.

10. Adams, *The History of Eureka College*, 25.

11. William Davenport to Ben Major, November 28, 1850, Major Family Private Collection.

12. "Catalogue of the Officers and Students of Walnut Grove Academy, Eureka, Woodford Co., Illinois, for the Session Ending July 4, 1852." Found in a scrapbook belonging to Ben Major's granddaughter, Major Family Private Collection.

13. Adams, *The History of Eureka College*, 11.

14. Dickinson, *A History of Eureka College*, 45.

23. I Am a Free Man in a Free Country

1. This letter is long and disjointed; the sequence of a few sentences has been shifted to improve readability. A verbatim transcription appears in the appendix.

2. Wiley, *Slaves No More*, 323; Joseph Major to Ben Major, November 27, 1837, February 26, 1839, and September 13, 1839, Major Family Private Collection.

3. Ben Major's notebook, Major Family Private Collection.

4. Thomas Hersey, ed., "Ravages of Cholera at Campeachy [*sic*]," *Thomsonian Recorder* 2, no. 15 (April 26, 1834): 232; L. S. Major to Ben Major, May 28, 1849, Major Family Private Collection.

5. Robert M. Page to Charles W. Andrews, October 28, 1849, in Wiley, *Slaves No More*, 112.

6. "Liberia as It Is," *Boston Recorder*, June 15, 1838.

7. Wiley, *Slaves No More*, 133; Sion Harris to William McLain, September 20, 1850, *African Repository* 27, no. 1 (January 1851): 18, HathiTrust.org, https://hdl.handle.net/2027/hvd.hwrchp.

8. Kleber, ed., *Kentucky Encyclopedia*, s.v. "Land Between the Lakes," 534.

9. Wiley, *Slaves No More*, 6.

10. "Late Intelligence from Liberia" (a reprint of a June 30, 1848, article from the *Liberian Herald*), *African Repository* 24, no. 9 (September 1848): 282.

11. Wiley, *Slaves No More*, 8.

12. Joseph Jenkins Roberts to Don Jose Zerresti, December 22, 1847, *African Repository* 24, no. 4 (April 1848): 103.

13. "Relations between the American Colonization Society and the Republic of Liberia," *African Repository* 24, no. 9 (September 1848): 257–259.

14. John N. Lewis to Reverend William McLain, April 5, 1848, in Svend Holsoe Collection, Liberian Collections, Indiana University Libraries, Bloomington, Indiana. (A note on the copy reads ACS, reel 154, no. 99345, which may refer to the American Colonization Society collection in the Library of Congress.) "Citizens of Liberia in the United States" and "Movements among the Colored People," *African Repository* 24, no. 9 (September 1848): 259–263.

15. "Citizens of Liberia in the United States," *African Repository* 24 (September 1848): 260, HathiTrust.org, https://hdl.handle.net/2027/hvd.hwrch9.

16. Wiley, *Slaves No More*, 2.

24. Send Me Some Carpenter Tools (and Bonnets)

1. Wiley, *Slaves No More*, 154; Stephen A. Benson to American Colonization Society, October 22, 1849, Liberian Collections, Indiana University Libraries, Bloomington, Indiana. A note on the copy indicates the original is in American Colonization Society microfilm, reel 154, series IB, vol. 32, letter no. 125, doc. No. 99567, American Colonization Society Collection at the Library of Congress, Washington, D.C. Murray, "Whiteness in Africa," 297.

2. Clegg, *Price of Liberty*, 171; "From Liberia," *Louisville Courier-Journal*, May 26, 1849.

3. Benson to American Colonization Society, October 22, 1849, Liberian Collections, Indiana University Libraries, Bloomington, Indiana.

4. The ages cited in this book are based on those recorded in the roll of emigrants to Liberia ("Brig *Luna*'s Company," 269–271).

5. Annual rainfall on the Liberian coast is more than four times that of Seattle, Washington.

6. *African Repository* 24, no. 11 (November 1848): 351.

7. John Marston to F. H. Gregory, April 8, 1850, Liberian Collections, Indiana University, Libraries, Bloomington, Indiana.

8. Wiley, *Slaves No More,* 53, 78.

9. J. N. Lewis to Reverend William McLain, December 23, 1847, Liberian Collections, Indiana University Libraries, Bloomington, Indiana.

10. G. and C. Merriam to Joseph J. Roberts, April 30, 1851, *African Repository* 27, no. 2 (February 1852): 51, Liberian Collections, Indiana University Libraries, Bloomington, Indiana.

11. Sanneh, *Abolitionists Abroad,* 215.

12. Peter Ross and Robert Carter to John Ker, March 23, 1848, in Wiley, *Slaves No More,* 157.

25. We Have Not Lived in Vain

1. Margaretta Major, "Faith, Hope and Charity," March 4, 1846, Major Family Private Collection.

2. Radford, *Autobiography.*

3. Ben Major's account with Henkel Danforth, May 1846; receipt for chairs from Henkel Danforth, November 23, 1841; account with Gaunt Willard, 1848; all from Major Family Private Collection; also accounts from J. D. Gaunt, in estate records, Circuit Clerk's Office, Woodford County, Illinois, reel 103, record 322.

4. Sue E. Grant to Elmira Dickinson, March 2, 1893, in Dickinson, *A History of Eureka College,* 217; Dickinson, *A History of Eureka College,* 114–115.

5. Major Family Private Collection; Dickinson, *A History of Eureka College,* 115.

6. William T. Major to William Davenport, July 7, 1849, Major Family Private Collection.

26. He Was Killed by Those Barbarous People

1. Murray, "Whiteness in America," 179.

2. Joseph J. Roberts to Reverend Ralph Gurley, December 24, 1843, *African Repository* 20 (1844): 134, Liberian Collections, Indiana University Libraries, Bloomington, Indiana.

3. Joseph J. Roberts to Reverend William McLain, March 18, 1845, *African Repository* 21 (1845): 215, Liberian Collections, Indiana University Libraries, Bloomington, Indiana.

4. "Late and Important," *Southern Press* (Washington, D.C.), February 9, 1852, reprinting an article that originally appeared in the *New York Commercial Advertiser;* Wiley, *Slaves No More,* 319.

5. "Recent Intelligence from Liberia," *African Repository* 28, no. 3 (March 1852): 92–94.

6. Ibid., 94; "Late and Important," *Southern Press,* February 9, 1852.

7. "Late and Important," *Southern Press,* February 9, 1852.

8. Ibid.

9. "Recent Intelligence from Liberia," 92.

10. Ibid., 93.

11. Ibid., 93–94; "Late and Important," *Southern Press,* February 9, 1852. The *Lark* was donated to Liberia by the British government specifically to help suppress the slave trade (*African Repository* 26, no. 7 [July 1850]: 203).

12. Shick, *Behold the Promised Land,* 106.

13. Matilda Skipwith Lomax to John H. Cocke, January 27, 1852, in Wiley, *Slaves No More,* 74.

14. "Liberia," *American Baptist,* January 27, 1852, republished by the *Herald of Freedom* (Wilmington, Ohio), April 9, 1852.

15. B. J. Campell to Ben Major, February 17, 1852, Major Family Private Collection.

27. I Thirst to Meet You in Bright Glory

1. Dickinson, *A History of Eureka College,* 121–122.

2. Copy of an undated newspaper clipping, signed "Old Timer." The newspaper name is not known. Provided to the author by Annie Major-Dillard.

3. Roy L. Moore, *History of Woodford County: A Concise History of the Settlement and Growth of Woodford County* (Eureka, Ill.: Woodford County Republican, 1910), 37.

4. New York Passenger Lists, 1820–1957, Ancestry.com, https://search.ancestry.com/cgi-bin/sse.dll?indiv=1&dbid=7488&h=1321064&tid=&pid=&usePUB=true&_phsrc=HOk9&_phstart=successSource; *African Repository* 32, no. 8 (August 1856): 229; "Intelligence from Liberia," *Philadelphia Inquirer,* August 19, 1856. When Wesley left America as a nine-year-old in 1836, his name was recorded on the roll of emigrants as Wesley Harland (see "Brig *Luna*'s Company," 269–271), and he used the spelling "Harland" when he signed his name in letters he wrote in 1843 and 1844. In the 1846 letters published in the *African Repository,* his name was recorded as Wesley Horland and W. J. Horland. Perhaps he adopted the name John Wesley in honor of the founder of Methodism or maybe his name had always been John Wesley, but he had not previously used his first name.

5. Dickinson, *A History of Eureka College,* 118.

6. Murray, "Whiteness in Africa," 23, 25, 51, 68. Murray's dissertation presents an excellent discussion of perceptions and understanding of "whiteness," the effect that migration to Africa had on those who migrated, and how it altered how they perceived themselves and how they were perceived by others.

7. "Peoria Conference," *African Repository* 34, no. 10 (October 1858): 310.

8. Dickinson, *A History of Eureka College,* 118.

9. Ibid., 118. By 1858, Tolbert, his older sons, Austin's sons, and all of Wesley's brothers were dead. The only living Major males old enough to travel to America would have been Austin and Wesley. Wesley's departure from Liberia and his arrival in New York are documented, as is his involvement in the colonization movement; New York

Passenger Lists, 1820–1957; *African Repository* 32, no. 8 (August 1856): 229; "Intelligence from Liberia," *Philadelphia Inquirer*, August 19, 1856.

10. "The Next Legislature," *African Repository* 49, no. 8 (August 1873): 249; "American Relations with Liberia," *African Repository* 50, no. 8 (August 1874): 252.

Conclusion

1. Harrison, *Antislavery Movement in Kentucky*, 84; Jack Glazier, *Been Coming through Some Hard Times: Race, History, and Memory in Western Kentucky* (Knoxville: Univ. of Tennessee Press, 2012), 38–47.

2. Wiley, *Slaves No More*, 8, 11.

3. Tolbert Major to Ben Major, June 23, 1848, Major Collection of Letters from Liberia, McLean County Museum of History, Bloomington, Illinois.

Afterword

1. Joseph Jenkins Roberts, Dispatch to American Colonization Society, August 31, 1842, *African Repository* 19, no. 1 (January 1843): 21.

2. The town's name has also appeared in print as Harlansville or Harlingsville.

3. Bill of appraisement and estate inventory, Circuit Clerk's Office, Woodford County, Illinois, reel 103, record 322.

4. Estate auction flyer dated September 3, 1852, Melick Library, Eureka College, Eureka, Illinois.

5. US census, 1860.

6. *Past and Present of Woodford County, Illinois* (Chicago: Wm. Le Baron, Jr. and Co., 1878), 604–605; obituary in scrapbook of Ben Major's granddaughter, Major Family Private Collection; US census, 1870.

7. E. Duis, *The Good Old Times in McLean County, Illinois* (Bloomington, Ill.: Leader Publishing and Printing House, 1874), https://books.google.com/books?id=j U40AQAAMAAJ&printsec=frontcover&dq=The+Good+Old+Times+in+McLean+C ounty,+Illinois&hl=en&sa=X&ved=0ahUKEwj2_OOitdnUAhVBRyYKHdtnDicQ6 AEIKDAA#v=onepage&q=The%20Good%20Old%20Times%20in%20McLean%20 County%2C%20Illinois&f=false.

8. Joseph Major to Ben Major, April 29, 1839, Major Family Private Collection.

9. "Amount and articles sold at sale on 22 & 23 of November 1864 by J. A. Catlett, exc. of Joseph Major Deceased," Christian County Deed Book T, 188–200; "Settlement of the estate of Joseph Major," Christian County Will Book T, 374–377, June 9, 1866; will of Joseph Major, dated October 3, 1863, Christian County Will Book T, 446–448; "Valuable Christian County Farm for Sale," *Clarksville (Tenn.) Weekly Chronicle*, September 8, 1865.

10. Davenport, handwritten notes found at Kentucky Historical Society, Frankfort, Kentucky.

11. *The Biographical Record of Livingston and Woodford Counties, Illinois* (Chicago: S. J. Clarke Publishing, 1900), 522; William Davenport, notes in his family Bible, transcribed by his son, Benjamin Major Davenport, and found on file at the Kentucky Historical Society, Frankfort, Kentucky; William Davenport to Ben Major, January 16, circa 1844, Major Family Private Collection.

12. Haynes, *Disciples of Christ in Illinois,* 503; William Davenport obituary, June 28, 1869.

13. "Historical Pageant to Be Given on Eureka College Anniversary," *Pantagraph* (Bloomington, Ill.), June 8, 1930.

14. Ted Olsen, "Disciples of Christ Board Apologizes for Not Doing More to Oppose Slavery," *Christianity Today,* May 1, 2001, http://www.christianitytoday.com/ct/2001/mayweb-only/5-7-44.0.html.

15. Harlan, *History and Genealogy of the Harlan Family,* 268–269.

16. US General Land Office Records, 1776–2015, Ancestry.com, https://www.ancestry.com/search/collections/blmlandpatents/?name=George_Harlan&event=_macoupin-illinois-usa_1849&name_x=s_s, and Illinois Public Land Purchase Records, 1800–1900, on Ancestry.com.

17. *Portrait and Biographical Record of Macoupin County, Illinois* (Chicago: Biographical Publishing, 1891).

18. Harlan, *History and Genealogy of the Harlan Family,* 268–269.

19. Miller, *"Dear Master,"* 28–29.

20. "To the Clergy of All Denominations," *African Repository* 21, no. 5 (May 1845): 147.

21. Number of expeditions to Liberia in Burin, *Slavery and the Peculiar Solution,* 110.

22. Burin, *Slavery and the Peculiar Solution,* 29–30.

23. *African Repository* subscription book, American Colonization Society Records, microfilm volumes 28 and 35, reel 297, Library of Congress Manuscript Collection, Washington, D.C.; "Illinois State Colonization Society Annual Meeting," *African Repository* 34, no. 4 (April 1858): 122.

24. "Illinois State Colonization Society Annual Meeting," 122.

25. Radford, *Autobiography,* 15; also see Alison Davis Wood, producer and writer, *Lincoln: Prelude to the Presidency,* WILL Public Media (Urbana, Ill.: Illinois Public Media, 2009), and related online information, http://will.illinois.edu/lincoln.

26. Eugenia Jones Hunt (granddaughter of William T. Major) to the editor of the *Bloomington (Ill.) Daily Pantagraph,* May 30, 1944; William Davenport obituary, *Daily Nebraska Press,* June 28, 1869.

27. Lowell H. Harrison and James C. Klotter, *A New History of Kentucky* (Lexington: Univ. Press of Kentucky, 1997), 180.

28. Ibid.

29. Wiley, *Slaves No More,* 3.

30. Coleman, "Kentucky Colonization Society," 8; J. H. T. McPherson, "History of

Liberia," Ph.D. diss., Johns Hopkins University Studies in Historical and Political Science, 1891, electronic ed., edited by Herbert B. Adams, chapter 5, http://www.fullbooks.com/History-of-Liberia.html.

31. "Advocate Dispatches," *Baton Rouge (La.) Daily Advocate*, April 15, 1870.

32. Wiley, *Slaves No More*, 3; Clegg, *Price of Liberty*, 6, 266.

33. "Certain Cavilings against Colonization Replied To," *African Repository* 24, no. 4 (April 1848): 117, 118.

34. Buchanan to Wilkeson, December 13, 1840, 81; Burin, *Slavery and the Peculiar Solution*, 80.

35. *Colonization Herald*, February 1851, cited by Burin, *Slavery and the Peculiar Solution*, 89.

36. Innes, *Liberia*, 103.

37. Jessica Farrell, Department of History, University of Minnesota, drew this distinction in her presentation "The Ambiguities of Colonization: A Historical Literary Analysis of 'Colonize' in 19th Century Relations between Liberia and the United States," Liberian Studies Association annual meeting, Concordia University, Chicago, Illinois, May 28–30, 2015.

38. "Annual Report of the American Colonization Society," 1843, 70.

39. J. W. Lugenbeel, "Colonization of Free Blacks," October 2, 1845. First published in the *National Intelligencer* and reprinted in the *Lexington (Ky.) True American*, May 13, 1846.

40. "The World Factbook: Africa: Liberia," Central Intelligence Agency, https://www.cia.gov/library/publications/the-world-factbook/geos/li.html (accessed June 11, 2017).

41. Helene Cooper, *The House at Sugar Beach: In Search of a Lost African Childhood* (New York: Simon and Schuster, 2008), 6.

42. Martin Meredith, *The Fate of Africa: From the Hopes of Freedom to the Heart of Despair: A History of 50 Years of Independence* (New York: Public Affairs [Perseus Book Group], 2005), 545.

43. D'Azevedo, "Tribal Reaction to Nationalism, Part 1," 19.

44. Clegg, *Price of Liberty*, 95–96.

45. Allen, "Liberia and the Atlantic World," 31–33, 39, 40.

46. July, *Origins of Modern African Thought*, 209.

47. Ibid., 210–233.

48. Greene, *Journey without Maps*, 222.

49. Ibid., 224.

50. Leymah Gbowee and Carol Mithers, *Mighty Be Our Powers: How Sisterhood, Prayer, and Sex Changed a Nation at War* (New York: Beast Books, 2011), 5–6.

51. Cooper, *House at Sugar Beach*, 139, 140; Huffman, *Mississippi in Africa*, 185.

52. Cooper, *House at Sugar Beach*, 143–144.

53. Gbowee and Mithers, *Mighty Be Our Powers*, 16; Cooper, *House on Sugar Beach*, 164–165, 181–186; Leon Dash, "Liberian Soldiers Taunt, Shoot 13 Former

Leaders," *Washington Post,* April 23, 1980, http://www.washingtonpost.com/wp-dyn/content/article/2006/07/28/AR2006072800581_pf.html.

54. Theodore Dalrymple [Anthony Daniels], *Monrovia Mon Amour: A Visit to Liberia,* Kindle ed. (Cheltenham, UK: Monday Books: 2012), chapter 10 (first published under author's real name by John Murray [Publishers] Ltd., 1992).

55. Gbowee and Mithers, *Mighty Be Our Powers,* 167–168.

56. Marlise Simons, "Former Liberian President Convicted of War Crimes," *New York Times,* April 26, 2012; Laura Smith-Spark, "Charles Taylor: War Crime Conviction, 50-year Sentence Upheld," September 26, 2013, http://www.cnn.com/2013/09/26/world/africa/netherlands-charles-taylor-verdict/.

Bibliography

Archives and Collections

Information for this book was drawn from a number of archives and collections in addition to the sources listed below. These collections include the American Colonization Society Records, Library of Congress Manuscript Collection, Washington, D.C.; the Disciples of Christ Historical Society, Bethany, West Virginia; Eureka College, Melick Library, Eureka, Illinois; Kentucky Historical Society, Frankfort, Kentucky; Liberian Collections, Indiana University, Bloomington, Indiana; Major Collection of Letters from Liberia, McLean County Museum of History, Bloomington, Illinois; Major Family Private Collection; National Archives, Washington, D.C.; and National Museum of American History, Washington, D.C.

African Repository Sources

African Repository and Colonial Journal. Washington, D.C.: American Colonization Society. (Copies accessed at the Library of Congress, the Liberian Collections at Indiana University in Bloomington, HathiTrust.org, and original copies in the Major Family Private Collection.)

African Repository 11, no. 1 (January 1835): 29.

African Repository 11, no. 3 (March 1835): 85.

African Repository 11, no. 10 (October 1835): 319.

African Repository 23, no. 5 (May 1847): 152–153.

African Repository 24, no. 11 (November 1848): 351.

African Repository 26, no. 7 (July 1850): 203.

African Repository 32, no. 8 (August 1856): 229.

"American Relations with Liberia." *African Repository* 50, no. 8 (August 1874): 252.

"Annual Report of the American Colonization Society." *African Repository* 19, no. 3 (March 1843): 88.

"Annual Report." *African Repository* 11, no. 7 (July 1835): 221.

"Another Expedition Sailed for Liberia." *African Repository* 20, no. 7 (July 1844): 220.

Bell, Charles H., to Reverend Alfred Chester, April 3, 1840. *African Repository* 16 (October 1840): 294.

Benson, Stephen A., to Reverend William McLain, April 7, 1846. *African Repository* 22 (1846): 306.

Blackford, Abraham, to Mary B. Blackford, February 14, 1846. *African Repository* 22, no. 8 (August 1846): 261. HathiTrust.org. https://hdl.handle.net/2027/hvd.hwrch7.

Buchanan, Thomas, to Sam Wilkeson, August 10, 1839, *African Repository* 14 (1839): 283.

——— to the Honorable Council of Liberia, September 5, 1839. *African Repository* 16 (1840): 36–37.

——— to board of American Colonization Society, November 6, 1839. *African Repository* 16 (1840): 71–72, 74–75.

——— to Samuel Wilkeson, July 1, 1840, *African Repository* 16 (September 1840): 277.

———. Dispatch to the board of the American Colonization Society, September 1, 1840. *African Repository* 16 (1840): 334.

——— to Samuel Wilkeson, December 13, 1840. *African Repository* 17 (March 1841): 81–89.

——— to Samuel Wilkeson, June 10, 1841. *African Repository* 17 (September 1841): 258.

"Celebration of the Twenty-fourth of August" and "The Twenty-fourth." *African Repository* 24, no. 1 (January 1848): 14–17.

"Certain Cavilings against Colonization Replied To." *African Repository* 24, no. 4 (April 1848): 117–118.

"Citizens of Liberia in the United States" and "Movements among the Colored People." *African Repository* 24, no. 9 (September 1848): 259–263.

"The Colony and Colonization." *African Repository* 11, no. 11 (November 1835): 321.

"Colonization Meeting." *African Repository* 11, no. 1 (January 1835): 16.

Coppinger, William. "Methodist Episcopal Missions in Liberia." *African Repository* 24, no. 10 (October 1848): 293. (Republished from *Christian Repository*.)

"Departure of the Emigrants by the *Luna*." *African Repository* 12, no. 7 (July 1836): 226–229.

"Dr. Hall's Answers to Mr. Key's Questions." *African Repository* 28, no. 13 (November 1842): 342.

"Dr. Proudfit's Address to Emigrants." *African Repository* 11, no. 10 (October 1835): 306–308.

"Emancipation." *African Repository* 11, no. 12 (December 1835): 335–336.

"Expeditions to Liberia." *African Repository* 11, no. 12 (December 1835): 373.

"Forty-First Annual Report of the American Colonization Society." *African Repository* 34, no. 3 (March 1858): 68.

"Governor Roberts' Annual Message." *African Repository* 21, no. 5 (May 1845): 132.

Bibliography

"Governor Thomas Buchanan's Dispatch, May 17, 1839." *African Repository* 16 (1840): 50–52.

"Gradual Emancipation in Kentucky." *African Repository* 11, no. 8 (August 1835): 256.

Hall, James. "Voyage to Liberia," *African Repository* 33, no. 8 (August 1857), 272–273. HathiTrust.org, https://hdl.handle.net/2027/hvd.hwrchv.

———. "Voyage to Liberia." *African Repository* 34, no. 4 (April 1858): 110–111.

Harris, Sion, to William McLain, September 20, 1850. *African Repository* 27, no. 1 (January 1851): 18. HathiTrust.org, https://hdl.handle.net/2027/hvd.hwrchp.

Horland [Harlan], Wesley. "Letters from Bassa Cove." *African Repository* 23, no. 9 (September 1847): 279–281.

Hoyt, W. B., to the editors, December 15, 1845. *African Repository* 21 (1845): 143–144.

"Illinois State Colonization Society Annual Meeting." *African Repository* 34, no. 4 (April 1858): 122.

"The Late Expedition for Liberia." *African Repository* 26, no. 4 (April 1850): 103–106.

"Late Intelligence from Liberia" (reprinted from *Liberian Herald*, June 30, 1848). *African Repository* 24, no. 9 (September 1848): 282.

"Latest from Liberia." *African Repository* 11, no. 11 (November 1835): 337–339.

Lists of contributors. *African Repository* 18, no. 13 (November 1842): 34–35; 19, no. 2 (February 1843): 67–68; 19, no. 3 (March 1843): 85.

Lugenbeel, J. W., to Rev. R. R. Gurley, January 17, 1844. *African Repository* 20 (1844): 146.

——— to Reverend William McLain, February 8, 1847. *African Repository* 23 (May 1847): 139–140.

———. "Religion among the Congoes by the *Pons*." *African Repository* 24, no. 2 (February 1848): 37.

———. "Sketches of Liberia. No. 3." *African Repository* 26, no. 8 (August 1850): 230.

———. "Sketches of Liberia. No. 4." *African Repository* 26, no. 9 (September 1850): 279.

———. "Sketches of Liberia. No. 7." *African Repository* 26, no. 12 (December 1850): 377–378.

"Marine List." *African Repository* 11, no. 11 (November 1835): 341.

"Massachusetts Colonization Society." *African Repository* 20, no. 7 (July 1844): 212.

Mercer, Samuel, to Elliot Cresson, May 12, 1848. *African Repository* 24, no. 10 (October 1848): 290–292.

Merriam, G. and C., to Joseph J. Roberts, April 30, 1851. *African Repository* 27, no. 2 (February 1852): 51.

Minor, James C., to John Minor, February 11, 1833. *African Repository* 9 no. 6 (June 1833): 127. HathiTrust.org, https://hdl.handle.net/2027/hvd.32044010585735.

"Monument to Governor Buchanan." *African Repository* 26, no. 11 (November 1850): 338.

"Munificent Donations." *African Repository* 11, no. 7 (July 1835): 211.

"The Next Legislature." *African Repository* 49, no. 8 (August 1873): 249.

"Outfit for Emigrants." *African Repository* 24, no. 4 (April 1848): 119.

"Peoria Conference." *African Repository* 34, no. 10 (October 1858): 310.

"Proceedings of the American Colonization Society." *African Repository* 11, no. 2 (February 1835): 50.

"Recent Intelligence from Liberia." *African Repository* 28, no. 3 (March 1852): 92–94.

"Relations between the American Colonization Society and the Republic of Liberia." *African Repository* 24, no. 9 (September 1848): 257–259.

Roberts, Joseph Jenkins, to the executive committee of the American Colonization Society, June 9, 1842. *African Repository* 19, no. 1 (January 1843): 10–11.

———. Dispatch to American Colonization Society, August 31, 1842. *African Repository* 19, no. 1 (January 1843): 21.

——— to Reverend Ralph Gurley, December 24, 1843. *African Repository* 20 (1844): 134.

——— to Reverend William McLain, March 18, 1845. *African Repository* 21 (1845): 215.

———. Letter dated January 4, 1847. *African Repository* 23, no. 5 (May 1847): 152–153.

——— to Don Jose Zerresti, December 22, 1847. *African Repository* 24, no. 4 (April 1848): 103.

"Sentiments in London on African Colonization." *African Repository* 24, no. 2 (February 1848).

"The Slave Trade." *African Repository* 26, no. 12 (December 1850): 361.

Starkey, James R. Correspondence with Reverend W. N. Hawks and the American Colonization Society, May to October 1850. *African Repository* 26, no. 12 (December 1850): 366–368. (Also see Wrial, James.)

Teage, Hilary. "Extract from a letter from the Hon. H. Teage to Rev. J. B. Pinney." *African Repository* 29 no. 1 (January 1853): 17. HathiTrust.org, https://hdl.handle.net/2027/hvd.hwrchr.

"Things Which Every Emigrant to Liberia Ought to Know." *African Repository* 24, no. 4 (April 1848): 111–114. (Also published as a pamphlet.)

"To the Clergy of All Denominations." *African Repository* 21, no. 5 (May 1845): 147.

Wilson, Beverly. Letter dated November 1833. *African Repository* 11, no. 8 (August 1835): 244.

Wrial, James, to the American Colonization Society, May 29, 1848, and James Rial Starkey to the American Colonization Society, July 12, 1848. *African Repository* 24, no. 10 (October 1848): 304–305. (Also see Starkey, James R.)

"Young Men's Colonization Society of Pennsylvania." *African Repository* 12, no. 4 (April 1836): 125.

Other Sources

Adams, Harold. *The History of Eureka College*. Eureka, Ill.: Board of Trustees of Eureka College, 1982.

Bibliography

Allen, William E. "Liberia and the Atlantic World in the Nineteenth Century." *History in Africa* 37 (2010): 7–49.

Amemasor, James. "A Taste of Freedom: The Benjamin Major Collection of Letters from Emancipated American Slaves in Liberia, 1836–1851." Master's thesis, Illinois State University, 2004.

American Colonization Society. "The Constitution of the American Society for Colonizing the Free People of Colour of the United States." Library of Congress digital archives. http://www.log.gov/item/91898198.

———. *Memorial of the Semi-centennial Anniversary of the American Colonization Society.* Washington, D.C.: American Colonization Society, 1867. https://books.google.com/books?id=QC4OAAAAIAAJ.

———. "Census of the Colony of Liberia." In *Tables Showing the Number of Emigrants and Recaptured Africans Sent to the Colony of Liberia . . . Together with A Census of the Colony.* Washington, D.C.: American Colonization Society, 1845. https://books.google.com/books?id=tK4EJoPvb70C&printsec=frontcover&dq=%22Tables+Showing+the+Number+of+Emigrants%22&hl=en&newbks=1&newbks_redir=0&sa=X&ved=2ahUKEwiro5egwN_lAhVErlkKHQmtD_EQ6AEwAHoECAIQAg#v=onepage&q=%22Tables%20Showing%20the%20Number%20of%20Emigrants%22&f=false. (Referred to as the 1843 census.)

———. *Twentieth Annual Report of the American Colonization Society for Colonizing the Free People of Colour of the United States, with the Proceedings of the Annual Meeting, December 13, 1836.* Washington, D.C.: American Colonization Society, 1837. https://books.google.com/books?id=lscCAAAAYAAJ&pg=RA3-PA21&lpg=RA3-PA21&dq=Donelson+and+Liberia&source=bl&ots=A890EM3lQB&sig=-NS5Qt0P_R—SgICU5cEOIIYqao&hl=en&sa=X&ved=0ahUKEwjHvan1zOrJAhVK5yYKHUeZBOkQ6AEILzAE#v=twopage&q=Donelson&f=false.

Apple, Lindsey. *The Family Legacy of Henry Clay: In the Shadow of a Kentucky Patriarch.* Lexington: Univ. Press of Kentucky, 2011.

Armistead, Wilson. *Calumny Refuted by Facts from Liberia.* London: Charles Gilpen, 1848.

The Biographical Record of Livingston and Woodford Counties, Illinois. Chicago: S. J. Clarke Publishing, 1900.

Breckinridge, John, and Thomas Buchanan. "The Massacre at Bassa Cove." *Religious Intelligencer,* October 31, 1835, American Periodicals, 347.

"Brig *Luna's* Company, Arrived at Bassa Cove, August 1836." *Senate of the United States, Second Session of the Twenty-Eighth Congress,* vol. 9, no. 150 (Washington, D.C.: Gales and Seaton, 1845), 269–271. (Referred to in text as the passenger list.) https://books.google.com/books?id=N4lHAQAAIAAJ.

Burin, Eric. *Slavery and the Peculiar Solution: A History of the American Colonization Society.* Gainesville: Univ. Press of Florida, 2005.

Burrowes, C. Patrick. *Between the Kola Forest and the Salty Sea: A History of the Liberian People before 1830*. Bomi County, Liberia: Know Your Self Press, 2016.

Campbell, Alexander, and W. K. Pendleton. "Our Tour to the West." *Millennial Harbinger* 3 (1846): 204.

Campbell, Alexander. "The Crisis." *Millennial Harbinger* 3 (1832): 86.

Carey, Mathew. *Letters on the Colonization Society; and on Its Probable Results . . .* 7th ed. Philadelphia, Pa.: I. Johnson, 1833.

Channing, W. C. "What is Education?" *Millennial Harbinger* 4, no. 9 (September 1840): 430.

Chesnut, Mary Boykin. *Mary Chesnut's Civil War*. Edited by C. Vann Woodward. New Haven, Conn.: Yale Univ. Press, 1981. https://books.google.com/books?isbn=0300024592.

Christian County Deed Book F. Hopkinsville, Kentucky.

Christian County Genealogical Society. *Family Histories: Christian County, Kentucky, 1797–1986*. Nashville, Tenn.: Turner, 1986.

Christian County Order Book F, Hopkinsville, Kentucky.

Christian County Will Book T. Hopkinsville, Kentucky.

Clegg, Claude A., III. *The Price of Liberty: African Americans and the Making of Liberia*. Chapel Hill: Univ. of North Carolina Press, 2004.

Clinton, Catherine. *The Plantation Mistress: Woman's World in the Old South*. New York: Pantheon, 1982.

Coleman, J. Winston, Jr. "The Kentucky Colonization Society." *Register of the Kentucky State Historical Society* 39, no. 26 (January 1941): 1–9.

———. *Slavery Times in Kentucky*. Chapel Hill: Univ. Press of North Carolina, 1940.

Colonization and Abolition Contrasted. Philadelphia: Herman Hooker, n. d.

Cooper, Helene. *The House at Sugar Beach: In Search of a Lost African Childhood*. New York: Simon and Schuster, 2008.

Dalrymple, Theodore [Anthony Daniels]. *Monrovia Mon Amour: A Visit to Liberia*. Kindle ed. Cheltenham, UK: Monday Books, 2012. First published under the author's real name by John Murray (Publishers) Ltd., 1992.

Darsie, George. "Mrs. Emily H. Tubman." In *Churches of Christ: A Historical, Biographical, and Pictorial History of Churches of Christ*, edited by John T. Brown. Louisville, Ky.: Morton, 1904.

Davenport, William. Notes written by William Davenport in the flyleaf of his Bible; transcribed by his son Benjamin Major Davenport. Kentucky Historical Society, Frankfort, Kentucky.

d'Azevedo, Warren. "Tribal Reaction to Nationalism, Part 1." *Liberian Studies Journal* 1, no. 2 (spring 1969): 1–22.

Dickinson, Elmira J., ed. *A History of Eureka College with Biographical Sketches and Reminiscences*. St. Louis, Mo.: Christian Publishing Company, 1894.

Douglass, Frederick. *On Slavery and the Civil War: Selections from His Writings*. New York: Dover Thrift Editions, 2003.

Duis, E. *The Good Old Times in McLean County, Illinois.* Bloomington, Ill.: Leader Publishing and Printing House, 1874. https://books.google.com/books?id=jU40AQ AAMAAJ&printsec=frontcover&dq=Good+old+times+in+McLean+County&h l=en&sa=X&ved=0ahUKEwiL3v7i7OTSAhUFKyYKHcv8DmIQ6AEIHDAA #v=onepage&q=Good%20old%20times%20in%20McLean%20County&f=false.

Dunnigan, Alice A., ed. *The Fascinating Story of Black Kentuckians: Their Heritage and Tradition.* Washington, D.C.: Associated Publishers, 1982.

Eastman, Zebina. "Black Code of Illinois." *Illinois Historical Survey.* Learning Lincoln Online. http://learningabe.info/Black_Code_Text_Portion.html. Accessed May 22, 2019.

Fox, Early Lee. "The American Colonization Society: 1817–1840." Ph.D. diss., Johns Hopkins University, 1919, 33. https://archive.org/stream/americancoloniza00f-oxe/americancoloniza00foxe_djvu.txt.

Fox-Genovese, Elizabeth. *Within the Plantation Household: Black and White Women of the Old South* (Chapel Hill: Univ. of North Carolina Press, 1988).

"From Liberia." *Niles Weekly Register,* December 26, 1835, American Periodicals, 288.

Gates, Henry Louis, Jr., host and executive producer. "The Stories We Tell." *Finding Your Roots,* season 3, episode 1. Public Broadcasting Service, 2016.

Gbowee, Leymah, and Carol Mithers. *Mighty Be Our Powers: How Sisterhood, Prayer, and Sex Changed a Nation at War.* New York: Beast Books, 2011.

Gebhardt, Kristine. "The Major Family Collection of Letters: An Examination of Colonization and These and Other Letters from Liberia." Senior Capstone, Bloomington, Illinois, 1995.

Georgia Wills and Probate Records, 1742–1992, from Wills, vol. A–B, 1798–1853, Will of Richard Tubman. https://search.ancestry.com/cgi-bin/sse.dll?indiv=1& dbid=8635&h=499393&tid=&pid=&usePUB=true&_phsrc=oNP1&_phstart =successSource.

Georgia Women of Achievement. "Emily Harvie Thomas Tubman." Georgia Women of Achievement. http://www.georgiawomen.org/copy-of-thomas-ella -gertrude-clanto.

Glazier, Jack. *Been Coming through Some Hard Times: Race, History, and Memory in Western Kentucky.* Knoxville: Univ. of Tennessee Press, 2012.

Greene, Graham. *Journey without Maps.* New York: Penguin, 2006. (First published in Great Britain by William Heinemann, 1936.)

Harlan, Alpheus H. *History and Genealogy of the Harlan Family and Particularly the Descendants of George and Michael Harlan.* Baltimore, Md.: Gateway, 1914.

Harrison, Lowell H. *The Antislavery Movement in Kentucky.* Lexington: Univ. Press of Kentucky, 1978.

Harrison, Lowell H., and James C. Klotter. *A New History of Kentucky.* Lexington: Univ. Press of Kentucky, 1997.

Haynes, N. S. "The Disciples of Christ in Illinois and Their Attitudes toward Slavery." *Transactions of the Illinois State Historical Society for the Year 1913.* Springfield, Ill.: Board of Trustees, Illinois State Historical Society, 1913: 52–59.

Haynes, Nathaniel S. *History of the Disciples of Christ in Illinois, 1819–1914.* Cincinnati: Standard Publishing, 1915.

Hersey, Thomas, ed. "Ravages of Cholera at Campeachy [*sic*]." *Thomsonian Recorder* 2, no. 15 (April 26, 1834): 232.

Hinds, Charles F. "Migration Routes from Kentucky." Martin F. Schmidt Research Library, Kentucky Historical Society Library, Frankfort, Kentucky.

History of Tazewell County. Chicago: Chas. C. Chapman and Co., 1879.

"The House Gag Rule." US House of Representatives, History, Art and Archives. http://history.house.gov/Historical-Highlights/1800-1850/The-House-of-Representatives-instituted-the-%E2%80%9Cgag-rule%E2%80%9D/. Accessed May 8, 2019.

Huffman, Alan. *Mississippi in Africa: The Saga of the Slaves of Prospect Hill Plantation and Their Legacy in Liberia Today.* New York: Gotham, 2004.

Illinois Public Land Purchase Records, 1800–1900. Ancestry.com.

The Independent Republic of Liberia: Its Constitution and Declaration of Independence; Address of the Colonists to the Free People of Color in the United States. Philadelphia: William F. Geddes, Printer, 1848. https://babel.hathitrust.org/cgi/pt?id=mdp.351 12104975158&view=1up&seq=12.

Innes, William. *Liberia; or the Early History and Signal Preservation of the American Colony of Free Negroes on the Coast of Africa.* Edinburgh, UK: Waugh and Innes, 1831.

Jefferson, Thomas. Autobiography draft fragment, January 6 through July 27, 1821. From the Thomas Jefferson and William Short correspondence, transcribed and edited by Gerard W. Gawalt. Manuscript Division, Library of Congress. https://www.loc.gov/collections/thomas-jefferson-papers/?q=Thomas+Jefferson%2C+July+27%2C+1821.

Johnson, Walter. *Soul by Soul: Life inside the Antebellum Slave Market.* Cambridge, Mass.: Harvard Univ. Press, 1999.

July, Robert W. *The Origins of Modern African Thought: Its Development in West Africa during the Nineteenth and Twentieth Centuries.* New York: Praeger, 1967.

Kentucky Pension Roll of 1835. Ancestry.com. https://www.ancestry.com/search/collections/flhg-kypensionroll/?name=George_Harlan&name_x=s_s.

Kleber, John E., ed. *The Kentucky Encyclopedia.* Lexington: Univ. Press of Kentucky, 1992.

Lewis, John N. Letter dated December 8, 1848. First published in the *Philadelphia Ledger* and republished in the *Maryland Colonization Journal* 4, no. 20 (February 1849): 314–315.

Liberian Constitution of 1839. http://liberianforum.com/articles/constitution1839.htm.

Liberian Declaration of Independence. https://emansion.gov.lr/doc/Presidential%20Declaration.pdf.

Library of Congress, Prints and Photographs Division: Staten Island Quarantine Grounds, view of Bassa Cove, "Fish Town at Bassau," coffee tree illustration from

Arbre du café dessiné en Arabie sur le naturel, "Liberian Senate," "President Robert's House," and images of Joseph Jenkins Roberts, Jane Roberts, and Stephen Benson,

McDowell, R. "Miscellaneous Information: Attack on Bassa Cove." *Religious Monitor and Evangelical Repository,* January 1836, American Periodicals, 251.

McPherson, J. H. T. "History of Liberia." Ph.D. diss., Johns Hopkins University, 1891. Electronic ed., edited by Herbert B. Adams, http://www.fullbooks.com/History-of-Liberia.html.

Meredith, Martin. *The Fate of Africa: From the Hopes of Freedom to the Heart of Despair: A History of 50 Years of Independence.* New York: Public Affairs (Perseus Book Group), 2005.

Miller, Randall M. *"Dear Master": Letters of a Slave Family.* Ithaca: Cornell Univ. Press, 1978.

Moore, Roy L. *History of Woodford County: A Concise History of the Settlement and Growth of Woodford County.* Eureka, Ill.: Woodford County Republican, 1910.

"Mrs. Emily H. Tubman." *Christian Standard,* June 1885.

Murray, Robert P. "Whiteness in Africa: Americo-Liberians and the Transformative Geographies of Race." Ph.D. diss., University of Kentucky, 2013. Theses and Dissertations—History, 23. https://uknowledge.uky.edu/history_etds/23/.

New York Passenger Lists, 1820–1957. Ancestry.com. https://www.ancestry.com/cs/offers/join?sub=281479271972864&dbid=7488&url=https%3a%2f%2fsearch.ancestry.com%2fcgi-bin%2fsse.dll%3findiv%3d1%26dbid%3d7488%26h%3d1321064%26usePUB%3dtrue%26_phsrc%3dHOk9%26_phstart%3dsuccessSource%26requr%3d281479271972864%26ur%3d0&gsfn=&gsln=&h=1321064.

Nunnelly, Donald. "Emily Tubman: A Disciple Wonder Woman." Disciples of Christ Historical Society.

Olsen, Ted. "Disciples of Christ Board Apologizes for Not Doing More to Oppose Slavery." *Christianity Today,* May 1, 2001. http://www.christianitytoday.com/ct/2001/mayweb-only/5-7-44.0.html.

Past and Present of Woodford County, Illinois. Chicago: Wm. Le Baron, Jr. and Co., 1878.

Pennsylvania Colonization Society. *Annual Report of the Board of Managers of the Young Men's Colonization Society of Pennsylvania.* Philadelphia: Pennsylvania Colonization Society, 1837.

Perrin, William Henry, ed. *Counties of Christian and Trigg, Kentucky: Historical and Biographical.* Chicago: F. A. Battey Publishing Co., 1884. https://archive.org/details/countiesofchrist00perr/.

Pope, Clayne L. "Adult Mortality in America before 1900: A View from Family Histories." In *Strategic Factors in Nineteenth Century American Economic History,* edited by Claudia Goldin and Hugh Rockoff. Chicago: Univ. of Chicago Press, 1992. http://www.nber.org/chapters/c6965.

Portrait and Biographical Record of Macoupin County, Illinois. Chicago: Biographical Publishing, 1891.

Portrait and Biographical Record of Tazewell and Mason Counties, Illinois. Chicago: Biographical Publishing, 1894.

Radford, B. J. *History of Woodford County.* Peoria, Ill.: W. T. Dowdall, Printer, 1877.

Radford, Benjamin Johnson. *Autobiography of Benjamin Johnson Radford.* Eureka, Ill.: N.p., 1928.

Rechenbach, Russell R., II. "Emily Tubman of Kentucky." An address given in commemoration of Emily Tubman's 200th birthday, March 19, 1994, at Augusta First Christian Church, Augusta, Georgia.

Reef, Catherine. *This Our Dark Country: The American Settlers of Liberia.* New York: Clarion, 2002.

Rosten, Leo, ed. *Religions of America: Ferment and Faith in an Age of Crisis.* New York: Simon and Schuster, 1975.

Sanneh, Lamin. *Abolitionists Abroad: American Blacks and the Making of Modern West Africa.* Cambridge, Mass.: Harvard Univ. Press, 1999.

Seifman, Eli. "The United Colonization Societies of New York and Pennsylvania and the Establishment of the African Colony of Bassa Cove." *Pennsylvania History: A Journal of Mid-Atlantic Studies* 35, no. 1 (January 1968): 24.

Sherwood, Henry Noble. "The Formation of the American Colonization Society." *Journal of Negro History* 2, no. 3 (July 1917). https://www.gutenberg.org/files/20752/20752-8.txt.

Shick, Tom W. *Behold the Promised Land: A History of Afro-American Settler Society in Nineteenth-Century Liberia.* Baltimore, Md.: Johns Hopkins Univ. Press, 1977, 1980.

———. "Emigrants to Liberia, 1820–1843: An Alphabetical Listing. Liberian Studies Research Working Paper No. 2." University of Delaware, 1971 (referred to as the roll of emigrants).

Simmons, John D. "A Memorial to Emily Thomas Tubman, 1794–1885." *Augusta Chronicle,* July 1985.

"Slavery and the Making of America." Public Broadcasting Service. http://www.pbs.org/wnet/slavery/.

Smith-Spark, Laura. "Charles Taylor: War Crime Conviction, 50-year Sentence Upheld." September 26, 2013. http://www.cnn.com/2013/09/26/world/africa/netherlands-charles-taylor-verdict/.

Stone, Barton W. *Biography of Eld. B. W. Stone, Written by Himself, with Additions and Reflections from Elder John Rogers.* Cincinnati: J. A. and U. P. Jones, 1847. HathiTrust.org. https://babel.hathitrust.org/cgi/pt?id=chi.26752889;view=1up;seq=7.

"Struggles over Slavery: The Gag Rule." National Archives. http://www.archives.gov/exhibits/treasures_of_congress/text/page10_text.html.

Tallant, Harold D. *Evil Necessity: Slavery and Politics in Antebellum Kentucky.* Lexington: Univ. Press of Kentucky, 2003.

Trabue, Daniel. *Westward into Kentucky: The Narrative of Daniel Trabue,* edited by

Chester Raymond Young. Lexington: Univ. Press of Kentucky, 1981; paperback ed., 2004.

Trefzger, John D. "Our People, Our Pastors, 1837–1987." Bloomington, Ill.: First Christian Church (Disciples of Christ), 1987.

———. "Pioneer Disciple: William T. Major." *Discipliana* (October 1967).

Tyler-McGraw, Marie. *An African Republic: Black and White Virginians in the Making of Liberia*. Chapel Hill: Univ. of North Carolina Press, 2007.

———. "Patrick Bullock: Abandoned in Liberia." Virginia Emigrants to Liberia, Virginia Center for Digital History, University of Virginia. www.vcdh.virginia.edu/ liberia/index.php?page=Stories&section=Patrick%20Bullock.

US Congressional Documents and Debates, 1774–1874. Library of Congress, American Memory. http://memory.loc.gov/ammem/hlawquery.html.

US Federal Census data, 1810–1870. www.census.gov and Ancestry.com.

US General Land Office Records, 1776–2015. Ancestry.com, https://www.ancestry.com/search/collections/blmlandpatents/?name=George_Harlan&event=_ macoupin-illinois-usa_1849&name_x=s_s.

Walker, Charles A., ed. *History of Macoupin County, Illinois: Biographical and Pictorial*, vol. 1. Chicago: S. J. Clarke Pub., 1911.

Watts, Isaac. Lyrics, "When I Can Read My Title Clear," 1707. http://library.timelesstruths.org.

Wiley, Bell I., ed. *Slaves No More: Letters from Liberia, 1833–1869*. Lexington: Univ. Press of Kentucky, 1980.

Wilkeson, Samuel. *A Concise History of the Commencement, Progress and Present Condition of the American Colonies in Liberia*. Washington, D.C.: Madisonian Office, 1839. https://books.google.com/books?id=J8sNAAAAQAAJ.

Williamson, Samuel H., and Louis P. Cain. "Measuring Slavery in 2009 Dollars." http://www.measuringworth.com/slavery.php. Figure 5, "Real Price of Owning a Slave in 2009 Dollars."

Wood, Alison Davis, producer and writer. *Lincoln: Prelude to the Presidency*. WILL Public Media, Urbana, Ill.: Illinois Public Media, 2009, and related online information. http://will.illinois.edu/lincoln.

Woodford County Circuit Clerk's Office. Ben Major's estate records. Eureka, Illinois.

"The World Factbook: Africa: Liberia." Central Intelligence Agency. https://www.cia.gov/library/publications/the-world-factbook/geos/li.html. Accessed June 11, 2017.

Yates, William, ed. *Woodford County History*. Woodford County, Ill.: Woodford County Board of Supervisors, 1968.

Zwass, Maurice. "Unpublished Letter from Bassa Cove in 1847 from a Black American Missionary: Political and Medical Significance." A paper presented at the Liberian Studies Association annual meeting, April 1976, Bloomington, Indiana.

Index

Index

Weller, Royal, 43
Wheatly, Francis, 36, 41, 191
widows in Liberia, 52, 56, 67, 68, 80, 119, 120, 121, 147, 157, 161
Wilkeson, Samuel, 28, 29, 221n8
women settlers in Liberia, 66–69, 120, 149

Woodford County, Illinois, 173, 219n13
Wrial, James (James Rial Starkey), 102

Young Men's Colonization Society of Pennsylvania, 27

CPSIA information can be obtained
at www.ICGtesting.com
Printed in the USA
LVHW090215130421
684247LV00001B/64

9 780813 179339